His Name is Yahweh

by Neil Snyder

Registration number, United States Copyright Office: TXu1-156-444

Bible quotes in this book are from the New American Standard Bible unless otherwise indicated. God's personal Name, Yahweh, is used in this book instead of "the LORD," "the Lord GOD," or "LORD of hosts" as it is translated in the New American Standard Bible, and the first letter in any word is capitalized if it refers to God, the Messiah, or His Name.

Your comments are welcomed. To correspond with the author, please use the following address:

Dr. Neil H. Snyder
100 Paradise Circle
Townville, SC 29689

Contents
His Name is Yahweh

Acknowledgements

The members of my family were a constant source of inspiration as I worked on this book, and I am indebted to all of them: my wife Katie, my daughters Melanie and Rebekah, my brother Craig, my mother and father Mary and Ed Snyder, my sister Carol Labarre, and my wife's parents Dan and Sue Plaster. I love them will all my heart.

Many other people assisted me, some of them without even knowing it: Andrew Roth, Sid Roth, Pat Parks, Charles Stewart, Ralph Motsinger, John Welborn, Ed Rose, Kay and Mac Snyder, Bill Shenkir, Elias Awad, Bernie Morin, Tony Crunk, Ann Rought and her mother-in-law Jean Rought, and a woman whose name I will not mention. She is the mother of one of my former Jewish students, and she read every chapter of this book while I was writing it. Her comments were invaluable to me.

I want to thank several of my former students who helped me: Macon Hubard, Allyn Dabkowski, Lindy Blevins, Josh Johnson, Kristin Braggins, Josh Paulson, Ed Deng, Lauren Franzel, Adrianne Walvoord, Kristin Rogus, Patricia Lopez, Dave Chattleton, Reece Hale, Lili Hyder, Devon Pearce, Key Richardson, Andy Jaspen, and Jenny Phillips.

Finally, I want to thank Noam Avraham. She is an Israeli girl who lived with my wife and me for several months in 2002. While Noam was with us, I was working on PowerPoint presentations to deliver the content of this book, and I was adding details to the text that are critically important. She helped me by explaining the meanings of many Hebrew words that are not easily translated into English. She is like a daughter to my wife and me, and we love her very much.

I know I failed to mention everyone who helped me, and I apologize to anyone I left out. I am truly grateful to Yahweh for giving me so many people for support.

Neil Snyder
Townville, SC

About the Author

Neil Snyder earned a Ph.D. degree in strategic management from the University of Georgia in 1979 and taught leadership and strategy at the University of Virginia for 25 years. He is the author of numerous books including Vision, Values & Courage (The Free Press, 1994) and The Will to Lead (Irwin Professional Publishing, 1997), and he has published more than 100 articles and business case studies. Dr. Snyder retired from UVA in 2004, and currently he is the Ralph A. Beeton Professor Emeritus at the University of Virginia.

During his tenure at UVA, he served as Policy Advisor for Regulatory Reform to Governor Charles S. Robb of Virginia (1982-1985), and he was co-chairman in 1985 and chairman in 1986 of the Governor's Conference on Small Business in Virginia. In 1985, he received the Small Business Advocacy Award of the Virginia Chamber of Commerce.

He served as deacon at Milledge Avenue Baptist Church in Athens, Georgia while working on his doctorate and at Crozet Baptist Church in Crozet, Virginia while teaching at the University of Virginia.

Chapter 1
God Said It and That Makes It So

Recently, I heard a disturbing statistic. According to a Gallup poll taken in May 2006, fewer than 30 percent of Americans believe the Bible is the Word of God.[1] Since God gave us the Scriptures to direct our path toward Him, the fact that more than 70 percent of the people in this so-called "Christian nation" say they do not believe His Word is alarming.

God is not an abstract idea or a theological concept. He is the Sovereign of the universe. To avoid any confusion, I want you to understand at the outset that I accept the truth of the Bible without reservation or qualification. I make no apologies for standing on God's Word, and my goal in this book is to show you what the Bible actually says about the Name of God — Yahweh.

Yahweh is God

It took me almost a decade to do the research required to write this book. I studied Hebrew and Greek, and I read ancient documents that few people have ever seen. I also made hundreds of presentations about the importance of God's Name to groups ranging in size from 3 or 4 people to more than 500 people. All told, I have talked with thousands of people about this subject, and my personal experience has taught me an invaluable lesson. We have a long way to go before the Christian community understands what God said in the Scriptures about the importance of His Name.

It's tragic that most Christians don't know God's Name and that He commanded us to declare the Name "Yahweh" to the world. It may surprise you to discover that "Yahweh" is the only Name God told us to proclaim to the world. This is an irrefutable fact—a fact you will understand perfectly by the time you finish reading this book. Even more, most Christians have no idea that Jesus is Yahweh and that we have salvation in the Name "Yahweh." Think about it and let it sink in. Jesus is Yahweh—our only Savior.

Occasionally, when Christians hear this message for the first time, they become indignant because they haven't heard a preacher say it from the pulpit. I'm confused too. It's difficult for me to understand why so many preachers don't have a grip on the importance of this message—especially since it comes straight from the Bible and it's repeated so often in the Scriptures. A few years ago, I told a friend that God's Name is Yahweh and that Yahweh is the Name in which we have salvation. These are irrefutable facts, yet my friend was visibly angry. With a harsh tone in his voice, he said, "That can't be true because if it were I would have heard it a long time ago."

My friend was more than 50 years old at the time, and he had attended church regularly since he was a small boy. During more than five decades of attending church, he never heard God's Name mentioned from the pulpit—not even once. Interestingly, my friend will tell you in a heartbeat that he is a Bible-believing Christian and that he attends a Bible-preaching church. That's all the more reason to be confused.

Given what God says in the Scriptures about His Name, how can so many Christians fail to grasp its significance? Why do Bible scholars tolerate the longstanding tradition of replacing God's Name in the Scriptures with titles that Yahweh never intended as substitutes for His holy Name? Even more, why have preachers as a group not made a fuss about this editorial tradition? These are important questions that I hope you will ponder as you read this book.

The Name "Yahweh" is Concealed in the Scriptures

It's regrettable that the Name "Yahweh" doesn't appear even once in the text of the three most popular Bible translations on the market today. The King James Bible, the New American Standard Bible, and the New International Version leave God's Name out completely, and they substitute the titles "LORD" and "GOD" where the Name "Yahweh" belongs in the Scriptures.

There are two significant problems with this editorial tradition. First, "LORD" and "GOD" are titles—not names, and Yahweh commanded us to declare His Name to the world. He never even hinted that we should declare His titles to the world.

Second, the titles "lord" and "god" can be applied appropriately to wood, rock, or metal, and Yahweh Himself refers to anything that has been fashioned into an idol for worship as either a "god" or a "lord." In other words, these titles don't distinguish between Yahweh and inanimate objects or false deities. Once more,

Yahweh did not tell us to declare His titles to the world. He did command us to tell the world who He is by Name.

In the Old Testament, the Name "Yahweh" should appear where you see the phrase "the LORD" where all the letters in the word "LORD" are capitalized. It should also appear where you see the phrase "the Lord GOD" where all the letters in the word "GOD" are capitalized. Many times Yahweh's Name is translated as "LORD of hosts" where all the letters in the word "LORD" are capitalized. In Hebrew, this phrase is Yahweh Sabaoth, and it means "Yahweh Master of legions." It refers to Yahweh as the Supreme Sovereign in the universe—the ruler of everyone and everything including the forces of nature.

According to Charles Ryrie, author of Ryrie Study Bible, Yahweh's Name appears in Hebrew manuscripts of the Old Testament exactly 6,823 times.[2] That number probably seems large to you, and I hope it raises questions in your mind about why you haven't heard a lot about God's Name in church. And we know this, too. The New Testament is loaded with direct quotes and paraphrased passages from the Old Testament and many times those Old Testament verses contain the words "LORD" and "GOD" in capital letters. The Name "Yahweh" belongs there, but it's not always easy to identify where God's Name should be in the New Testament because most Bible translations don't pay enough attention to the case of the letters brought from the Old Testament to the New Testament.

It makes sense to me that somewhere along the way in their studies of the Scriptures most preachers would have picked up on all the commands in the Bible associated with God's Name and would have pointed them out to their congregations, but it hasn't happened on a large scale, at least until now. The fact that so few preachers tell their congregations about Yahweh by Name is troubling.

The systematic removal of God's Name from the Scriptures and from daily use by His people has had serious repercussions. God tied His promises, His covenant, His Law, and salvation to His Name. Moreover, He commanded us to know His Name, to seek His Name, to bless His Name, and to share His Name with everyone. In fact, these are unambiguous commands that come straight from the Bible, but it is evident that most Christians simply read past them without giving it a second thought. It's as if they think it doesn't matter, even though Yahweh said it matters—a lot.

There is only one person I can think of who has a fanatical interest in hiding Yahweh's Name (and the promises associated with it) from the human population. He is none other than Satan himself. The Holy Spirit may have allowed him to do it, but He certainly did not condone it. You need to keep this fact in mind as you read this book. The Holy Spirit may permit Satan to lead us into gross errors, but that does not mean He approves of all our actions. Despite our disobedience where Yahweh's Name is concerned, He has blessed us as a testament to His own generosity, kindness, patience, and love, but now it is time for us to obey Yahweh.

Try this experiment. When you read the Bible and see the phrase "the LORD," insert the Name "Yahweh;" when you see the phrase "LORD of hosts," insert the Name "Yahweh Master of legions;" and when you see the phrase "the Lord GOD," insert the Name "Lord Yahweh." These are accurate translations from Hebrew to English. If you make these changes, you will see what God actually says in the Scriptures about His Name, and it will awaken you to insights that will amaze you, and maybe even shock you. It will also help you to appreciate what God meant when He said,

"In every place where I cause My Name to be remembered, I will come to you and bless you."[3]

Jesus is Yahweh

This book presents what Yahweh said about Himself in the Bible, and it shows clearly that Yahweh identified Himself as the Messiah from the beginning. The Person[4] Christians call Jesus is Yahweh. For example, in Philippians 2: 9-11, the apostle Paul was referring to the Name Yahweh when he said,

"God...bestowed on Him (Jesus) the Name which is above every name, that at the Name of Jesus every knee should bow, of those who are in heaven and on earth, and under the earth, and every tongue should confess that Jesus Christ is Lord, to the glory of God the Father."[5]

"Yahweh" is the Name God bestowed on Jesus; it is the Name that is above every name; and it is the Name to which every knee will bow when He returns. Regrettably, most of the time, Paul didn't reference the Old Testament when he quoted Scripture. In this instance, we know for a fact that Paul said God bestowed the Name "Yahweh" on Jesus because he is paraphrasing Isaiah 45: 21-24 in Philippians 2: 9-11.

This is what Yahweh told Isaiah:

"And there is no other God besides Me, a righteous God and a Savior; there is none except Me. Turn to Me, and be saved, all the ends of the earth; for I am God, and there is no other. I have sworn by Myself, the Word has gone forth from My mouth in righteousness and will not turn back, that to Me every knee will bow, every tongue will swear allegiance, they will say of Me, 'Only in Yahweh are righteousness and strength.' Men will come to Him and all who were angry with Him shall be put to shame."[6]

Jesus said the same thing a little differently in John chapter 17. Take a look at John 17: 6, 11-12, and 26 and you can see for yourself:

- John 17: 6—"I have manifested Your Name to the men whom You gave Me out of the world...."

- John 17: 11-12—"...Holy Father, keep them in Your Name, the Name which you have given Me, that they may be one even as We are. While I was with them, I was keeping them in Your Name which you have given Me."

- John 17: 26 — "I have made Your Name known to them, and will make it known...."

In John 8: 58, Jesus said plainly that He is Yahweh: "Truly, truly, I say to you, before Abraham was born, I Am."[7] That's about as clear as it gets. "I Am" is the definition of the Name Yahweh. Later, I'll explain why He used the definition of the Name instead of the Name itself in John 8: 58.

When Jesus was with us in Person 2000 years ago, the three most common names for boys in Israel were Yohanan (translated as Jonathan or John), Yaakov (translated as Jacob or James), and Yeshua (Joshua in modern English but transliterated as "Jesus"). In other words, His Name was never Jesus. In fact, the Greek Name for Jesus is "Iesous," and it has been transliterated into many languages. "Jesus" is just the English transliteration of His Name.

This is my point. The Messiah is called by many Names, but Yahweh is the only Name God commanded us to declare to the world. Even more, Yahweh is the only Name that distinguishes between God and anyone or anything else in existence.

Yahweh is Our Only Savior

I think the most significant problem with leaving God's Name out of the Scriptures is the simple fact that we have one Savior, and His Name is Yahweh. Take a look at these verses:

- "I, even I, am Yahweh, and there is no savior besides Me."[8]

- "And it will come about that whoever calls on the Name of Yahweh will be saved."[9]

In Acts 4: 12, Peter said, "...there is no other name under heaven that has been given among men by which we must be saved." By the time you finish reading this book, you'll know that every verse in the New Testament referring to salvation either makes direct reference to the Name "Yahweh" or it alludes to the Name "Yahweh." In reality, the Scriptures make it clear that "everyone who calls on the Name of Yahweh will be saved."[10] This isn't my opinion and I'm not speculating. That's what the Bible says, and the fact that most Christians have never heard this message before is shocking.

I Will Use Endnotes Extensively as I Present My Case

In this book, I won't try to impress you with my wisdom and my opinions. I spent my adult life as a university professor so you can rest assured that I have opinions but they aren't relevant to my message in this book. My sole purpose here is to show you what the Scriptures say about the Name "Yahweh." I know this is a controversial message, but it's true nonetheless, and you need to know it.

I use endnotes extensively throughout this book to document my points so you will have the opportunity to look at the Scriptures and compare what I say about them with the words as they appear in the Bible. My reason for doing this is simple. I want you to know that I minimized my interpretation of God's Word, and in so doing, I let Yahweh speak for Himself.

Since some of the information in this book will be new to many of you, you should do what the Jewish people in Berea did when the apostle Paul preached the Gospel to them:

"...they received the word with great eagerness, examining the Scriptures daily, to see whether these things were so."[11]

Please take your time as you read this book and examine what I say. I know this is a controversial message because most Christians haven't heard it before, but when you finish reading this book, you will realize that the controversy should revolve around the fact that such an important message has been ignored for so long by so many Christian people—especially preachers. As I said, it's troubling that so few Christians know the Name of their God, and it's time to do something about it.

God Said It and that Makes It So

Many years ago, I heard a preacher deliver a sermon titled "God said it; I believe it; and that makes it so." Later, I remember thinking that something was wrong with the message, but I couldn't put my finger on it. Then it dawned on me that God saying it makes it so and that my believing what He said has no bearing on the truth of God's Word. His Word would still be true even if no one believed Him.

As you read this book, please resist the temptation to lay it aside when you see things for the first time. The fact that some of the information in this book may be new to you says a great deal about how powerful and well-entrenched Christian traditions are, but it says absolutely nothing about the accuracy of the information I'm presenting. Take the time to examine the Scriptures and determine if I have attempted to mislead you in any way. When all is said and done, God's Word is true no matter what anyone says.

The Scriptures tell us beyond any shadow of a doubt that we have One God and that His Name is Yahweh. Yahweh is our Redeemer and our Savior, and the One most Christians call Jesus is Yahweh.

Chapter 2
His Name is Yahweh

Yahweh is God's personal Name, or His Divine Name. Yahweh is called the Tetragrammaton,[12] or four-letter word, because it has four letters in Hebrew. Orthodox Jews won't say Yahweh. Instead, they say HASHEM which is a Hebrew word that means "The Name." Also, Yahweh is called the Ineffable Name, or the unspeakable Name, but God's Name is not unspeakable. In fact, according to the Bible, Yahweh commanded us to tell the world who He is by Name. Make no mistake. Not declaring God's Name is an act of disobedience, and it is wrong.

Yahweh Means "I AM"

Yahweh means I was, I am, and I will be,[13] and "I AM" is one of His Names. "I AM" is also the definition of His Name. God's Name sets Him apart by distinguishing between Him and anything or anyone else. When Moses asked Yahweh to tell him His Name so he could let the Children of Israel know who sent him to lead them out of Egypt, God said, "I AM WHO I AM; thus you shall say to the sons of Israel, 'I AM has sent me to you.'"[14] Then immediately He added this command:

> "Say to the Israelites, 'Yahweh, the God of your fathers—the God of Abraham, the God of Isaac, and the God of Jacob—has sent me to you.' This [Yahweh] is My Name forever, the Name

by which I am to be remembered from generation to generation."[15]

Since "forever" means without end, it's obvious that Yahweh didn't intend for us to substitute titles for His Name in the Scriptures. Also, since He instructed Moses to tell the Children of Israel to remember Him by the Name Yahweh "from generation to generation," it's crystal clear that Yahweh wants us to know His Name, to call on Him by Name, and to tell the world about Him by Name.

The Correct Pronunciation of God's Name

Some people believe that the correct pronunciation of God's Name was lost, but according to the Encyclopedia Judaica, that's not so.[16] However, because people use it so infrequently, the correct way to pronounce God's Name remains a source of considerable debate.

Many people believe that all the letters in Yahweh's Name are consonants, but that is not the case either. In fact, each letter in His Name is a vowel-consonant or semivowel.[17] The Hebrew spelling of Yahweh, yod-hey-vav-hey, appears below. Since Hebrew reads right to left, "yod" is the letter on the far right:

Most Bible scholars and Hebrew linguists believe that "Yahweh" is the correct way to pronounce God's Name.[18] The Y-a-h in His Name sounds like "Yah," and the w-e-h in His Name sounds like "way." That said, considerable debate persists about whether to enunciate the second syllable in God's Name with a "v" sound or with a "w" sound, but compelling evidence proves that the "w" sound is correct.[19]

God's Name is Not Jehovah

Between the years 500 A.D. and 1000 A.D., vowel markings were invented and introduced in the Hebrew language. To prevent Jewish people from accidentally saying Yahweh, the rabbis decided to place the vowel markings for the word "Adonai" (which means lord) on the Name "Yahweh." That produced a word with this sound: YeHoVah.[20]

In 1520 A.D., a Bible scholar named Galatinus[21] mistakenly called God by the name "Jehovah,"[22] and in 1611 A.D., the translators of the original King James Bible explained in a footnote that God's Name is Jehovah. That's why so many people today believe that God's Name is Jehovah.[23] Of course, they're wrong, but most of them know only what they have been told, and they have been given incorrect information.

Yahweh Commanded Us to Declare His Name to the World

In this book, as a rule I avoid criticizing any Bible translation. Clearly, translating from one language to another is difficult since words may have multiple meanings and because colloquial expressions can change the natural meanings of words. However, in this and in one other instance I'll make an exception to my rule.

The New American Standard Bible translates Genesis 4: 26 in the following way:

"To Seth, to him also a son was born; and he called his name Enosh. Then men began to call upon the Name of Yahweh."[24]

The King James Version and the New International Version differ only slightly from the NAS translation. However, The Septuagint Tanach (a version of the Tanach, or the Jewish Old Testament, that was translated from Hebrew to Greek in 285 B.C. by a team of 70 rabbis) and The New Jerusalem Bible tell us in Genesis 4: 26 that Enosh (not men as the NAS, KJV, and NIV suggest) was the first person in history "to invoke the Name of Yahweh."[25]

Below is a literal translation of the Hebrew in Genesis 4: 26:

"And to Seth also was born a son, and he called his name Enosh. Then he (Enosh) began to call on the Name of Yahweh."[26]

The Hebrew word translated in this verse as "to call" is qara (kaw-raw'). It means to call upon, to cry unto, or to proclaim. Obviously, Yahweh had a reason for including this information in the Bible. He wanted us to know who invoked His Name the first time and when he did it.

Clearly, this verse in Genesis challenges the Jewish tradition forbidding the use of God's Name, and it should raise serious questions about the legitimacy of that tradition. In spite of this, in

The Stone Edition Tanach, The ArtScroll Series®, a highly regarded version of the Tanach, Rabbi Nosson Scherman translates Genesis 4: 26 in the following way:

"And as for Seth, to him also a son was born, and he named him Enosh. Then to call in the Name of HASHEM (Yahweh) became profaned."[27]

Rabbi Scherman's translation of Genesis 4: 26 contradicts most Bible translations on the market today, and it also disagrees with The Septuagint Tanach. Moreover, his translation is internally inconsistent because the Psalms, the prophets, and the Torah that he translates make it perfectly clear that Yahweh commanded us to declare His Name to the world.

I bring this up to make a critical point. It is dangerous and irresponsible to mistranslate God's Word deliberately in an attempt to make it comply with our traditions. If God's Word contradicts our traditions, then we should abandon our traditions. Yahweh will not give anyone permission to alter the plain meaning of His Word.

God forbids the misuse of His Name or the use of it in a deceitful or duplicitous manner. In his translation of Genesis 4: 26, Rabbi Scherman has distorted the true meaning of God's Word to make it comply with a Jewish tradition that contradicts His Word. Jewish people need to know this, and Rabbi Scherman should correct his error.

I used strong words in criticizing Rabbi Scherman's translation of Genesis 4: 26, and later you will see that I used strong words to criticize his translation of Proverbs 30: 4. Thus, I felt compelled to let him read what I said about his work before publishing this book. I telephoned him and asked him if he would read the sections of this book that are critical of his work, and he agreed. I mailed him the manuscript for *His Name is Yahweh* and identified the sections he should read. One week later, I received this response from him:

> "My translation is based on Talmudic and Rabbinic sources going back hundreds—indeed, according to our faith—thousands of years. Judaism rejects your contention that the recipients of the Torah doctored its meaning, which pre-dates the Common Era."[28]

Rabbi Scherman did not challenge my interpretation of the Hebrew words used in Genesis 4: 26 and Proverbs 30: 4. Instead, he defended his translation by referencing "Talmudic and Rabbinic sources" that interpret the Tanach differently. Later, I will show that these non-Scriptural sources have been the source of much difficulty for the Jewish people. The Talmud, the Mishnah, and other non-Scriptural sources present and discuss Judaic laws and traditions, many of which defy Yahweh's written Word.

Jesus condemned the practice of relying on these "non-Scriptural sources" by saying that Jewish religious leaders had "invalidated the Word of God for the sake of tradition."[29] In other words, the tradition I'm addressing in this book is the same problem Jesus confronted almost 2000 years ago. It affects both Jews and

Gentiles because Yahweh's Name has been edited out of virtually every English Bible translation on the market today.

Although we must be respectful when saying or writing God's Name, He commanded us to declare His Name to the world, and in the end, His Name is Yahweh. For instance, Isaiah 12: 4 tells us to declare Yahweh's Name and to make His acts known among people everywhere so that His Name will be exalted. Declaring Yahweh's Name means more than simply saying it. Declaring His Name means to shout it out boldly so people everywhere can hear it and know that Yahweh is God.

The Bible is overflowing with instructions to declare Yahweh's Name. For example, it commands us to shout out His Name[30] and to tell the world about His righteousness,[31] His truth,[32] His works,[33] His mighty acts,[34] and His greatness.[35] It orders us to proclaim Yahweh's Name when we assemble together,[36] to our children,[37] and to heathen peoples.[38] It directs us to call on His Name,[39] to seek His Name,[40] to fear His Name,[41] to confess His Name,[42] to glorify His Name,[43] to sing praises to His Name,[44] and to bless His Name.[45]

It is absolutely clear that Yahweh commanded us to cry out with a loud voice and say, "Yahweh is our God! Look and see what He has done!" God wants us to know Him and His Name and to declare His Name to the world, and it is impossible to reconcile the unambiguous commands in the Bible with Rabbi Scherman's translation of Genesis 4: 26.

We Have Salvation in Yahweh's Name

Throughout the Scriptures, Yahweh made it clear that we have salvation in His Name. For example, consider these verses:

- Isaiah 12: 2—"Behold, God is my salvation, I will trust and not be afraid; for Adonai Yahweh is my strength and song, and He has become my salvation."

- Isaiah 43: 3—"For I am Yahweh your God, the Holy One of Israel, your Savior."

- Isaiah 43:11—"I, even I, am Yahweh, and there is no savior besides Me."

- Proverbs 18: 10—"The Name of Yahweh is a strong tower; the righteous runs into it and is safe."

- Joel 2: 32, Acts 2: 21, and Romans 10: 13—"And it will come about that whoever calls on the Name of Yahweh will be saved."

As you can see, in the Bible, we are told repeatedly that we have salvation in Yahweh's Name. Now consider Acts 4: 12:

"And there is salvation in no one else; for there is no other name under heaven that has been given among men by which we must be saved."

Since the Bible is consistent from Genesis to Revelation, the Name to which this verse refers must be Yahweh, and no other name. This assertion contradicts nothing God said in the Old Testament or the New Testament. In fact, as you read this book you will realize that both the Old and New Testaments make this point again and again, and due to its unparalleled importance, this is the most redundant message in the Scriptures.

Misguided Editorial Tradition Concealed Yahweh's Name in the Scriptures

You already know that the Name "Yahweh" has been edited out of most English Bible translations and that the titles "LORD" and "GOD" have been substituted where the Name "Yahweh" belongs. This misguided tradition prevents us from understanding the true meaning of many important Bible passages. The New Jerusalem Bible is a rare exception because it uses Yahweh's Name correctly most of the time.[46]

In this book, I have abandoned the practice of substituting "the LORD" for "Yahweh," "the Lord GOD" for "Lord Yahweh," and "LORD of hosts" for "Yahweh Master of legions." Thus, for the first time many of you will see what Yahweh told us in the Bible about His Name, and it will be an eye-opening experience.

How Did This Tradition Begin?

Yahweh's Name was used extensively in Israel until the mid-second century B.C., but during the reign of the Seleucid king Antiochus Epiphanes (175-164 B.C.) its use was abandoned.[47]

Epiphanes ruled the Syrian empire (or the Seleucid empire) that included Israel, and he tried to Hellenize the Jewish people (i.e., he tried to turn them into good Greeks) against their will. As a part of his Hellenization program, Epiphanes compelled the Jews under penalty of death to abandon Yahweh's Law. Additionally, he renamed the Temple of Yahweh and called it Zeus Olympius. Prostitution was commonplace inside the Temple during his reign.

Epiphanes' actions led to the Maccabean (or Hasmonaean) revolt and that led to the rise to prominence of three Jewish religious sects: the Pharisees, the Sadducees, and the Essenes. With the emergence of these three groups, new religious philosophies began to take hold. The Pharisee sect is the one most responsible for today's Rabbinic or Talmudic Judaism.[48]

The Pharisees were justifiably appalled by the persecution of Law-abiding Jews and by the attempts of Hellenizers to profane anything having to do with Yahweh and His Law. They decided to build "a wall around the Torah" to keep people from violating God's decrees. By this I mean they forbade things Yahweh did not prohibit in order to keep Jewish people from even coming close to breaking one of Yahweh's commands.

One of the so-called "walls" they constructed was the prohibition against saying the Name "Yahweh." To keep people from blaspheming God's Name or from using it in vain, the rabbis simply forbade its use except on special occasions—and then only by highly educated, religious Jews. Thus, Yahweh's Name never was lost. There have been people who knew the correct pronunciation of

God's Name all along, but over time His Name was lost for most people.

The rabbis in the mid-second century B.C. believed their actions were reasonable and justifiable. The Mishnah explains their rationale:

"In times of emergency it may be right to set aside or amend the commandments of God enjoined in His Law: the Law may best be served by breaking it."[49]

While their motives may have been pure, their ruling made illegal something Yahweh requires and had far-reaching consequences. It prevented people from using God's Name at all — the Name He commanded us to declare openly and loudly throughout the world and the Name in which we have salvation. They were not the first people to do this. The false prophets of Jeremiah's day did something similar, and this is what Yahweh said about them:

"How long are there to be those among the prophets who prophesy lies and are in fact prophets of their own delusions? They are doing their best, by means of the dreams that they keep telling each other, to make My people forget My Name, just as their ancestors forgot My Name in favour of Baal. Let the prophet who has had a dream tell it for a dream! And let him who receives a Word from Me, deliver My Word accurately!"[50]

Clearly, Yahweh was not pleased with the false prophets of Jeremiah's day, and He certainly did not condone the actions of the rabbis who took it upon themselves about 300 years later to remove His Name from circulation. Their ruling caused most people to forget God's Name, and some very knowledgeable Bible scholars have argued that it locked away the key to properly understanding the Scriptures. Some of them even suggest that Jesus was addressing this very problem when He said,

> "But woe to you scribes and Pharisees, hypocrites, because you shut off the kingdom of heaven from people; for you do not enter yourselves, nor do you allow those who are entering to go in."[51]

In Luke's Gospel, Jesus' statement reads this way:

> "Woe to you lawyers! For you have taken away the key of knowledge; you yourselves did not enter, and you hindered those who were entering."[52]

According to the Mishnah, "The blasphemer is not considered culpable unless he exactly pronounces the Name,"[53] and violating the ban against saying the Name "Yahweh" was considered a capital offense—i.e., punishable by death. The prescribed manner of death for people committing "blasphemy" was a combination of stoning and being hung on a tree.[54] As you will see later, the Bible reveals that Jesus was crucified for violating this prohibition or for simply saying the Name "Yahweh."

Yahweh Did Prohibit One Group From Using His Name—As Punishment

Although Yahweh commanded us to declare His Name to the world, there was a time when He forbade the use of His Name by the Jewish refugees in Egypt following the Babylonian captivity in 597 B.C.[55] But He intended this prohibition as punishment.

When Nebuchadnezzar conquered Judah, he allowed some of the poorer Jewish people to remain in the Promised Land rather than deporting them to Babylon.[56] He also appointed Gedaliah as governor,[57] but in a short while Baalis, the Ammonite king, sent Ishmael son of Nethaniah to murder Gedaliah.[58] Fearful that Nebuchadnezzar would retaliate by annihilating the Jewish people remaining in the land, they thought about fleeing to Egypt, but instead they asked Jeremiah to intercede with Yahweh on their behalf.[59]

Jeremiah did as they asked, and this is what Yahweh said:

"If you will only stay in this country, I shall build you and not overthrow you; I shall plant you and not uproot you, for I am sorry about the disaster I have inflicted on you. Do not be afraid of the king of Babylon, whom you fear now; do not fear him, Yahweh declares, for I am with you to save you and rescue you from his clutches. I shall take pity on you, so that he pities you and lets you return to your native soil.

But if you say: 'We will not stay in this country;' if you disobey the voice of Yahweh your God, and say: 'No, Egypt is where we shall go, where we shall not see war or hear the trumpet-call or go short of food; that is where we want to live;' in that case, remnant of Judah, listen to Yahweh's word: Yahweh Sabaoth, God of Israel, says this: If you are determined to go to Egypt, and if you do go and settle there, the sword you fear will overtake you there in Egypt, and there you will die."[60]

When Jeremiah gave them Yahweh's reply, they accused him of lying[61] and set off for Egypt, taking Jeremiah with them. In Egypt, they worshiped false gods thinking that they were prosperous in Israel while they venerated idols.[62] They did not realize that Yahweh inflicted the Babylonian disaster on them for worshipping false gods, among other things.

Jeremiah confronted them in Egypt and warned them to abandon this vile practice, but they were stubborn and refused to listen. Thus, Yahweh said,

"I swear by My great Name…that My Name will no longer be uttered by any man of Judah throughout Egypt; no one will say: 'As Lord Yahweh lives.'"[63]

As you can see, Yahweh prohibited a specific group of people from using His Name for a particular time. He was punishing them for disobeying Him, for worshipping false gods, and for profaning His Name. Eventually, most of the Jewish people who fled to Egypt for safety were killed in Egypt by Nebuchadnezzar's army, just as Yahweh foretold. It should be clear that God will not tolerate our willful disobedience or our profaning His great Name—Yahweh.

With this information as background, consider this perspective on the prohibition against writing or saying Yahweh. The writers of the "Talmudic and Rabbinic sources" referred to by Rabbi Scherman institutionalized a punishment Yahweh imposed on an idolatrous group of Jewish people who were violating His Word and His specific commands delivered to them by His prophet Jeremiah. Read Yahweh's Word and search for even a hint that He intended for them to do that. If you do, you will not find it because it does not exist. Whether or not their motives were pure, they dishonored, distorted, and defiled God's Word by incorporating as an integral part of their tradition a punishment from Yahweh intended for a specific group for a particular time. What's more, virtually every modern English Bible translation on the market today has repeated this dreadful error.

Prohibiting the Use of God's Name is Wrong

As you now know, the prohibition against saying or writing God's Name is a man-made tradition that has been handed down through the generations for more than 2000 years, ostensibly to show honor and respect for His Name. It is NOT a directive from Yahweh, and you can be certain of this fact. It is not respectful to ignore God's Word, and it is dangerous, reckless, and foolish to impose an injunction against something Yahweh explicitly commands us to do. To believe otherwise makes no sense.

Even so, many people believe that saying or writing Yahweh's Name puts a person at risk of violating the third Commandment. Exodus 20: 7 says,

"You shall not take the Name of Yahweh your God in vain, for Yahweh will not leave him unpunished who takes His Name in vain."[64]

The Hebrew word translated as "vain" in this verse is shav (shawv). It means to use God's Name in a destructive, deceptive, or false manner. It can also mean to misuse His Name. This is not a prohibition against saying it or writing it. It simply means that we must be careful and honest when using the Name "Yahweh." Additionally, Leviticus 24: 11 says that the penalty for blaspheming His Name is death. The Hebrew word translated as "blaspheme" in this verse is naqab (naw-kab'), and it means to curse God's Name or to use it in a way that is incomplete, dishonest, or deceptive. These two verses tell us that even though Yahweh bestowed upon us the privilege of sharing His Name with the world, we must do it properly.

Tradition is a Huge Obstacle

I have talked with many Jewish people about Yahweh. With few exceptions, those who recognize His Name refuse to say it because of tradition, and they are not shy about admitting that tradition is the only reason they refrain from using God's Name.

I searched for a way to depict their logic, and this is what I came up with. At the top of the next page I have shown how I think most Jewish people see their tradition placed side-by-side with Yahweh's indisputable commands in the Tanach concerning the use of His Name:

Tradition

For most Jewish people, tradition is bigger, bolder, and more important than Yahweh's Word. They ignore Yahweh's commands and hold fast to tradition apparently without giving the consequences any consideration at all.

The notion that tradition plays a more important part in the daily lives of Jewish people than the Tanach is deeply embedded in the Mishnah. It contains the Talmudic laws that govern every aspect of Jewish life, and this is what the Mishnah says about this question:

"Greater stringency applies to the words of the Scribes than to the Torah. If a man said, 'There is no obligation to wear phylacteries,' so that he transgresses the word of the Torah, he is not culpable; but if he said, 'There should be in them five partitions,' so that he adds to the words of the Scribes, he is culpable."[65]

According to Bible scholar Herbert Danby,

"The Mishnah, in other words, maintains that the authority of those rules, customs, and interpretations which had accumulated around the Jewish system of life and religion was equal to the authority of the Written Law itself, even though they found no place in the Written Law. This, again, is but an assertion...that side by side with the written code there exists a living tradition with power to interpret the written code, to add to it, and even at times to modify it or ignore it as might be needed in changed circumstances, and to do this authoritatively. Inevitably the inference follows that the living tradition...is more important than the Written Law, since the 'tradition of the elders,' besides claiming an authority and continuity equal to that of the Written Law, claims also to be its authentic and living interpretation and its essential complement."[66]

Yahweh will not condone our willful disobedience and our attempts to edit His Word to make it comply with our personal preferences and traditions. To believe otherwise is foolish. And make no mistake about this fact. Removing God's Name from the Scriptures and substituting titles in its place are just as wrong. So be careful before criticizing Jewish people for their disobedience in this regard because Christians are just as guilty as they are, and neither group has a good excuse.

Excuses People Use to Justify Not Calling God by His Name

Reducing the risk of using God's Name in vain or blaspheming His Name are the two most logical reasons advanced for not saying it or writing it. However, over the centuries people have come up with many more so-called "justifications" for not using His Name. They include the following:

- It is too sacred.
- We are not required to use it.
- It has no real value.

- Yahweh is a Hebrew Name, and people who do not speak Hebrew are not required to use it.
- Only Jews are required to use the Name "Yahweh."
- Jesus and His disciples did not use the Name "Yahweh" so we are not required to use it either.
- The correct pronunciation of God's Name has been lost over time.
- Jehovah is the Name for God most commonly used today, and it is sufficient and appropriate.
- God knows when we are addressing Him so the name we use is unimportant.
- God has not convicted me personally about the importance of using the Name "Yahweh."
- Moses was the first person to use the Name "Yahweh" so the Name itself is not eternal.[67]

These are just a few of the many excuses people have come up with to defend their practice of not using God's Name, and none of them stand up under careful scrutiny. For instance, while it is true that Moses took Yahweh's Name to the Children of Israel when they were in bondage in Egypt, Enosh—Seth's son and Adam's grandson—invoked His Name shortly after the creation. In chapter 10, you will see that Jesus and His disciples used Yahweh's Name, and the Psalms talk repeatedly about the importance of declaring His Name. Further, no one should require Yahweh to convict them personally about the importance of obeying each explicit command in the Scriptures. We should obey Him because we love Him. In fact, there is no good excuse for disobeying God, and He commanded us to declare His Name to the world. That much is certain.

Are You Ready to Embrace Yahweh's Clear Instructions?

Misguided tradition concealed Yahweh's Name from us for centuries, but it was right in front of us all the time shrouded by titles that Yahweh never intended as substitutes for His Name. God's Word makes it clear that we are supposed to know His Name, to call Him by His Name, and to tell others about Him by Name.

The Scriptures make it clear that Yahweh condemns anything that contradicts His Word. Therefore, not using God's Name is one tradition we should abandon—and the sooner the better. I'll go even further. Since the Bible says repeatedly that "everyone who calls on the Name of Yahweh will be saved"[68] and that "there is no other name under heaven that has been among men by which we must be saved,"[69] ignoring this message is foolish and dangerous.

Other Names for Yahweh

Exhibit 2.1 presents several Names for Yahweh and their meanings.[70] Each Name reveals an attribute of His character. For example, He is Elohim (God), Adonai (Lord), and El Shaddai (God Almighty). But His Name is Yahweh. Further, Yahweh will share the title "god" with anything—even a piece of wood or a rock. He will share the title "lord" with anyone. Some of the most evil people in the history of the world were called "lord." But Yahweh will not share His Divine Name with anyone. In due course, the importance of distinguishing between Yahweh and any so-called "god" will become obvious to everyone. There is One God, and His Name is Yahweh.

Exhibit 2.1
Several Names for Yahweh Found in the Bible

- **Elohim**—Strong One. It is used when referring to Yahweh or to a pagan god. When it refers to Yahweh, it is translated as "God," and when it refers to a pagan god it is translated as "god." Elohim is a plural word that suggests majesty.

- **Adonai**—Lord or Master of all. It is used when referring to Yahweh or to men. When it refers to Yahweh, it is translated as "Lord," and when it refers to men it is translated as "lord." Adonai suggests a master-servant relationship.

- **El Gibbor**—Mighty God. A powerful Warrior God who protects and defends His people.

- **El Elyon**—God Most High or strongest Strong One.

- **El Roi**—the Strong One who sees.

- **El Shaddai**—Almighty God. It means sufficient or enough and refers to God as the One who sets constraints or limits in the universe.[71]

- **El Olam**—Everlasting God.

- **Yahweh Yireh**—Yahweh will provide.

- **Yahweh Nissi**—Yahweh our Banner.

- **Yahweh Shalom**—Yahweh our Peace.

- **Yahweh Sabaoth**—This Name is translated in most Bibles as "LORD of hosts," and it refers to Yahweh as the Leader of a great army. The Tanach interprets this Name as "HASHEM Master of Legions."

- **Yahweh Maccaddeshcem**—Yahweh our Sanctifier.

- **Yahweh Raah**—Yahweh our Shepherd.

- **Yahweh Tsidkenu**—Yahweh our Righteousness.

- **Yahweh El Gmolah**—Yahweh God of Recompense or Yahweh our Reward.

- **Yahweh Shammah**—Yahweh who is present.

- **Yahweh Raphah**—Yahweh our Healer. A literal translation of this Name is Yahweh our doctor.

Chapter 3
Yahweh Declares Himself to the World

The primary purpose of the Exodus was to tell the world who God is by Name. It was no coincidence that He chose Egypt as the country from which to deliver His people. At that time, Egypt was the lone superpower; pharaoh was the most powerful person in the world; and Egypt's many gods were recognized throughout the known world. Yahweh wanted to establish a written record about Him and His sovereignty. During the Exodus, He was going to make it clear that nations, leaders of nations, so-called "gods," viruses, bacteria, insects, and even the forces of nature are subservient to Him. Jewish people call that written record the Torah and Christians refer to it as the Pentateuch, or the five books of Moses: Genesis, Exodus, Leviticus, Numbers, and Deuteronomy.

The Exodus also illustrates Yahweh's salvation. By delivering His people from bondage in Egypt, Yahweh demonstrated His power to save under the most adverse conditions imaginable. Literally, He can reach down and pluck His people out of danger and then inflict punishment on His enemies with laser-guided precision. Nothing is impossible for Him.

The Exodus Begins

As the book of Genesis comes to an end, the Children of Israel are moving to Egypt because of a famine in the Promised Land. Joseph had been brought to Egypt as a slave, and he eventually became viceroy or prime minister, a position that was second only to Pharaoh. In that capacity, he was able to provide for the Children of Israel, and they were treated well and prospered while Joseph was alive.

According to Rabbi Phillip Sigal, the pharaoh in Egypt at the time of Joseph's arrival was probably from the Hyksos line, and many Hyksos were Semites—as were the Children of Israel. Sigal says,

> "It is conceivable that the pharaoh of Joseph's period welcomed the Hebrews to his kingdom because he was one of the Hyksos and a Semite like themselves. When the Hyksos were overthrown, the new Egyptian monarch, regarding the Hebrews as consorts of the Hyksos, and therefore enemies, proceeded to enslave them."[72]

Yahweh Initiates the Exodus

The events described in the book of Exodus take place about 300 years after Joseph's death. As Exodus begins, a pharaoh had come to power in Egypt who had not known Joseph. He was concerned because he thought the Hebrews, who had grown in number to several million people, could turn against Egypt if enemies invaded the country and possibly could help to bring about her defeat. Thus, he decided to enslave the Children of Israel, and he put them to work making bricks to build cities and temples that were needed as Egypt grew and prospered.

The Hebrew people continued to increase rapidly in number despite their difficult circumstances. Thus, Pharaoh decided to kill their male children at birth. Moses was born during this time, and Pharaoh's daughter spared his life when she found him floating in a basket in the Nile River. She brought him into Pharaoh's house and raised him as her own son.

Yahweh protected Moses, and He arranged things so that his real mother became his wet nurse. She must have taught Moses about his heritage as an Israelite because when he was 40 years old, Moses decided to forego the life of luxury that he could have lived as the son of Pharaoh's daughter, and he attempted to rescue his Hebrew relatives.

One day he got involved in a dispute between an Egyptian taskmaster and a Hebrew slave, and he killed the taskmaster. When news of the incident reached Pharaoh, he ordered Moses' execution. Thus, Moses fled to the Land of Midian which is known today as Saudi Arabia.

While living in Midian, Moses married the daughter of the priest of Midian and began raising a family. He worked for his father-in-law (Jethro) as a shepherd of his flocks, and he spent long hours in the wilderness grazing sheep. When he was 80 years old, Moses met Yahweh on Mount Sinai.

Yahweh Meets Moses on Mount Sinai

Exodus 3: 2 says that the Angel of Yahweh appeared to Moses as a blaze of fire in a bush that was not consumed, and Exodus 3: 4

says that the Angel of Yahweh is Yahweh. Keep this fact in mind because the Angel of Yahweh is the personification and manifestation of Yahweh, and we refer to Him as the Messiah.

Moses turned aside to take a close look at the bush. He could have simply looked at it from a distance in amazement, or he could have run away from it since it was such an unusual, and possibly frightening, sight. Instead, he walked right up to the bush, and he got so close to it that Yahweh stopped him and told him to take off his shoes because he was walking on holy ground.[73] The ground was holy because of Yahweh's presence.

Yahweh called out to Moses from the burning bush and said,

"I am the God of your father, the God of Abraham, the God of Isaac, and the God of Jacob."[74]

When he realized who was talking to him, Moses hid his face because he was afraid to gaze at God. Moses' mother had probably taught him about God's awesome power and about His absolute purity. He knew that compared to God he was a filthy wretch.

Yahweh told Moses that He was sending him as His emissary to the Children of Israel and to Pharaoh. He also told Moses that He would deliver the Israelites from bondage in Egypt personally and take them to the land He promised to give Abraham and his descendants.

At first Moses was reluctant to assume this responsibility perhaps because he had tried to help his Hebrew relatives 40 years earlier, and they had asked Him, "Who made you a prince or a judge over us?"[75] When they asked him this question, Moses did not know how to respond.

In all likelihood, Yahweh had been working in Moses' life at that point, and he understood what he was supposed to do. However, he did not understand the details. He did not know who was giving him the job or when he was supposed to do it. Forty years later on Mount Sinai speaking from a burning bush, Yahweh told Moses about the role he would play in the redemption of the Children of Israel.

Yahweh Gives Moses His Orders and Reveals His Name

God ordered Moses to return to Egypt and tell the Children of Israel,

"Yahweh, the God of your fathers, the God of Abraham, the God of Isaac, and the God of Jacob, has sent me to you."[76]

Once the Children of Israel knew who had sent him, God assured Moses they would respond positively to his message. Then He said,

"...this (Yahweh) is My Name forever, the Name by which I am to be remembered from generation to generation."[77]

This is an important point. The very first command Yahweh gave Moses was to tell the Children of Israel His Name. Obviously, He never intended for us to forget it because forever means "without end." God certainly did not want us to conceal His Name in the Scriptures by substituting the titles "LORD" and "GOD" in its place. People did that on their own initiative, and as I said before, Satan must have inspired them to do it.

At that moment, Yahweh could have instructed Moses to tell the Children of Israel not to say His Name, and if saying His Name had been a problem, He would have. He must have known how they would respond when they learned that Moses had come in His Name and that Yahweh was going to rescue them. His Name was about to spread through their community faster than a brush fire in the desert.

Yahweh's Name is important. It draws a sharp distinction between Him and every god created by men, and it identifies Him as the God of Abraham, Isaac, and Jacob. It also distinguishes between Him and any human being called lord. Yahweh is not a god or a lord. He is the One true God and the Lord and Master of all creation.

Moses Goes to Pharaoh

After Moses delivered God's message to the Israelites, he went to Pharaoh and told him that Yahweh, "the God of Israel,"[78] had said to let His people go to serve Him. Pharaoh must have been amused with Moses because he had fled from Egypt 40 years earlier, and now he was back giving orders. The Egyptians believed Pharaoh was god on earth. In his eyes, Moses was nothing and the Children of Israel were less than nothing, except for the fact that he wanted them to continue making bricks.

Pharaoh looked at Moses and arrogantly said,

"Who is Yahweh that I should obey His Voice and let Israel go? I do not know Yahweh."[79]

Pharaoh was right. He did not know Yahweh, and that was the problem. If he had known Yahweh, he never would have treated the Hebrew people so harshly, and now he decided to teach Moses a lesson by imposing an even heavier burden on them.

From that moment forward, he proudly proclaimed, they would be required to gather the straw used in brick making, but their daily quota would remain the same. Until that time, the Egyptians provided the straw, and the Hebrews made the bricks. Thus, Pharaoh made their backbreaking task even more difficult. He did not realize it, but he was begging Yahweh to teach him a lesson.

The Children of Israel were incensed when Pharaoh increased their workload, and they let Moses know it. They blamed him because he was God's emissary. He had told them that God would deliver them, but instead of setting them free, God allowed Pharaoh to punish them severely even though they had done nothing wrong.

Moses was dumbfounded, and he presumptuously told God,

"Ever since I came to Pharaoh to speak in Your Name, he has done harm to this people, and You have not delivered Your people at all."[80]

Yahweh's response to Moses is revealing. He simply told Moses to give the Children of Israel this explanation:

"I am Yahweh, and I will bring you out from under the burdens of the Egyptians, and I will deliver you from their bondage. I will also redeem you with an outstretched arm and with great judgments. Then I will take you for My people, and I will be your God; and you shall know that I am Yahweh your God, who brought you out from under the burdens of the Egyptians. I will bring you to the land which I swore to give to Abraham, Isaac, and Jacob, and I will give it to you for a permanent possession; I am Yahweh."[81]

The essence of God's explanation is this: "I am Yahweh." In truth, "I am Yahweh" says it all. These verses hint at the importance of God's Name. In some ways, the significance of His Name is a mystery because most of us don't place much weight on names, but God does. He wants us to know that His Name sets Him apart. Yahweh is the Sovereign Lord of the universe—a fact that Pharaoh is about to learn.

The Ten Plagues

The ten plagues were a ten-part lesson designed to teach Pharaoh, everyone in Egypt including the Israelites, and the rest of the world that Yahweh is the One and only God. Additionally, according to Charles Ryrie, they demonstrated Yahweh's power and the utter uselessness of these Egyptian gods:

- Plague 1—Hapi (thought to be the spirit of the Nile) and Khnum (thought to be the guardian of the Nile).
- Plague 2—Heqt (thought to have the form of a frog) and Hapi.
- Plague 3—It's not clear in this plague which Egyptian god Yahweh is mocking.
- Plague 4—Uatchit (a god thought to appear as a fly).
- Plague 5—Ptah (thought to be the creator), the Apis bull (thought to be the incarnation of Ptah), and sacred cows in general.
- Plague 6—Sekhmet (a goddess thought to have healing powers) and Serapis (another god thought to have healing powers).
- Plague 7—Seth (thought to be the protector of crops) and Nut (thought to be the goddess of the sky).
- Plague 8—Isis (thought to be the goddess of life) and Seth.
- Plague 9—Ra (thought to be the sun god).
- Plague 10—Osiris (thought to be the giver of life) and Pharaoh (thought to be god on earth).[82]

Yahweh spoke the universe into existence,[83] and He could have destroyed Egypt by simply saying the word. But He did not. Yahweh wanted to teach this lesson, and He told Moses to write it down as a permanent record and as a warning to the world that disobedience is costly. At the end of the lessons, Pharaoh would die.

The First Plague—Turning Water Into Blood

God introduced the first plague with these words:

"By this you shall know that I am Yahweh."[84]

Moses instructed his brother Aaron to strike the Nile River with his staff, and it turned into blood. Then he told Aaron to stretch out his staff over the waters of Egypt, and all the streams and ponds in Egypt turned into blood. Pharaoh responded by asking his magicians to perform a similar sign through trickery, which they did. So Pharaoh hardened his heart, and he did not let God's people go.

The Second Plague—Frogs

Seven days later, God instructed Moses to deliver this message to Pharaoh:

"Let My people go, that they may serve Me. But if you refuse to let them go, behold, I will smite your whole territory with frogs."[85]

Pharaoh refused to obey God so Aaron stretched out his staff over the rivers, ponds and streams, and frogs came up out of the water and covered the whole land of Egypt. Pharaoh asked his magicians to perform a similar feat, and they did. But he summoned Moses immediately and promised him that he would let God's people go if Moses would ask Yahweh to remove the frogs from the land.

Moses allowed Pharaoh to choose the specific time the frogs would be removed to show him that "there is no one like Yahweh our God."[86] Pharaoh said tomorrow, and the next day the frogs were gone. Still, he refused to obey God.

The Third Plague—Gnats

God told Moses to instruct Aaron to stretch out his staff and strike the dust on the ground, and it would turn into gnats. He did it, and gnats covered the whole land of Egypt. Pharaoh's magicians tried unsuccessfully to copy this plague, and they went to Pharaoh and said, "This is the finger of God."[87] Even though Pharaoh's servants were beginning to understand that Yahweh is God, Pharaoh did not believe it, and he did not let God's people go.

The Fourth Plague—Flies

The first three plagues showed Pharaoh that Yahweh is God, and they were inflicted on the entire land of Egypt. However, Yahweh made an important distinction between the Israelites and the Egyptians during the fourth plague. He instructed Moses to tell Pharaoh that if he did not let His people go, swarms of insects would cover Egypt, but they would not swarm in Goshen where the Children of Israel lived. God said,

> "But on that day I will set apart the land of Goshen, where My people are living, so that no swarms of insects will be there, in order that you may know that I, Yahweh, am in the midst of the land. I will put a division between My people and your people. Tomorrow this sign shall occur."[88]

Once again, Pharaoh refused to let God's people go so insects swarmed throughout Egypt and devastated the land, but they did not swarm in Goshen. Pharaoh softened his position a bit after he saw the damage caused by the insects. He summoned Moses and told him that he could sacrifice to Yahweh, but he would have to do it in Egypt.

Moses responded by reminding Pharaoh that they intended to sacrifice cattle to Yahweh, and since the Egyptians believed cattle were gods, they might be attacked. Pharaoh reluctantly agreed to let them go, and Moses warned Pharaoh not to renege on his promise again. But it was no use. Pharaoh changed his mind and refused to let God's people go.

The Fifth Plague—Disease on the Livestock

Yahweh told Moses to warn Pharaoh that if he refused to let His people go "the hand of Yahweh will come with very severe pestilence on your livestock,"[89] but He said that the plague would affect none of the Hebrew livestock. God gave Pharaoh a day to make up his mind, but he still refused to let God's people go.

The next day, Yahweh inflicted a disease on the livestock in Egypt, and many of them died. Pharaoh sent his scouts to Goshen to find out if any of the Hebrew livestock had survived, and they reported back to him that all of their animals were alive and well. Still Pharaoh hardened his heart and refused to let God's people go.

The Sixth Plague—Boils on Men and Animals

God told Moses to take soot from a kiln and to throw it into the air in front of Pharaoh. Immediately, it became a fine dust that covered the land of Egypt, and it caused boils to break out on men and animals. Boils broke out so badly on Pharaoh's magicians that they could not stand in his presence. Still, he refused to accept Yahweh's authority. Pharaoh had a stubborn, unyielding heart, and Yahweh was furious with him. For the first time, Yahweh hardened Pharaoh's heart, and he did not let God's people go.

The Seventh Plague—Hail

God's anger was growing by the moment, and He said,

"This time I will send all My plagues on you and your servants and your people, so that you may know that there is no one like Me in all the earth. For if by now I had put forth My hand and struck you and your people with pestilence, you would then have been cut off from the earth. But, indeed, for this cause I have allowed you to remain, in order to show you My power, in order to proclaim My Name (Yahweh) through all the earth."[90]

God instructed Moses to tell Pharaoh and his servants to bring their animals in from the fields to safety because the next day He would send a hailstorm the likes of which they had never seen. By now, many Egyptians believed Moses and feared Yahweh, and they quickly brought their animals inside for cover. Those who did not believe God turned a deaf ear to His merciful warning, and they were destined to suffer great loss.

The next day the storm began, but it was not a typical hailstorm. Hail and fire (not lightning) mixed together rained down from heaven. Ordinarily, water and fire cannot coexist, but this time they did. In the deutero-canonical[91] book "Wisdom" that is included in Catholic Bibles, King Solomon[92] said this about the seventh plague:

> "Even more wonderful, in the water—which quenches all—the fire raged fiercer than ever[93]....For the whole creation, submissive to your commands, had its very nature re-created, so that your children should be preserved from harm[94]....A new attuning of the elements occurred, as on a harp the notes may change their rhythm, though all the while preserving the same tone; and this is just what happened[95]....fire reinforced its strength in water, and water forgot the power of extinguishing it...."[96]

What a sight that must have been. But in the land of Goshen where the Hebrew people lived there was no storm at all, and for the first time Pharaoh feared Yahweh. Hurriedly he sent for Moses and pleaded with him to ask Yahweh to call off the storm. He said, "I have sinned this time; Yahweh is the righteous one, and I and my people are the wicked ones."[97] Pharaoh told Moses that if Yahweh would stop the storm, he would let His people go.

Moses did as Pharaoh requested, but he knew Pharaoh's fear of Yahweh was normal human fear—not fear leading to obedience to

God. Sure enough, when the storm ended Pharaoh broke his word again.

With these plagues, Yahweh was demonstrating His sovereignty over the forces of nature and nature itself. He was also displaying His superiority over the most powerful principality in the world. No king or god can prevent from happening anything that God wills to happen. Yahweh is in control, and the Exodus experience became an enduring lesson for all of mankind about the omnipotence of Yahweh.

The Eighth Plague—Locusts

God told Moses,

"Go to Pharaoh, for I have hardened his heart and the heart of his servants, that I may perform these signs of Mine among them, and that you may tell in the hearing of your son, and of your grandson, how I made a mockery of the Egyptians and how I performed My signs among them, that you may know that I am Yahweh."[98]

This would not be a normal locust infestation. They would come in such a massive swarm that they would literally cover the ground. Nothing is beyond Yahweh's reach: not insects, not bacteria, and not viruses. By this time, Pharaoh's servants were afraid of Yahweh, and they begged him to let God's people go. Pharaoh called for Moses and told him he could take the Hebrew men with him but that he would have to leave the women and children behind to ensure their return. Moses rejected Pharaoh's offer, and the locusts descended on Egypt.

The locusts devastated the remaining vegetation, and Pharaoh begged Moses to remove them. Again, he admitted he had sinned, and he promised to let God's people go. Yahweh caused a strong wind to blow the locusts out of Egypt, but when they were gone Yahweh hardened Pharaoh's heart. He did not let God's people go.

The Ninth Plague—Darkness

Without notifying Pharaoh in advance, God told Moses to stretch out his hands and darkness would cover Egypt for three days. It was not ordinary darkness, though. It might have been a severe sandstorm, and it could have been darkness along with thick, moist air. Some people have speculated that ashes from the volcano on the Greek island of Santorini may have caused the darkness following a stunning eruption at about the time of the Exodus, but no one knows for sure. This much is certain. Pharaoh knew that his chief god, Ra the sun god, was obliterated for three days and that the people of Egypt were angry with him for exposing them needlessly to Yahweh's unrelenting hand.

Pharaoh called for Moses and told him to take all his people with him, but to leave the animals in Egypt. Again, Moses refused Pharaoh's offer because they needed the animals to make sacrifices to Yahweh. God hardened Pharaoh's heart once more, and he did not let His people go.

The Tenth Plague—The Death of the First-Born or Passover

The tenth plague was different from all the others because this time Yahweh targeted the first-born of every living creature. It would touch every home in Egypt, including Pharaoh's house. The tenth plague was different in these respects as well:

- Yahweh came in Person to execute it.[99] He used the tenth plague to demonstrate His sovereignty over life and death and to show Pharaoh, Egypt, and the rest of the world that there are consequences for rebellion against Him.

- Yahweh used it to re-emphasize that He "makes a distinction between Egypt and Israel."[100] In a broader sense, He was showing that He differentiates between His people and everyone else.

- Yahweh used the tenth plague, or Passover, to teach us a lesson about redemption, and He commanded us to celebrate Passover yearly forever.[101]

Passover is the day Yahweh redeemed His people, when He passed over their houses and spared them from the death penalty. But the penalty for sin is death. God told Adam that he would surely die if he disobeyed Him,[102] and God cannot go back on His Word. The blood of the Passover lamb on the doorposts and lintels of their houses was, and still is, symbolic of the sacrifice Yahweh made to secure our salvation. In other words, Passover is not just about redemption from bondage in Egypt. In a larger sense, it is about redemption from bondage to sin, and that is why He commanded us to celebrate it every year forever.

God told Moses,

"This month shall be for you the beginning of months, it shall be for you the first of the months of the year. Speak to the entire assembly of Israel, saying: On the tenth of this month they shall take for themselves—each man—a lamb or a kid for each father's house, a lamb or a kid for the household. But if the household will be too small for a lamb or kid, then he and his neighbor who is near his house shall take according to the number of people; everyone according to what he eats shall be counted for the lamb or kid. An (singular) unblemished lamb or kid, a male, within its first year shall it be for you; from the sheep or goats shall you take it. It shall be yours (your lamb) for examination until the fourteenth day of this month; the entire congregation of the assembly of Israel shall slaughter it in the afternoon. They shall take some of its blood and place it on the two doorposts and on the lintel of the houses in which they will eat it. They shall eat the flesh on that night—roasted over a fire—and matzos; with bitter herbs shall they eat it."[103]

Yahweh refers to the Passover lamb as "a lamb" three times. He told them to take "a lamb" for each household, and if a household was too small for "a lamb," He told them to combine families and share "a lamb." Everyone will have enough, and no one will have too much. This is fundamental to God's plan for redemption and salvation. Next, God refers to it as "the lamb"—the unblemished lamb. Then, God refers to "the lamb" as "your personal lamb":

"It (the lamb) shall be yours (your lamb) for examination until the fourteenth day of this month."[104]

Yahweh told the Children of Israel to take "the lamb" into their houses for four days. During the four-day period, it becomes "your lamb." You get to know it. It becomes part of your family. You learn about its character and disposition. In every sense of the word, it becomes "your lamb." Yahweh's redemption is personal as well. He made a sacrifice for you, and He is your Lamb.

Finally, Yahweh told them to slaughter their personal lamb on the afternoon of the 14th. It was as if they were slaughtering a member of their own family. The children knew and loved their lamb, and they probably cried when it was slaughtered. Yes, this lamb is your lamb, and it is dying for your salvation. Your Lamb's blood is the only thing that saves your life.

To redeem us and to atone for our sins, the unblemished Passover Lamb of God had to die. He had to pay the price for our sins in order to save us. This is the most important message contained in the Scriptures. Yahweh explained the literal meaning of Passover to Isaiah this way: "Yahweh inflicted on Him the iniquity of us all,"[105] and He is our "guilt offering."[106] The Person about whom Yahweh is speaking in Isaiah is the Messiah, and He took the penalty for our sins upon Himself. As you will see later, this Person is the personification and manifestation of Yahweh.

Yahweh is Sovereign

Pharaoh ignored God again and again, and finally God had enough of his rebellion and disobedience. He came down from heaven and went through the land of Egypt killing the first-born of men and animals in homes that were not covered by the blood of the Passover lamb.

As I said at the beginning of this chapter, the Exodus tells about Yahweh revealing His sovereignty and His salvation to the world. His Name is the Name that is above every name and in His Name alone there are redemption and salvation. That is exactly what Isaiah meant when he said,

> "Give thanks to Yahweh, declare His Name, make His acts known among the peoples; declare that His Name is exalted. Make music to Yahweh, for He has acted with grandeur; make this known throughout the world. Exult and shout for joy, O inhabitant of Zion, for the Holy One of Israel is great in your midst!"[107]

An Ancient Egyptian Document May Describe the Exodus

An Egyptian who lived during the time of the Exodus may have preserved a record of the Exodus for us. A document called The Ipuwer Papyrus describes a time in Egypt when the country was in total chaos. It was written shortly after the Exodus as a poem, and many people believe it is a work of fiction, and it may be. However, it reads as though it were an eyewitness account of the Exodus, and it describes what life in Egypt must have been like after Yahweh finished demonstrating His awesome power to the Egyptians. For example,

- It mentions a large group of "foreigners" who lived and worked in the delta region of Egypt, or Goshen. The Children of Israel were foreigners, and they lived in Goshen.

- It says that the Nile River turned into blood and that many Egyptians died as a result.

- It laments the destruction of the land, including all the timber and grain in Egypt, and it grieves about a severe shortage of building material and food.

- It talks about the sudden and unexpected death of the king and a large number of noblemen, a possible reference to the destruction of Pharaoh and his army in the Red Sea.

- It talks about Egypt being a leaderless society and about crime being out of control throughout the country. If Pharaoh and his army had been destroyed, we would expect criminal activity in Egypt to increase because the army, which was also the police force, was not around to prevent it.

- It says, "What the ancestors foretold has happened."[108] Joseph foretold the Exodus hundreds of years in advance, and he instructed his brothers to take his bones with them when they left Egypt. It is reasonable to assume that the

Egyptians were familiar with Joseph's prophecy and his instructions to his brothers.

Probably the most interesting statement in The Ipuwer Papyrus is this chilling refrain: "If I knew where god is I would serve him." This line is remarkable because the Egyptians did not believe in a god. They believed in many gods. Only Joseph and the Children of Israel believed in One God.

It is reasonable to assume that the people in Egypt were thoroughly familiar with Yahweh by the time the Children of Israel departed, because He had destroyed their land and their leaders. He had upset their world in ways we can't imagine, and everyone alive in Egypt, Hebrew or Egyptian, knew that the God of Israel is sovereign. Thus, it should come as no surprise to anyone that after the Exodus some of the Egyptians who survived the onslaught from Yahweh longed to know more about Him.[109]

Yahweh's Message is Crystal Clear

After examining Yahweh's message in the book of Exodus, it's impossible for me to understand the logic of those who took it upon themselves to remove His Name from the Scriptures. The rabbis who built a wall around the Torah in the mid-2nd century B.C. must have thought they were doing a good thing when they forbade the use of God's Name, but in reality, they prevented His people from obeying Him. Likewise, the editors of the King James Version, the New American Standard Bible, the New International Version, and most other English Bible translations must have believed they were following a good precedent, but they were not. At this moment, most

Christians don't even know the Name of their God. This is not just unfortunate. It is wrong.

The excerpts from the book of Exodus that I've discussed in this chapter make it clear that Yahweh never intended for us to take His Name out of circulation or to substitute titles where it belongs in the Bible. He always wanted us to know Him by Name as our Savior, our Redeemer, and our God. Based on what the Bible says, arguing against these facts makes no sense at all. It's time for us to tell the world who God is by Name.

Tradition is a powerful force, but Yahweh's commands pertaining to His Name are as plain as day. So the question is this. Will we obey Yahweh or hold fast to tradition despite what He says? I know my answer. Do you know yours?

Chapter 4
Yahweh is Holy

After the tenth plague and the death of his own son, Pharaoh finally agreed to let Moses take the Children of Israel out of Egypt along with all their animals. He must have been confused or in a state of shock because he asked Moses to bless him before leaving.[110] Even though it appeared as if Pharaoh had finally come to his senses, he was destined to change his mind again and pay the ultimate price.

Yahweh had promised Moses that the Hebrew people would not depart empty-handed so they asked the Egyptians for gold, silver, and garments. After experiencing Yahweh's devastating wrath, including the loss of at least one member in each family, the surviving Egyptians must have been thrilled that the Children of Israel were finally leaving because they complied with their request.

At the time of the Exodus, there were at least 2 or 3 million men, women, and children traveling with Moses. They had spent 430 years to the day in Egypt,[111] and they were leaving as a very rich people. One day earlier, they had been poor slaves. Some people mistakenly believe that Yahweh has no sense of humor, but He certainly does.

The shortest way to the Promised Land was along the coast of Egypt. At most, the journey should have taken two weeks, but

Yahweh was concerned that they would encounter hostility along that route and return to Egypt.[112] Thus, He instructed Moses to take them out by way of the wilderness which is the Sinai Peninsula. Yahweh accompanied the Children of Israel on their journey. By day He appeared as a pillar of smoke and by night as a pillar of fire to give them light. Thus, they could travel day and night without difficulty.[113]

The Trip to Mount Sinai

Yahweh warned Moses that He would cause Pharaoh to change his mind and pursue his former slaves, but He also told him,

"I will be glorified through Pharaoh and his entire army, and Egypt will know that I am Yahweh."[114]

Within a few days, Pharaoh and his servants regretted letting the Israelites go. Pharaoh decided to rally his troops, hunt the Jews down, and bring them back.

The chase was on. Pharaoh and his entire army were in hot pursuit while Moses and the Children of Israel, unaware that Pharaoh was following them, marched to Mount Sinai to meet Yahweh. Finally, after traveling miraculously for several days, both day and night, through the barren Sinai Peninsula, they reached the Red Sea. No sooner had they arrived than they saw Pharaoh and his army.

The Children of Israel were terrified when they saw the Egyptians approaching, and they blamed Moses for their predicament. They screamed at him in horror:

"Were there no graves in Egypt that you took us to die in the Wilderness? What is this that you have done to us to take us out of Egypt? Is this not the statement that we made to you in Egypt, saying, 'Let us be and we will serve Egypt'?—for it is better that we should serve Egypt than that we should die in the Wilderness!"[115]

For several days, Yahweh had led them through a desert wilderness. He was a column of smoke by day and a column of fire by night. This was not normal, and they knew Yahweh was traveling with them personally. Even more, they knew what He had done in Egypt. They had witnessed first-hand some of the most remarkable events in the history of mankind as Yahweh inflicted ten plagues on Egypt in rapid-fire succession.

They should have felt secure and confident because of Yahweh's presence and a great sense of anticipation as they traveled to meet Him. Instead, they were angry with Moses for endangering their lives. Yahweh had a lot of work to do teaching them to trust Him, and the story of Israel told in the Bible is the story of God teaching His children who He is and that we can trust Him.

Trapped Between Pharaoh and the Deep Red Sea

Moses was in a real bind. Pharaoh was pressing in on him from the rear, and the Red Sea prevented him from moving forward. On either side of him, mountains blocked any escape route, and to make matters worse, he had several million frightened men, women, and children screaming at him. Under these conditions, what could he do?

It was time to call on Yahweh, and that is exactly what Moses did. Yahweh's response was intriguing. He said, "Why are you crying out to Me? Tell the sons of Israel to go forward."[116] By posing a question, Yahweh was actually telling Moses that there was no need to ask for His help. Did God care about Moses and the Children of Israel? Of course He did. Then why did He not do something dramatic and save the day?

He would in the end, but first God wanted Moses to understand that He had already given him all the power and authority he needed to take care of the situation himself. To Yahweh, it was as if Moses were asking Him if he should provide assistance to an injured person. The answer was obvious. Yahweh expected Moses to exercise His power because He had delegated it to him.

Now that is worth knowing. Yahweh grants us His power and authority when we understand who gets the glory when we put them into effect. All He expects from us are faith in Him and obedience to His Word. Yahweh had done His part already, and it was Moses' turn to do his. Even in the face of tremendous adversity, Moses could be bold and confident because Yahweh was with him.

God said, "Tell the sons of Israel to go forward," and that is exactly what Moses did. Moses looked at the obstacle in front of him, raised his hands high in the air, and the Red Sea parted.

That must have been an amazing sight. The night was black as coal, and the only light came from the glow of Yahweh's Shekinah in the pillar of fire. Then suddenly a strong wind blew, and walls of water formed on either side of an underwater land bridge. The parting water revealed a gentle slope that everyone traveling with Moses could traverse. At that moment, the pillar of fire moved from in front of the Children of Israel to the rear blocking the path of the pursuing Egyptian army, and the Children of Israel strolled across the Red Sea on dry ground.

After they were safe on the other side, Yahweh inspired Pharaoh and his army to follow them into the depths of the sea. This is the way God explained it to Moses:

"As for Me, behold, I will harden the hearts of the Egyptians so that they will go in after them; and I will be honored through Pharaoh and all his army, through his chariots and his horsemen. Then the Egyptians will know that I am Yahweh...."[117]

When Pharaoh and his army were at the bottom of the sea, Yahweh told Moses to stretch out his hands over the sea again, and the waters came crashing down on them. They did not have Yahweh's protection, so all of them died—every single one of them.

That day, Yahweh saved the Children of Israel. They witnessed God performing a miraculous work, and they had faith in Him and in Moses, His servant.[118] They were ecstatic so they sang Yahweh a song. Below are a few lines from that song:

"I will sing to Yahweh, for He is highly exalted; the horse and its rider He has hurled into the sea. Yahweh is my strength and song, and He has become my salvation; this is my God, and I will praise Him; my father's God, and I will extol Him. Yahweh is a warrior; Yahweh is His Name[119]....In your lovingkindness You have led the people whom You have redeemed[120]....Yahweh shall reign forever and ever."[121]

Yahweh Teaches the Children of Israel Lessons on Holiness

It took Moses almost three months to lead the Children of Israel to Mount Sinai, and during that time Yahweh taught them several lessons. Actually, He taught the first lessons while they were in Egypt. The ten plagues He inflicted on Pharaoh and the Egyptians taught them that Yahweh is the One true God, that He is sovereign over everything in the universe including man and nature, and that He alone is in control of life and death. The tenth plague taught them that He is their Redeemer and their Savior.

The Red Sea crossing taught them that Yahweh is their Protector and that He will do extraordinary things to secure their safety if they have faith in Him. Before they reached Mount Sinai, they learned that Yahweh is their Provider. He turned bitter water into sweet drinking water to quench their thirst; He gave them manna from heaven every day to satisfy their hunger and taught them that they must learn to rely on Him daily for their provisions; and He showed them that He is their Warrior by defeating Amalek when he attacked the Children of Israel at Rephidim.

Finally, He poured out a river of water from a rock near the base of Mount Sinai so they had ample water to drink. All these lessons demonstrated that they could have faith in Yahweh, but they were mere preparation for a more advanced lesson. Yahweh was about to teach them what being holy means.

Moses was prepared to meet Yahweh when they reached Mount Sinai. He had spent 40 years in the Land of Midian as a shepherd quietly learning about God and His holiness. Then at the end of 40 years, Yahweh introduced Himself to Moses personally at the burning bush. The Children of Israel did not have 40 years to get ready. They were about to receive a crash course in God's holiness.

At Mount Sinai, Yahweh instructed Moses to tell the Children of Israel that He would descend on the mountain in two days[122] and that they should wash their clothes and prepare to witness His magnificent arrival. Washing their clothes was important and symbolic. During their time in Egypt, they had become dirty. They had picked up Egyptian traditions, customs, and beliefs, and they needed to be clean before Yahweh's arrival. God also told Moses to set up boundaries around the mountain so no one could touch it. When Yahweh's presence descended on Mount Sinai, only Moses was prepared to enter into close proximity with Him.[123]

Yahweh Descends on Mount Sinai and Gives the Ten Commandments

At the crack of dawn two days later, there was thunder and lightning, and a thick, dark cloud appeared over Mount Sinai. The people could hear a shofar (a ram's horn that has been hollowed out so it can be blown like a trumpet) sounding in the distance as the cloud descended to the top of the mountain.

The shofar grew louder and louder as the cloud approached, and the people were in awe of Yahweh. Many of them trembled in fear. The whole mountain was engulfed in smoke as Yahweh descended with fire and tremendous heat. Smoke billowed into the air while the mountain quaked and the sound of the shofar grew even louder. No one dared go near the mountain except Moses, and he spoke to Yahweh. God responded to him audibly with words that everyone could hear and understand.[124]

From the cloud Yahweh summoned Moses to the top of the mountain, and Moses climbed up to meet with Him. After Yahweh finished speaking with Moses, He told him to go back down and warn the people not to go near the mountain lest they die. When Moses reached the bottom of Mount Sinai, God proclaimed the Ten Commandments.

Jewish tradition states that everything was silent when Yahweh declared the Ten Commandments. This is the description of that moment in the rabbinic writings:

"When the Holy One, Blessed is He, presented the Torah at Sinai, not a bird chirped, not a fowl flew, not an ox lowed, not an angel ascended, not a seraph proclaimed, Holy. The sea did not roll and no creature made a sound. All the vast universe was silent and mute. It was then that the Voice went forth and proclaimed, I am HASHEM, your God!"[125]

In fact, Yahweh did not say, "I am HASHEM." He said, "I am Yahweh, your God!"[126] What came next may be the most powerful statements ever made, and they came directly from the mouth of Yahweh in the hearing of all the people gathered at the base of Mount Sinai. The only statements that even compare with the Ten Commandments are the ones Yahweh made when He created the universe. His Voice echoed through the air while the people listened in fear and awe.

The Ten Commandments are not suggestions. They are, in fact, commandments. The words themselves and the Voice of God annunciating them made that clear to everyone. Yahweh commanded us to obey His Law, and the Ten Commandments are the foundation of that Law. They are much more than edicts to follow, though. The Ten Commandments tell us about God's character and His holiness, and they are the stipulations of the covenant God made with us at Mount Sinai. He said,

"If you will indeed obey My Voice and keep My covenant, then you shall be My own possession among all the peoples, for all the earth is Mine."[127]

The second half of the book of Exodus (chapters 19 through 40) tells about God revealing Himself and His Law to His people, and it explains what it means to be God's people. Yahweh is holy, and if we want to be His people and have a personal relationship with Him, then we must be holy as well.

The book of Leviticus expands on God's Law by explaining in detail what we must do if we violate any portion of it. If we transgress even the smallest stipulation in the Law, we cease to be holy. Therefore, at the end of the day, the Law teaches us that our holiness depends entirely on God because no one except Yahweh can keep all the stipulations in the covenant without fail, and it teaches us that we need a redeemer. Only Yahweh is qualified to be our Redeemer.

The Ten Commandments, along with God's introductory declaration, are presented below. Read them carefully and understand that it is impossible for you or anyone else to obey them—any of them:

1. "I am Yahweh your God, who brought you out of the land of slavery. You shall have no other gods before Me.
2. You shall not make for yourself an idol.
3. You shall not take the Name of Yahweh your God in vain.
4. Remember the Sabbath day, to keep it holy.
5. Honor your father and your mother.
6. You shall not murder.
7. You shall not commit adultery.
8. You shall not steal.

9. You shall not bear false witness.
10.You shall not covet."[128]

The first five commandments focus on our relationship with Yahweh, and they conclude with the commandment to honor our father and mother. Clearly, God places great weight on honoring our parents, and every one of us is guilty of breaking this command. But we are guilty of worshipping other gods as well. You may be thinking, "I have never done that," but let me assure you that you have.

Consider this. When we get caught up in earning a living and making money, it is very easy to let our desire to create wealth become our idol. Today, many people who are facing retirement spend more time tracking their net worth than they spend with God. When this happens, money becomes our idol, and we are guilty of violating a commandment. Money cannot save us. Only Yahweh can do that. The assets we possess can depreciate to nothing, or virtually nothing, in a matter of days. Thus, we must place our faith in Yahweh and trust Him to take care of all our needs. Yahweh alone is our Provider.

Additionally, in the last few years scientific studies have shown that more than 66 percent of the people in the United States are overweight and that more than 33 percent of them are obese.[129] When our craving for food consumes our thoughts and actions, then food becomes our idol. How many people living in the United States today spend more time thinking about their next meal or snack than they spend thinking about God?

But anything can become an idol. The clothes we wear or our desire to be popular can consume our thoughts and energy just as easily as money and food. Yes, every one of us has worshiped other gods, and we need a redeemer.

The fourth commandment deals with the Sabbath, or Shabbat in Hebrew, and we are told to remember it and to keep it holy. To keep the Sabbath holy means "to consecrate it" or "to treat it as sacred." While most Christians recognize Sunday as the Sabbath, Jewish people identify Saturday as the Sabbath day. This is a controversial issue and one that deserves attention. However, it is not my purpose in this book to examine it, but others have addressed it in detail already.[130]

Laying aside the controversy surrounding the Sabbath day, you must admit that most people in the United States do not consecrate Saturday or Sunday, and they treat neither day as sacred. Life goes on as usual, and we do not give it a second thought. Rest assured that Yahweh gives it His attention, and He included this commandment for a reason. One day He will make this point clearly so that everyone understands.

The last five commandments focus on our relationship with each other. Looking at them, it is easy to conclude, for example, that I have not murdered so I am all right on that one. But Yahweh did not mean just the act of murder. He included our thoughts and attitudes as well. The command not to murder includes anger. If you are angry with someone, you are just one step away from committing the act of murder, so an angry thought makes you guilty of murder.[131]

Similarly, slander is a form of stealing. When you commit slander, you are taking one of the most precious possessions a person has—a good name. If you follow this logic and carry it through the prohibitions against adultery and coveting, for instance, you will see that every one of us has broken every commandment. Yes, each one of us needs a redeemer, and Yahweh is our only hope. He is the only One who has never violated any stipulation in His covenant with us, and He is the only One qualified to be our Redeemer.

The Children of Israel Instruct Aaron to Make a Golden Calf

After God spoke the Ten Commandments, Moses went back up on the mountain to receive additional instruction. He was with God for forty days and forty nights. When several days had passed, the people became concerned that Moses might never return, and they told Aaron to build a golden calf for them to worship.

It is preposterous to think that they believed the golden calf was Yahweh. They had witnessed God's mighty acts on their behalf, and they had heard Yahweh declare the Ten Commandments with their own ears. In all likelihood, they wanted Aaron to fashion an intermediary for them that could stand between them and God the way Moses had done. They probably asked Aaron to make a golden calf because they were familiar with the worship of cattle from their experience in Egypt. But the reason they asked Aaron to do it and the reason Aaron did it are unimportant. The fact is that within days of receiving the Ten Commandments, the whole congregation, including Aaron, had violated the first two commandments.

Yahweh was furious. The Children of Israel had not been able to keep His commandments for even a few days, and He was literally right there with them. His Shekinah was just a few hundred yards away from them on top of the mountain. God told Moses to stand aside so He could annihilate all of them and build a great nation through Moses' descendants.

Moses urged Yahweh to change His mind, to remember the covenant He made with Abraham, Isaac, and Jacob, and to have mercy on the people. In truth, Yahweh could have fulfilled every promise He made to the patriarchs by raising up a nation through Moses' seed, but Moses pleaded with God anyway. Then Moses presented an argument that demonstrated how much he loved God and how much he cared about protecting His holy Name:

> "Why should the Egyptians speak, saying, 'With evil intent He brought them out to kill them in the mountains and to destroy them from the face of the earth?'"[132]

In essence, Moses was reminding Yahweh that the ten plagues He inflicted on Egypt were a powerful message to Pharaoh and to the people of Egypt that Yahweh God is sovereign over everything in existence. If the Sovereign God and Creator of the universe were incapable of saving His people after He brought them out of Egypt, then the Egyptians (and people in other nations as well) would say about Him that He must not be a great God after all. They would also say about Him that He was not powerful enough to save them so He killed them instead, thus bringing dishonor to His Name.

God changed His mind partly because of Moses' plea and partly because He understood that no one can keep all of His commandments without fail. It is quite likely (in fact, it is almost certain) that He was simply testing Moses to see if he was up to the challenge of leading the Israelites. As their leader, he would have to stand in the gap between them and God many times. If Moses had failed to do it on this occasion, then he would not have been ready to lead God's people.

Those of us who have placed our faith in Yahweh are just like the Children of Israel. We want to go our own way and do our own thing. We would rather do what seems right to us than what we know God tells us to do. God calls this rebellion and disobedience — sin. Yahweh is holy, so His people must be holy and treat Him as holy. He set us apart for Himself, and He expects us to be distinct in the world—a people dedicated or consecrated to Him and recognizable because we are different. Yahweh expects us to be holy because He is holy, and when we behave in an unholy manner we profane His holy Name.

Yahweh actually told Ezekiel why He did not destroy the Children of Israel at the bottom of Mount Sinai:

"I acted for the sake of My Name, that it should not be profaned in the sight of the nations among whom they lived, in whose sight I made Myself known to them by bringing them out of the land of Egypt."[133]

God does not destroy us for the same reason—so that His Name will not be profaned in the sight of the nations. Yahweh is our only hope. He forgave us and He redeemed us because He loves us and because He wants to glorify His holy Name.

The Omnipotence of Yahweh on Display

The entire Exodus experience reveals the omnipotence of Yahweh. I can only speculate about many of the things He did for the Children of Israel as He led them out of Egypt and as He dwelt with them for 40 years in the wilderness, but a little speculation can be very helpful:

- While they traveled, the Children of Israel, who were at least 2 or 3 million strong, would have needed 1500 tons of food each day at a minimum. To bring them that much food, two freight trains each at least a mile long would have been required.

- They would have needed firewood for cooking and heating—or about 4000 tons of wood per day.

- If they only drank water, watered their animals, and washed a few dishes, they would have needed at least 11,000,000 gallons of water per day.

- If the Children of Israel had crossed the Red Sea in double file, it would have taken 35 days and nights to complete the crossing. For all of them to cross in one night, the land bridge had to be wide enough for them to walk across about 5000 abreast.

- When they camped, they needed an area about 750 square miles in size to handle all the people and the animals they had with them.[134]

Of course, these are just estimates, but they are reasonable given what we know. Neither Moses nor anyone else besides Yahweh could have provided everything the Children of Israel needed to survive in the wilderness for 40 years. That is why the Exodus remains such an important event in the history world to this day. It demonstrates that we serve the Omnipotent God who can, and will, take care of all our needs. The One who made water flow like a river from a rock in the desert will have absolutely no difficulty dealing with anything we encounter. We can have faith in Yahweh because nothing is impossible for Him.

The Wilderness Journey Comes to an End

When Yahweh led the Children of Israel out of Egypt, He could have taken them to the Promised Land in less than two weeks. Instead, the trip took 40 years. When they left Egypt, the Children of Israel were full of hope and anticipation about meeting Yahweh and entering the Promised Land. But only two Israelites (Joshua and Caleb) who were over the age of 20 when they started out got to their final destination. Why? The answer is sin.

The Israelites rebelled against Yahweh and broke His Laws again and again, but even more important than their willful disobedience was their lack of faith in Him. They simply would not trust Yahweh, and faith is the foundation of our relationship with Him.[135]

God allowed His people to die in the wilderness rather than permitting them to further pollute the Holy Land with their sinful ways. The people Yahweh drove out of the Promised Land to make room for the Israelites had polluted it already, and that is why they were being removed.[136] They had contaminated it with their "disgusting practices"[137] which had "filled it with filth from end to end."[138]

Joshua and Caleb were allowed to enter the Promised Land because they demonstrated faith in Yahweh, and that is what He requires. Since a single unfaithful act, no matter how insignificant it may seem, makes us guilty before Him and deserving of death, in the end the Bible teaches us that we need a redeemer and a savior.

Above all, Yahweh is holy. If we want to have an intimate relationship with Him, then we must be holy as well. To make us holy, Yahweh became a Man, suffered and died for us, and atoned for our sins by covering them with His own precious blood. He is our One and only Redeemer and Savior and our only hope.

Chapter 5
Yahweh has a Human Form

Yahweh has appeared to men and women in human form many times since the creation to declare His Word and to make certain that all of His promises are fulfilled. The first time we know Yahweh appeared in human form was when He walked in the Garden of Eden with Adam.[139] The Bible refers to Yahweh's human form as the Angel of the LORD. It refers to Him in other ways as well, but the fact that He has appeared in human form is evident from what He did and said and from people's reactions to Him. Further, since He never changes, Yahweh always has had a human form.

Later, I'll show that the human form of Yahweh is the Messiah, but in this chapter, I simply want to establish beyond any shadow of a doubt that according to the Bible many people throughout history have met with and spoken to Yahweh in Person. Abraham, Moses, and many others even shared meals with Him. If you believe God's Word, you'll find this information very compelling and impossible to refute.

There is some overlap between this chapter and the next one which deals with Yahweh's covenants and promises. Since Yahweh appeared in human form to make them, eliminating the overlap would have been virtually impossible, and besides, the Bible repeats

Yahweh's covenants and promises over and over again. I can think of no better example to follow.

Yahweh Appears to Abraham

Before Yahweh gave Abraham circumcision as a sign of the covenant, his name was Abram and his wife's name was Sarai. Later, He changed their names to Abraham and Sarah. I will refer to them by those names.

Abraham was born in Ur in the land of the Chaldees. Abraham's father took him, his wife Sarah, and his nephew Lot, and they went to Haran, a city that is located in Turkey. While he was in Haran, Yahweh told Abraham to take Sarah, Lot, and all his possessions and go to a land He would show him.[140] Abraham obeyed Yahweh, and when he arrived in the land of Canaan in a city called Shechem, Yahweh appeared to him in human form and said, "To your descendants I will give this land."[141]

Yahweh was talking about the land we know today as Israel, and that is why we call Israel the Promised Land. Yahweh promised to give Israel to Abraham and his descendants as a permanent possession. Although Abraham did not obey God perfectly, his heart was right before Him, and God used Abraham to bless all the nations of the world.

Yahweh Appears to Hagar

When Yahweh made the covenant with Abraham, Sarah had no children. She was desperate to have a child, and she asked Abraham to have intercourse with her maid, Hagar, so Hagar could give birth to a child for her. Abraham agreed. He had intercourse with Hagar, and she became pregnant.

When Hagar realized she had conceived, she despised Sarah and created a serious problem for Abraham. Evidently, Abraham was giving Hagar special attention because she was about to become the mother of his child (this child's name would be Ishmael), and Sarah believed Abraham's behavior was responsible for her attitude. She was furious, and she told Abraham,

> "May the wrong done me be upon you. I gave my maid into your arms, but when she saw that she had conceived, I was despised in her sight. May Yahweh judge between you and me."[142]

Not knowing exactly what to say, Abraham simply told Sarah that Hagar was still her maid and that she could do with her as she pleased. Afterwards, Sarah treated Hagar so harshly that she fled to the wilderness. Along the way, Yahweh appeared to her by a spring and said,

> "Hagar, Sarah's maid, where have you come from and where are you going?"[143]

She told Him she was running away from Sarah, and He said,

> "Return to your mistress and submit yourself to her authority[144] ....Moreover...I will greatly multiply your descendants so that

they shall become too many to count[145]....Then she called the Name of Yahweh who spoke to her, 'You are a God who sees (El Roi); for have I even remained alive after seeing Him?'"[146]

Did Yahweh actually appear to Hagar? Yes. First, He told her that He would greatly multiply her descendants. What angel can do that? Only Yahweh can. Furthermore, Hagar knew she had spoken directly to God. She called Him El Roi, the Strong One who Sees, and she seemed to be surprised that she did not die after having seen Him. Also, Hagar called the well at which He appeared to her "the well of the Living One who Sees me."[147] Yahweh did appear to Hagar, and she talked with Him in Person.

Yahweh Appears to Abraham Again

When Abraham was 99 years old, Yahweh appeared to him[148] and said,

"I am El Shaddai; walk before Me, and be blameless. I will establish My covenant between Me and you, and I will multiply you exceedingly."[149]

When Abraham saw Yahweh, he knew immediately that he was in the presence of the Almighty God, and he fell on his face before Him.[150]

Yahweh told Abraham that circumcision would be the sign of the covenant between them and that his wife Sarah would have a son through whom the covenant would pass to future generations. Abraham fell on his face and laughed[151] when God told him Sarah would have a son because Sarah was about 90 years old at the time—well past childbearing years. Ishmael, Abraham's son by Hagar, was 13 years old at the time, and Abraham asked Yahweh to fulfill His promise through Ishmael instead. But God said,

> "No, but Sarah your wife shall bear you a son, and you shall call his name Isaac; and I will establish My covenant with him...."[152]

Yahweh made it clear that His covenant would not pass through Ishmael. He was the product of Sarah's desire to have a son, Abraham's willingness to oblige Sarah, and Hagar's consent to become the mother of Abraham's child. They simply took it upon themselves to solve Sarah's problem. It is possible, even probable, that Abraham thought he needed to take matters into his own hands to fulfill Yahweh's promise to give the Promised Land to his descendants.

Isaac's birth was a miracle—a gift from God, and Yahweh spoke to Abraham face-to-face to emphasize that everything pertaining to the covenant was, and is, based on His promises and His desires. All God required from Abraham was faith in Him and obedience to His Word.

Although Yahweh made it clear that Isaac was the child of the covenant, He made several promises to Abraham about Ishmael:

> "As for Ishmael, I have heard you; behold, I will bless him, and will make him fruitful and will multiply him exceedingly. He

shall become the father of twelve princes, and I will make him a great nation. But My covenant I will establish with Isaac....When He finished talking with him, God went up from Abraham."[153]

Can there be any doubt that Yahweh appeared in Person to make these points? No.

Yahweh Tells Abraham about Isaac's Birth

Later, Yahweh and two angels appeared[154] to Abraham near Hebron, a city in present-day Israel. Abraham invited Yahweh to stay and share a meal with him, and He agreed. While they were eating,[155] Yahweh told Abraham that He would return in a year, and by that time Sarah would have a child.

Sarah was inside the tent listening, and she overheard the conversation. When she heard Yahweh say she would have a child, she laughed to herself saying,

> "After I have become old, shall I have pleasure, my lord being old also?"[156]

Yahweh knew Sarah's thoughts, and He said,

> "Why did Sarah laugh, saying, 'Shall I indeed bear a child, when I am so old?' Is anything too difficult for Yahweh? At the appointed time I will return to you, at this time next year, and Sarah shall have a son."[157]

Once again, Yahweh confirmed that He would fulfill His promises through Isaac—a child who had not been born yet. He concluded His conversation with Abraham by asking a question that every one of us should remember because the question is actually a statement. "Is anything too difficult for Yahweh?" The answer is NO.

Yahweh Appears to Isaac Twice

There was a famine in the land of Canaan, and Isaac was tempted to go down to Egypt where food was in abundant supply. But Yahweh appeared to Isaac in Person to confirm His promise and said,

> "Do not go down to Egypt; stay in the land of which I shall tell you. Sojourn in this land and I will be with you and bless you, for to you and to your descendants I will give these lands, and I will establish the oath which I swore to your father Abraham. I will multiply your descendants as the stars of heaven, and will give your descendants all these lands; and by your descendants all the nations of the earth shall be blessed; because Abraham obeyed Me and kept My charge, My commandments, My statutes and My Laws."[158]

Later, Isaac experienced problems with his neighbors who were concerned that his wealth was a threat to their security. They made life difficult enough for him to make him move on, and Isaac kept moving until he found a place where he and his family could live in peace. That place is called Rehoboth, and it means "plenty of room."[159]

From there Isaac went to Beersheba, and Yahweh appeared to him in human form and said,

> "I am the God of your father Abraham; do not fear, for I am with you. I will bless you, and multiply your descendants, for the sake of my servant Abraham."[160]

God told Isaac, "Do not fear." That statement suggests Isaac was afraid and that he needed reassurance from Yahweh. Thus, God appeared to him and repeated the message He has been giving His children since the beginning: "I am Yahweh, and I will watch over my Word to perform it. You can have faith in Me, and I will bless you if you obey Me."

Yahweh Appears to Jacob in a Dream

Isaac's first-born son, Esau, was willing to trade his birthright for a meal.[161] Since his birthright included the promise of the coming Messiah, in effect Esau traded the honor and privilege of being in the Messiah's lineage for a single meal because for a brief moment he was hungry. Self-gratification and sensual pleasure motivated Esau to trade away his part in the greatest gift ever bestowed on mankind, and God hated him for it before he was born.[162] Furthermore, God would not allow Esau to obtain the birthright of the first-born even though he wept bitterly when the time came for Isaac to bless his sons.[163] Obviously, he still wanted the blessing of the first-born, but he had treated it so lightly when he was younger that God would not allow him to have it.

Isaac loved Esau and intended to bestow the blessing of the first-born on him contrary to Yahweh's desire.[164] Rebekah, his wife, and Jacob, his second son, intervened to secure Isaac's blessing for Jacob. Many people have said that Rebekah and Jacob deceived Isaac and stole Esau's birthright, and maybe they did. But they did it with the blessing of God, and they kept Isaac from making a tragic mistake.

Before her sons were born, Yahweh told Rebekah that Jacob was the child of the promise,[165] not Esau. Consequently, Rebekah helped Jacob obtain the blessing of the first-born over Isaac's objections. When Esau learned what had happened, he was furious and threatened to kill his brother. Thus, Rebekah and Isaac urged Jacob to flee to Haran, to her relatives, and to take a wife from among her relatives. He obeyed his parents, and along the way he stopped to sleep at a place called Bethel. This Bethel is very likely Mount Moriah in Jerusalem,[166] not the town of Bethel in Israel today — a town about 12 miles north of Jerusalem.

While he was sleeping, Yahweh appeared to Jacob in a dream and said,

> "I am Yahweh, the God of your father Abraham and the God of Isaac; the land on which you lie, I will give it to you and to your descendants. Your descendants shall also be like the dust of the earth, and you shall spread out to the west and to the east and to the north and to the south; and in you and in your descendants shall all the families of the earth be blessed. Behold, I am with you and will keep you wherever you go, and

will bring you back to this land; for I will not leave you until I have done what I promised you."[167]

Yahweh Appears to Reassure Jacob

Many years later when Jacob returned to Canaan with his wives, his children, and all his belongings, he was afraid that Esau would still hold a grudge against him and kill his entire family. His faith in Yahweh at that time was not strong. He did everything that was humanly possible to protect his family from Esau, but he was still afraid that it would not be enough.

The night before he met Esau, Jacob separated himself from his family, and "a man wrestled with him until daybreak."[168] The Bible tells us that the Man was Yahweh and that He used this occasion to change Jacob's name to Israel.[169] Jacob knew that he had had a personal encounter, a wrestling match, with Yahweh, and he said, "I have seen God face to face, yet my life has been preserved."[170]

Yahweh allowed Jacob to win the wrestling match that night and said,

"....you have striven with God and with men and have prevailed."[171]

At that moment Jacob, whose name was now Israel, knew that God was on his side. If Yahweh had wanted to win the wrestling match, He could have with no trouble at all, but He was making a point. He was showing Jacob that he had nothing to fear because

God was with him. If Yahweh is involved, we can, and should, be fearless.

Yahweh Appears to Moses, Aaron, Nadab, Abihu, and 70 Elders of Israel

After Yahweh gave the Ten Commandments, He instructed Moses to bring his brother Aaron, Nadab, Abihu, and 70 elders from Israel up to meet with Him on Mount Sinai. They climbed to the top of the mountain, and they looked upon Yahweh[172] while they ate a meal in His presence.[173] The Tanach describes Yahweh's appearance this way:

> "They saw the God of Israel, and under His feet was the likeness of sapphire brickwork, and it was like the essence of the heaven in purity. Against the great men of the Children of Israel, He did not stretch out His hand—they gazed at God, yet they ate and drank."[174]

This depiction is almost identical to the description of the Messiah in the book of Revelation.[175] The significance of this fact will become apparent later when I discuss the Messiah.

Yahweh Appears to Balaam

When Moses led the Children of Israel out of Egypt, they were a very large group. At the very least there were 2 or 3 million people, and there may have been as many as 6 million people, traveling with Moses. The people in the nations through which the Children of Israel walked along with their herds and flocks were terrified. A group that large easily could consume virtually all the vegetation in the land and drink most of the available fresh water. The people in those nations did not know that Yahweh miraculously provided food and water for His children.

As they marched toward the land of Moab, which is in Jordan today, they fought with and defeated the King of Arad, the King of the Amorites, and the King of Bashan. When they reached Moab, the Moabite King, Balak, sent for Balaam because he was known far and wide as a man who possessed the ability to bless or to curse. Balak wanted Balaam to curse Israel and to destroy them. Yahweh appeared to Balaam in Person and said,

"You shall not curse the people, for they are blessed."[176]

However, Balak had offered to pay Balaam a large sum of money if he would curse the Children of Israel so he tried his best to get permission from Yahweh to curse them. Eventually, Yahweh appeared to Balaam with a sword in His hand ready to strike if Balaam did not change his mind.[177] Balaam went on to bless the Children of Israel to the disappointment of Balak, but Yahweh never forgave him for his evil intent and for his deceit and lustful desire to destroy God's chosen people for money.[178]

Yahweh Appears to Joshua

Before the Children of Israel conquered Jericho, Yahweh appeared to Joshua.[179] Based on what the Bible says, I am certain that Yahweh is the Person Joshua met and talked with at that time, but if you read the KJV, NAS, NIV, or the Tanach in English, it may not be crystal clear. However, if you understand Hebrew (or if you use a Strong's Concordance) it is as plain as day. According to the NAS,

> "Now it came about when Joshua was by Jericho, that he lifted up his eyes and looked, and behold, a Man was standing opposite him with His sword drawn in His hand, and Joshua went to Him and said to Him, 'Are you for us or for our adversaries?'
>
> He said, 'No; rather I indeed come now as Captain of the host of Yahweh.' And Joshua fell on his face to the earth, and bowed down, and said to Him, 'What has my Lord to say to His servant?' The Captain of Yahweh's host said to Joshua, 'Remove your sandals from your feet, for the place where you are standing is holy.' And Joshua did so."[180]

The first clue we have about the true identity of the Person Joshua met that day is the title the Man used: "the Captain of the host of Yahweh." The KJV also uses this title, but the NIV and the Tanach use another title: "the Commander of the host of Yahweh." The Hebrew word translated as "captain" or "commander" in this passage from Joshua is "Sar," but in Isaiah 9: 6, "Sar" is translated as "Prince" and refers to the Messiah as Prince of Peace, or Sar Shalom. Joshua's reaction when he learned the Man's identity is the next clue: he "fell on his face to the earth, and bowed down…"

The Man Joshua met gave us the final clue when He told Joshua to take off his shoes because he was standing on holy ground. That is what Yahweh told Moses to do at the burning bush, so there is no doubt that Joshua met and talked with Yahweh in Person.

Yahweh Speaks to the Children of Israel in the Promised Land

Yahweh told the Children of Israel to destroy all the inhabitants when they entered the Promised Land to avoid being perverted by them, and there were many groups of people already there when they arrived. Each group worshiped false gods, and many of them performed ritualistic sacrifices to their gods that included human sacrifices. It would be fair to say that the early inhabitants of the Promised Land had a smorgasbord[181] of gods from which to choose. Some people interpret this fact to mean that all the people living at that time were pagans, including the Israelites, because they performed sacrifices to many gods. But Yahweh is not a god. He is the One true God, and He does not require human sacrifices.

There is another way to interpret this information, though. You can conclude that Yahweh had been speaking to many people all along and that none of them understood His message correctly. All of them seemed to realize that God requires a sacrifice, but the sacrifices Yahweh required the Children of Israel to make were symbolic of the sacrifice He would make on our behalf.

The people living in the Promised Land when the Children of Israel arrived were so deluded that they were beyond hope. Yahweh told them to clear out the inhabitants so they could build a solid foundation for the nation of Israel based on faith in Him alone.

After they had been in the Promised Land for a number of years, Yahweh appeared to the Children of Israel and said,

"I brought you up out of Egypt and led you into the land which I have sworn to your fathers; and I said, 'I will never break My covenant with you, and as for you, you shall make no covenant with the inhabitants of the land; you shall tear down their altars.' But you have not obeyed Me; what is this you have done? Therefore I also said, 'I will not drive them out before you; but they shall become as thorns in your sides and their gods shall be a snare to you.'"[182]

Yahweh is telling the Children of Israel what will happen to them because of their lack of faith and their failure to obey Him. It makes no sense for anyone, especially a Christian, to ignore Yahweh's commands because He expects us to honor Him and His Word. Please keep this fact in mind as you think about the Messiah because He is Yahweh, and He told us to tell the world about Him by Name.

Yahweh Appears to Gideon

Just as Yahweh told them He would do, He removed His protective hedge from around the Children of Israel because of their sins. They had not obeyed Him so they had to defend themselves. During Gideon's day, God allowed Midian to invade Israel and steal their crops and flocks. Things were so bad in Israel that Gideon was forced to hide his wheat to keep the Midianites from taking it.

Yahweh appeared to Gideon in Ophrah. He sat down under an oak tree and said, "Yahweh is with you, O valiant warrior."[183] He meant it literally because He was with Gideon in Person at that moment, but it took Gideon by surprise since he was not a warrior. However, Yahweh saw what Gideon would become and declared that he was, in fact, a warrior.

Gideon did not realize he was talking to Yahweh in Person, and with a skeptical tone in his voice he asked,

"O my lord, if Yahweh is with us, why has all this happened? And where are all His miracles which our fathers told us about...?"[184]

Yahweh simply looked at him and told him to go and deliver Israel. Then He said,

"Surely I will be with you, and you shall defeat Midian as one man."[185]

Gideon remained doubtful, but he did not want to offend the Man so he invited Him to stay and share a meal. Yahweh accepted his invitation, and He waited patiently while Gideon prepared meat and bread. When Gideon brought the meal to Yahweh, He told him to place it on a nearby rock. Then Yahweh touched the food with the end of His staff, and fire came up out of the rock and consumed it. Immediately Yahweh vanished.

At that moment, Gideon knew he had been talking with God Himself, and he said, "Alas, O Adonai Yahweh! For now I have seen Yahweh face to face."[186]   Then Gideon heard Yahweh say these words: "Peace to you, do not fear; you shall not die."[187]

It took Gideon a little time to understand what Yahweh wanted him to do, and he needed constant reassurance. However, eventually Gideon delivered Israel from Midian under the miraculous guidance of Yahweh, and he turned the hearts and minds of the Children of Israel back to their God.

Yahweh Appears to Manoah and His Wife (Samson's Parents)

The Children of Israel reverted to evil ways again and again. During Manoah's time, Yahweh gave them over to the Philistines for 40 years, and they were so oppressed that they turned back to Him. Yahweh heard their pleas, and He came to Manoah's wife and told her that she would have a son who would "deliver Israel from the hands of the Philistines."[188]   Excitedly, she ran to tell her husband, and he prayed for God to return the Man who had spoken to her. God complied with his request and appeared again to Manoah's wife. Once more, she ran to get her husband.

When Manoah met the Man, he asked Him if He was the same Person who had spoken with his wife earlier, and He said, "I Am."[189] Then God repeated the message He had given her the first time He appeared, and Manoah asked Him His Name.[190]   Interestingly, Yahweh had alluded to His Name already because Yahweh means "I Am," but Manoah did not catch the subtle hint. Thus, God said, "Why do you ask My Name, seeing it is wonderful?"[191]

Some Bible translations of this verse use the word "hidden" or "secret" instead of "wonderful," and they read this way: "Why do you ask My Name, seeing it is 'hidden'?" or "Why do you ask My Name, seeing it is 'secret'?"   But the correct translation is "wonderful."

The Hebrew word for "wonderful" used in this verse is "piliy," and it comes from the prime root word "pala"—a Hebrew word that means wonderful beyond description. "Pele," another derivative of "pala," appears in Isaiah 9: 6 as a Name for the Messiah:

"For a Child will be born to us, a Son will be given to us; and the government will rest on His shoulders; and His Name will be called Wonderful (Pele), Counselor, Mighty God, Eternal Father, Prince of Peace. There will be no end to the increase of His government or of peace, on the throne of David and over His kingdom, to establish it and to uphold it with justice and righteousness from then on and forevermore. The zeal of Yahweh will accomplish this."[192]

Can we be certain that Yahweh was the Man talking with Manoah? Yes.

Manoah invited the Man to share a meal with them, and Yahweh said,

"Though you detain Me, I will not eat your food, but if you prepare a burnt offering, then offer it to Yahweh."[193]

For some reason, Yahweh would not eat their food, but He would accept it as a sacrifice. Manoah prepared a goat and grain for a burnt offering to Yahweh, but neither he nor his wife knew that Yahweh was with them in Person at that moment. As he prepared the sacrifice, the Man "performed wonders while Manoah and his wife looked on."[194] When he placed the offering on the altar, fire burst forth from the rocks, and the Man "ascended in the flame of the altar."[195] Instantly Manoah said, "We shall surely die, for we have seen God."[196] But his wife said,

> "If Yahweh had desired to kill us, He would not have accepted a burnt offering and a grain offering from our hands, nor would He have shown us all these things, nor would He have let us hear things like this at this time."[197]

Although we do not know what Yahweh told them, since He used the Name "Wonderful" it is reasonable to assume that He told them about the Messiah and about their own son—Samson. In a short while, Samson was born, and Yahweh delivered Israel from the Philistines through him. Even though Samson was a flawed human being, as we all are, Yahweh used him in a mighty way to bless His children.

Yahweh Appears to Samuel

Samuel was the last judge in Israel before God allowed the Jews to have a human king, and his birth was a miracle. His father, Elkanah, had two wives, Hannah and Peninnah. Hannah had no children, but Peninnah had many sons and daughters.

Each year Elkanah took his family to Yahweh's Tabernacle at Shiloh to worship and make sacrifices. The family's yearly pilgrimage to Shiloh, which should have been a festive occasion, was for Hannah a miserable experience. Year after year, Peninnah taunted and ridiculed[198] Hannah because she had so many children and Hannah had none. Finally, one year Hannah went into the Tabernacle and poured out her heart to Yahweh. With tears in her eyes,[199] she pleaded with Him to give her a son:

> "O Yahweh Sabaoth, if You will indeed look on the affliction of Your maidservant and remember me, and not forget Your maidservant, but will give Your maidservant a son, then I will give him to Yahweh all the days of his life, and a razor will never come on his head."[200]

Yahweh honored her prayer and gave her a son, and Hannah called him Samuel which means "the Name of God." When the boy was weaned she took him to the Tabernacle at Shiloh, dedicated him to Yahweh, and turned him over to Eli the priest to live out his years as God's servant.

Eli's sons, Hophni and Phinehas, were also priests who served at Shiloh, and they were "worthless men" who "did not know Yahweh."[201] Routinely, they stole sacrifices people made to God,[202] threatened to use force against them if they refused to surrender their sacrifices,[203] and had sex with the women who served at the doorway of the Tabernacle.[204] Eli knew about all of this and instructed his sons to change their ways, but he did not take appropriate steps to make sure they abandoned these repulsive practices.

Hophni and Phinehas ignored their father's warning, and one day Yahweh appeared to Samuel while he was in the Tabernacle and gave him this message for Eli:

> "I am going to do something in Israel which will make the ears of all who hear of it ring. I shall carry out that day against Eli everything that I have said about his family, from beginning to end. You are to tell him that I condemn his family for ever, since he is aware that his sons have been cursing God and yet has not corrected them. Therefore—I swear it to the family of Eli—no sacrifice or offering shall ever expiate the guilt of Eli's family."[205]

Yahweh was true to His Word, as He always is. Eli's sons were killed in a battle with the Philistines, and the Philistines took the Ark of the Covenant from Israel. When Eli learned that his sons had died and that the Ark of the Covenant had been taken, he died immediately, and his lineage was cut off.

Yahweh Appears to King David

David became a very successful king in Israel. He was Yahweh's anointed one,[206] and God blessed him mightily. The greatest blessing He bestowed on David was the promise that the Messiah would be One of his descendants. In fact, one of the Messiah's Names is Messiah Son of David. However, David behaved in sinful ways when Israel became prosperous.

One day Satan inspired David[207] to think about all the wealth and power he had accumulated, and he asked Joab, his military leader, to conduct a census of the people in his kingdom. According to Jewish tradition, David wanted to know how many troops he had,[208] as if it really mattered. Yahweh had put him on the throne, and everything he possessed was a result of God's blessings. It was sinful for David to think about those blessings as if they were the fruit of his own labor and to believe they could protect him in times of adversity. Joab knew he was asking for trouble and advised against it, but David insisted on the census anyway so Joab performed the count.

Yahweh instructed His prophet Gad to tell David that he was about to be punished and that he could choose what the punishment would be. He gave David three options: three years of famine, three months of being swept away before his enemies, or three days of the sword of Yahweh.[209]

The fact that God allowed David to choose the penalty was an indication of His love for him. David picked the third option and said,

> "I am in distress; please let me fall into the hand of Yahweh, for His mercies are very great. But do not let me fall into the hand of man."[210]

And so it was. For three days, Yahweh inflicted punishment on Israel because of David's sin. All told, 70,000 men in Israel died because of what David had done. After three days, Yahweh came to Jerusalem to destroy the city, and He changed His mind when He reached "the threshing floor of Ornan the Jebusite."[211] This is the site where Solomon built the Temple of Yahweh several years later. Today, this site is known as Mount Moriah, or the Temple Mount, and it is the epicenter of the dispute between Israel and the Palestinians.

David lifted up his eyes, and he saw Yahweh "standing between earth and heaven, with His drawn sword in His hand stretched out over Jerusalem. Then David and the elders, covered in sackcloth, fell on their faces,"[212] and David said,

> "Is it not I who commanded to count the people? Indeed, I am the one who has sinned and done very wickedly, but these sheep, what have they done?"[213]

Yahweh instructed Gad to tell David to build an altar on the threshing floor of Ornan the Jebusite.[214] David built the altar exactly where God told him to build it, and when he offered sacrifices to Yahweh the punishment ceased. This is an important fact. Before he built the altar, David bought Mount Moriah from Ornan the Jebusite. He paid Ornan 600 shekels of gold for the land,[215] or about 240 ounces of gold,[216] and then he made a sacrifice for his sins.

In other words, David did not "take the land," or using today's vernacular he did not "occupy the land." He purchased it for a sum certain from Ornan the Jebusite, and he had, and has, legal title to the land. Make no mistake. The Temple Mount is a very special place to

Yahweh, and anyone who believes God's Word would be foolish to ignore this fact.

Can we be certain that David saw Yahweh with a sword in His hand ready to destroy Jerusalem? Of course we can. 2 Chronicles 3: 1 talks about David's son Solomon preparing to build the Temple of Yahweh on Mount Moriah:

> "Then Solomon began to build the house of Yahweh in Jerusalem on Mount Moriah, where Yahweh had appeared to his father David, at the place that David had prepared on the threshing floor of Ornan the Jebusite."[217]

2 Samuel chapter 24 provides another account of David's sin in this matter, but in the 2 Samuel version of the incident Yahweh instructs David to purchase the threshing floor of Araunah the Jebusite[218] for 50 shekels of silver.[219] Many Bible scholars believe that 1 Chronicles chapter 21 and 2 Samuel chapter 24 talk about the same purchase of land, but this interpretation is less than satisfactory. It is possible for a person to have more than one name. For example, Solomon is referred to by several names in the Scriptures. Thus, Ornan and Araunah could be the same person. However, it is not logical to conclude that 50 shekels of silver and 600 shekels of gold are the same. Clearly they are not equal, and gold is far more valuable than silver.

Therefore, we must conclude that David acquired two pieces of property and that he paid different amounts of money for them. From Ornan he purchased a threshing floor on Mount Moriah for 600 shekels of gold, and from Araunah he bought another threshing floor for 50 shekels of silver. On both sites, David built altars for making sacrifices to Yahweh.

In *The Rod of an Almond Tree in God's Master Plan*, Peter Michas argues that Araunah's threshing floor was on the Mount of Olives directly across the Kidron Valley from Ornan's threshing floor on Mount Moriah. Michas says that Ornan's threshing floor is the site where Solomon eventually built the Temple of Yahweh, a fact about which Yahweh's Word is very clear, and that Araunah's threshing floor became the site where the Israelites sacrificed the Red Heifer to produce ashes for purification. I bring this up to emphasize that God's Word is accurate. We do not need to explain away or to rationalize about what might appear to be discrepancies or inconsistencies in the Bible. Our understanding is flawed—not God's Word.

Yahweh Appears to Solomon Twice

Solomon became king in Israel after David, and Yahweh blessed him mightily. Solomon's kingdom was unmatched in the world during his time. His wealth and power were immense, and people traveled from distant lands simply to hear him speak because of his wisdom.

Shortly after Solomon became king, Yahweh appeared to him in a dream and said, "Ask what you wish Me to give you."[220] Since he was young and inexperienced, Solomon asked Yahweh to give him "an understanding heart to judge Your people to discern between good and evil."[221] Obviously, God was pleased with

Solomon's request because He gave him what he asked for, but He also gave him great wealth and power that he could have asked for but did not.

Yahweh appeared to Solomon again when he dedicated the Temple[222] and said,

> "I have heard your prayer and your supplication, which you have made before Me; I have consecrated this house which you have built by putting My Name there forever, and My eyes and My heart will be there perpetually."[223]

This verse should cause alarm bells to ring out in the minds of people who believe Yahweh's Word. Anyone who thinks he can bargain with the Temple Mount is asking for trouble. Mount Moriah is not a bargaining chip. For reasons known only to Him, Yahweh chose Mount Moriah, and He made it perfectly clear that His Name will reside there forever.

God told Solomon He would bless him continually if he would simply obey His Word and follow after Him the way David had done. Wealth, power, and wisdom should have been enough for Solomon, but they were not. He turned his heart and his mind to other things, and it cost him dearly.

Solomon wrote the book of Ecclesiastes, and it describes his journey through life. He sought to discover anything that could be discovered, and Ecclesiastes is a litany of the things Solomon did and the things he learned. There was a great debate about whether to include Ecclesiastes in the Bible, but eventually it was included for only one reason, its conclusion. The last two verses in Ecclesiastes sum up what Solomon learned in his quest to know everything:

"The conclusion, when all has been heard, is: fear God and keep His commandments, because this applies to every person. For God will bring every act to judgment, everything which is hidden, whether it is good or evil."[224]

This conclusion is absolutely correct. It is a shame Solomon had to do the things he did to learn it. In 1 Kings 11: 9-11, Yahweh makes clear just how disappointed in Solomon He became:

"Now Yahweh was angry with Solomon because his heart was turned away from Yahweh, the God of Israel, who had appeared to him twice, and had commanded him concerning this thing, that he should not go after other gods; but he did not observe what Yahweh had commanded. So Yahweh said to Solomon, 'Because you have done this, and you have not kept My covenant and My statutes, which I have commanded you, I will surely tear your kingdom from you....'"[225]

You may be wondering what Solomon did that made Yahweh so angry. The details are in the Bible:

"Now King Solomon loved many foreign women along with the daughter of Pharaoh: Moabite, Ammonite, Edomite, Sidonite, and Hittite women, from the nations concerning which Yahweh had said to the sons of Israel, 'You shall not associate with them, neither shall they associate with you, for they will surely turn your heart away after their gods.' Solomon held fast to these in love. He had seven hundred wives, princesses, and three hundred concubines, and his wives turned his heart away."[226]

Before he died, Solomon built places of worship for Ashtoreth the goddess of the Sidonians, Milcom the god of the Ammonites, Chemosh the god of Moab, and Molech the god of the Ammonites.[227] He did these things to make his wives happy and to keep peace in his household, but there is no good excuse for what Solomon did. Idolatry was commonplace in Israel, and King Solomon set the example that many people followed to their own detriment.

Yahweh was true to His Word. When Solomon died, God tore Israel into two kingdoms: Israel in the north and Judah in the south. Eventually, the Assyrians took Israel into captivity and scattered the people throughout the world. Today, the Northern Kingdom is known as "the ten lost tribes of Israel." Most of the descendants of people from the Northern Kingdom are still scattered throughout the world. Later, the Babylonians took the Southern Kingdom into captivity. Most of them were allowed to return to Israel when Cyrus the Great conquered the Babylonian Empire.

Yahweh Appears to Isaiah

In about 740 B.C., Yahweh appeared to Isaiah and commissioned him to deliver His message to the Children of Israel. Isaiah's description of Yahweh is very interesting, and you can find it in Isaiah 6: 1-4. When he saw Yahweh, all Isaiah could say was this:

"Woe is me! I am lost, for I am a man of unclean lips and I live among a people of unclean lips, and my eyes have seen the King, Yahweh Sabaoth."[228]

The magnificence of Yahweh's appearance and His absolute purity were so striking that Isaiah was forced to see himself correctly. He was compelled to admit that he was a sinner and that he lived among sinners. That is exactly what each one of us must understand. Only then can we begin to appreciate who Yahweh is. He is the Holy One of Israel, the One and only God, and He will accept no blemishes.

Consider the Evidence

At the beginning of this chapter, I said that Yahweh has a human form and that He has appeared to people throughout history. The Bible provides abundant evidence to support this assertion. I also said that Yahweh intervenes in history to perform His Word and to fulfill His promises. Here again, there are many examples of God doing these things in Person, and I have discussed a few of them.

If you believe God's Word, by now you're convinced. Go to the Bible and see for yourself if I have misled you in any way. If you don't believe the Word of God or if you aren't sure it's true, then you may not be convinced, but at least I hope I have roused your curiosity.

I also said the human form of Yahweh is the Messiah. Glimpses of that fact were evident in this chapter, but as I said, the

Bible provides other compelling proofs to substantiate it. I'll discuss them later.

Once again, there is some overlap between this chapter and the next one because Yahweh appeared in human form to make most of His covenants and promises. Redundancy is a common practice used by engineers for our safety and protection. For instance, airplanes are equipped with redundant systems so that if one fails the pilot can still land the plane safely. Yahweh used this practice in the Scriptures for our protection, so I am following a precedent established by Yahweh Himself. Because of its unparalleled importance, Yahweh's role in the redemption and salvation of His people is the most redundant message in the Scriptures.

Chapter 6
Yahweh's Covenants and Promises

Yahweh tied His covenants and promises to His Name, and He will never do anything that contradicts His Word because it would defile His Name. The New Covenant is Yahweh's most important promise. It points to the Messiah and the completion of Yahweh's plan for His creation. It also demonstrates His deep and abiding love for us.

Yahweh Promises to Deal with Adam's Sin

Yahweh's first promise is found in Genesis 3: 14-15:

"Because you (the serpent) have done this, cursed are you more than all the cattle, and more than every beast of the field; on your belly shall you go, and dust shall you eat all the days of your life; and I will put enmity between you and the woman, and between your seed and her seed; He shall bruise you on the head, and you shall bruise Him on the heel."[229]

This promise is a foretelling of the battle Yahweh will wage with Satan to deal with the consequences of our sin. The battle between Yahweh and Satan over the redemption and salvation of His people is illustrated in every book in the Bible.

Although Yahweh promised to redeem and save His people, men and women are destined to suffer the physical consequences of sin. Yahweh told Eve,

"I will greatly multiply your pain in childbirth, in pain you shall bring forth children; yet your desire shall be for your husband, and he will rule over you."[230]

And to Adam God said,

"Cursed is the ground because of you; in toil you shall eat of it all the days of your life. Both thorns and thistles it shall grow for you; and you shall eat the plants of the field; by the sweat of your face you shall eat bread, till you return to the ground, because from it you were taken; for you are dust, and to dust you shall return."[231]

Sin upset the natural order Yahweh established in the beginning for men and women. He had intended for men and women to be associates and equals. But since Adam and Eve sinned, women have possessed a vain longing to rule their husbands, and men have struggled against a hostile environment to provide food for their families. Additionally, since that time both men and women have experienced sickness and physical death—something Yahweh mercifully permitted so we would not have to live eternally in a fallen state.[232]

By far, the most significant consequence of Adam's and Eve's sin was the immediate loss of intimacy with Yahweh. To restore what was lost, God had to become our Redeemer and Savior. Although Adam and Eve created a wide separation between God and the human race, man is incapable of bridging the gap. Yahweh had to do that Himself.

Yahweh's Covenant with Noah

Noah was the only righteous person in his generation, and Yahweh made a covenant with him and his family when He destroyed every living creature on the earth with the flood. Genesis 6: 8 says, "Noah found favor in the eyes of Yahweh."[233] The Hebrew word translated as "favor" in this verse is "chen," and it actually means "grace," or the "unmerited favor of a superior person to an inferior one."[234]

This is the first verse in the Bible that mentions "grace." In the next chapter, you will see that understanding grace is crucial in helping us grasp what Yahweh did for us through the Messiah. In a nutshell, grace means that our redemption and salvation are not dependent on anything we have done, will do, or even can do. They are gifts from God that are based on His righteousness, not ours.

Yahweh told Noah to build an ark, which took more than 100 years to complete, and he obeyed God. This may not sound like a big deal, but it was. During Noah's day, there was no rain. A mist rose from the ground every day and watered the earth,[235] so flooding was unheard of.

Building a huge boat on dry land made no sense to Noah's neighbors. For many decades, he endured their ridicule as he worked diligently to obey Yahweh's command. When the rain came, Noah, his family, and the animals Yahweh sent to him entered the ark, and God shut the door behind them. Literally, He sealed them in the ark and saved them. Their salvation was entirely dependent on Yahweh's grace since there was no way Noah could have known what would happen more than 100 years after God told him to build the ark.

After the flood, Yahweh made this promise:

"I will never again curse the ground on account of man, for the intent of man's heart is evil from his youth; and I will never again destroy every living thing, as I have done."[236]

Then God established a covenant between Himself and everything He created:

"'Now behold, I Myself do establish My covenant with you, and with your descendants after you; and with every living creature that is with you, the birds, the cattle, and every beast of the earth with you; of all that comes out of the ark, even every beast of the earth. I establish My covenant with you; and all flesh shall never again be cut off by the water of the flood, neither shall there again be a flood to destroy the earth.' God said, 'This is the sign of the covenant which I am making between Me and you and every living creature that is with you, for all successive generations. I set my bow in the cloud, and it shall be for a sign of a covenant between Me and the earth.'"[237]

Abraham's Call and Yahweh's Promise to Bless all the Families of the Earth

Yahweh told Abraham to leave his home and his country and go to a place He would show him,[238] and Abraham obeyed God. Then God said,

> "I will make you a great nation, and I will bless you, and make your name great; and so you shall be a blessing; and I will bless those who bless you, and the one who curses you I will curse. And in you all the families of the earth shall be blessed."[239]

Abraham's belief in Yahweh and his willingness to obey Him set the stage for our redemption and salvation. God's promise to bless all the families of the earth through Abraham refers to the Messiah and His redemptive work.

Repeatedly in history, we see that the willingness of individual men and women to ignore the odds against them and do what Yahweh told them to do has resulted in tremendous blessings for all of us. The next time you catch yourself thinking that nothing you do really matters, remember Noah and Abraham. They may have had similar thoughts, but they did not let their fear and insecurity prevent them from obeying God. They were ordinary people Yahweh used to do extraordinary things. Their lives made an enormous difference and yours can too.

The Promised Land

When Abraham entered the Promised Land he was traveling with his nephew, Lot. They were men of great wealth, and they had very large herds of animals. Since the land could not support the herds of both men, Abraham suggested that they separate, and he told Lot to take the land he wanted. Lot looked at the valley below the hills on which Jerusalem rests, and he saw that it was well watered and very fertile. Thus, he took the valley for his possession, and Abraham willingly accepted the hilly region that includes Mount Moriah—the hill beside which Jerusalem was built.

After Abraham and Lot parted company, Yahweh made this promise to Abraham:

> "Now lift up your eyes and look from the place where you are, northward and southward and eastward and westward; for all the land which you see, I will give it to you and to your descendants forever. I will make your descendants as the dust of the earth, so that if anyone can number the dust of the earth, then your descendants can also be numbered. Arise, walk about the land through its length and breadth; for I will give it to you."[240]

In Genesis 15: 18-21, Yahweh gave Abraham a more precise description of the Promised Land's boundaries:

> "To your descendants I have given this land, from the river of Egypt (the Nile River) as far as the great river Euphrates; the land of the Kenite and the Kenizzite and the Kadmonite and the

Hittite and the Perizzite and the Rephaim and the Amorite and the Canaanite and the Girgashite and the Jebusite."[241]

Later, Yahweh told Abraham that he would become the father of many nations, and He confirmed that the Promised Land would belong to his descendants forever:

"For My part, this is My covenant with you: you will become the father of many nations. And you are no longer to be called Abram; your name is to be Abraham, for I am making you father of many nations, and your issue will be kings. And I shall maintain my covenant between Myself and you, and your descendants after you, generation after generation, as a covenant in perpetuity, to be your God and the God of your descendants after you. And to you and to your descendants after you, I shall give the country where you are now immigrants, the entire land of Canaan, to own in perpetuity. And I will be their God."[242]

Then Yahweh explained that even though Abraham would become the father of many nations, His covenant would pass through Isaac's descendants:

"As regards your wife...Sarah....I shall bless her and moreover give you a son by her. I shall bless her and she will become nations: kings of peoples will issue from her....Yes, your wife Sarah will bear you a son whom you must name Isaac. And I shall maintain My covenant with him, a covenant in perpetuity, to be his God and the God of his descendants after him. For

Ishmael too I grant you your request. I hereby bless him and will make him fruitful and exceedingly numerous. He will be the father of twelve princes, and I shall make him into a great nation. But my covenant I shall maintain with Isaac, whom Sarah will bear you...."[243]

A "covenant in perpetuity" is binding for all eternity. That means the Promised Land belongs to Abraham's descendants through Isaac forever. In Genesis 26: 2-5, Yahweh confirmed His promise to Isaac:

"Do not go down to Egypt; stay in the land of which I shall tell you. Sojourn in this land and I will be with you and bless you, for to you and to your descendants I will give all these lands, and I will establish the oath which I swore to your father Abraham. I will multiply your descendants as the stars of heaven, and will give your descendants all these lands; and by your descendants all the nations of the earth shall be blessed; because Abraham obeyed Me and kept My charge, My commandments, My statutes and My Laws."[244]

In Genesis 28: 13-15, Yahweh said that the Promised Land belongs to Abraham's descendants through Jacob:

"I am Yahweh, the God of your father Abraham and the God of Isaac; the land on which you lie, I will give to you and your descendants. Your descendants shall also be like the dust of the earth, and you shall spread out to the west and to the east and to the north and to the south; and in you and in your descendants shall all the families of the earth be blessed. Behold, I am with you and will keep you wherever you go, and will bring you back to this land; for I will not leave you until I have done what I have promised."[245]

Yahweh repeated this promise in Genesis 35: 10-12:

"You shall no longer be called Jacob, but Israel shall be your name....I am God Almighty (El Shaddai); be fruitful and multiply; a nation and a company of nations shall come from you, and kings shall come forth from you. The land which I gave to Abraham and Isaac, I will give it to you, and I will give the land to your descendants after you."[246]

Later, Yahweh told Moses that He would rescue the Jewish people from bondage in Egypt and bring them to the Promised Land, and He tied the promise to His Name:

"I am Yahweh, and I will bring you out from under the burdens of the Egyptians, and I will deliver you from their bondage. I will also redeem you with an outstretched arm and with great judgments. Then I will take you for My people, and I will be your God; and you shall know that I am Yahweh your God, who brought you out from under the burdens of the Egyptians. I will bring you to the land which I swore to give to Abraham, Isaac, and Jacob, and I will give it to you for a permanent possession; I am Yahweh."[247]

As the Children of Israel were preparing to leave Mount Sinai and go to the Promised Land, Yahweh told them He would send His Angel before them. This Angel is the Angel of Yahweh who appeared to Moses in the burning bush, and He established Israel as a nation:

"Behold, I am going to send an Angel before you to guard you along the way and to bring you into the place which I have prepared. Be on your guard before Him and obey His Voice; do not be rebellious toward Him, for He will not pardon your transgression, since My Name is in Him. But if you will truly obey His Voice and do all that I say, then I will be an enemy to your enemies and an adversary to your adversaries. For My Angel will go before you and bring you in to the land of the Amorites, the Hittites, the Perizzites, and the Canaanites, the Hivites and the Jebusites; and I will completely destroy them. You shall not worship their gods, nor serve them, nor do according to their deeds; but you shall utterly overthrow them and break their sacred pillars in pieces. But you shall serve Yahweh your God, and He will bless your bread and your water; and I will remove sickness from your midst."[248]

In Exodus 23: 27-31, Yahweh explained how His Angel would drive out the early inhabitants of the Promised Land, and He gave another description of its boundaries:

"I will send My terror ahead of you, and throw into confusion all the people among whom you come, and I will make all your enemies turn their backs to you. I will send hornets ahead of you that they may drive out the Hivites, the Canaanites, and the Hittites before you. I will not drive them out before you in a single year, that the land may not become desolate and the beasts of the field become too numerous for you. I will drive them out before you little by little, until you become fruitful and take possession of the land. I will fix your boundary from the Red Sea to the sea of the Philistines (i.e., the Mediterranean Sea), and from the wilderness to the River Euphrates; for I will deliver the inhabitants of the land into your hand, and you will drive them out before you."[249]

The Covenant of Yahweh

If I were to make a list of the most important chapters in the Bible, Genesis chapter 15 would be at the top of my list because it presents Yahweh's covenant with His people. This covenant has never changed, and it points to the New Covenant to which I refer later. Furthermore, Genesis chapter 22 provides crucial insights into the New Covenant, and I will discuss them shortly as well.

Genesis chapter 15 begins with this statement: "The Word of Yahweh came to Abram in a vision...."[250] As you will see later, this verse does not mean Abraham only heard the spoken Words of Yahweh. In fact, the "Word of Yahweh" referred to here is the Messiah, and Genesis chapter 15 tells us that the Messiah ratified the covenant on which we all depend for our redemption and salvation.

Yahweh told Abraham, "Do not fear...I am a shield to you; your reward shall be very great."[251] Abraham responded by saying, in essence, "I have no children. How can this be?"[252]

Then Yahweh took Abraham outside and said, "Now look toward the heavens, and count the stars if you are able to count them...So shall your descendants be."[253] God was telling Abraham that despite the fact he was childless at that moment, he would have many descendants. Eventually, Abraham learned that he would have a son, the child of the covenant through whom the Messiah would come, and in Genesis chapter 22 he learned that the Messiah would become the sin offering for all mankind.

Genesis 15: 6 tells us that Abraham believed Yahweh and that God declared him righteous.[254] Clearly, Abraham's righteousness was based on his faith in Yahweh, and his obedience flowed from his faith. I need to mention this fact here because the covenant Yahweh made with His people is not dependent on our effort in any way. Faith in Yahweh and His sacrifice on our behalf are essential, and our willingness to obey Him simply proves that we have the kind of faith He expects and demands. Literally, nothing else will satisfy God. As unusual as this may sound, that is exactly what Yahweh said.

Ratification of the Covenant

Most Christians do not have a good understanding of the covenant Yahweh ratified with Abraham and his descendants. Thus, most of us do not fully appreciate what God did for us or what He expects from us in return. In Genesis 15: 9-10, God told Abraham,

"Bring me a three year old heifer, and a three year old female goat, and a three year old ram, and a young pigeon. Then he brought all these to Him and cut them in two, and laid each half opposite the other; but he did not cut the birds."[255]

In Abraham's day, people ratified covenants in the following way. First, they would slaughter animals and cut them in two. Next, they would place the parts of the slaughtered animals in two lines on the ground, and the people entering into the covenant would walk between the lines of animal parts together.

Ratification of a covenant signifies that the people walking between the animal parts are committing themselves to fulfill the covenant's terms—every one of them no matter what happens. For instance, if you and your friend enter into a covenant such as the one Yahweh entered into with Abraham, both of you are agreeing to live up to the covenant's terms even if the other one fails to keep his word. Ratifying a covenant this way also indicates that you are inviting Yahweh to slaughter you the way the animals were slaughtered if you break your promise.[256]

Today, we do not enter into covenants so most of us are unfamiliar with the concept. Instead, we enter into contracts, and covenants and contracts are very different. For instance, if you and your friend enter into a contractual relationship and you fail to discharge your commitments, then the contract's provisions are no longer binding on your friend. As I said, in a covenant the terms of the agreement never cease to apply.[257] This distinction is key.

Furthermore, the covenant Yahweh ratified with Abraham was not a typical covenant. Take a look at Genesis 15: 12 and Genesis 15: 17-18 and see what I mean:

"Now when the sun was going down, a deep sleep fell upon Abram; and behold, terror and great darkness fell upon him[258]....It came about when the sun had set, that it was very dark, and behold, there appeared a smoking oven and a flaming torch which passed between these pieces. On that day Yahweh made a covenant with Abram..."[259]

The "smoking oven" and the "flaming torch" mentioned in these verses were Yahweh's Shekinah. God caused Abraham to fall asleep when He made the covenant, and Yahweh the Father and Yahweh the Son walked between the lines of animal parts. Thus, the covenant we refer to as the covenant Yahweh made with Abraham is actually a covenant between the Father and the Son, and Abraham and his descendants are the beneficiaries of Yahweh's work on our behalf.

Since Abraham was asleep when Yahweh ratified the covenant, Yahweh assumed sole responsibility for fulfilling the covenant's terms. Stated another way, Yahweh's covenant with us is not dependent on our doing anything for Him. Please do not miss the significance of this point. The Children of Israel misunderstood it. They lacked faith in Yahweh, and as a result they had to spend 40 years in the wilderness instead of going directly to the Promised Land.[260]

Steve McVey, President of Grace Walk Ministries, has written several books dealing with the importance of grace in the lives of Yahweh's people.[261] In his book Grace Land, McVey explains the covenant's ratification this way:

> "When the time came for the covenant to be ratified, God caused Abraham to fall asleep....There was no way that Abraham could live up to the promises he would have been making....It was as if God were saying, 'Abraham, I know you have good intentions, but there is nothing you could ever do for Me. You would only break any promises you make. So for that reason, I want you to lie down and rest while I ratify the covenant. I'll do the work. You simply trust Me as the recipient of all I do.'"[262]

Yahweh's covenant is "a unilateral pact (between God and Abraham and his descendants), a divine initiative, a solemn promise sealed with an imprecatory oath."[263] In essence, God called down curses on Himself if He fails to deliver on every one of His promises. He knew that Abraham could not live up to the terms of the covenant no matter how hard he tried, and neither can we.

The Law requires the death of anyone violating even one of the covenant's provisions. Thus, every one of us deserves to die because all of us have violated the covenant. However, by ratifying it single-handedly Yahweh agreed to take upon Himself the penalty for our sins and to die[264] in our place. This fact is alluded to in Genesis chapter 22. When they nailed the Messiah to a tree, He paid the price for our sins, redeemed us, fulfilled the Old Covenant, and sealed the New Covenant with His own blood. Now that is true love.

Yahweh Tests Abraham's Faith and Promises the Messiah

Abraham knew that Yahweh's covenant and all His promises would pass to his descendants through Isaac, but one day God put him to the test. He said,

> "Take now your son, your only son, whom you love, Isaac, and go to the land of Moriah, and offer him there as a burnt offering on one of the mountains of which I will tell you."[265]

From Abraham's reaction to Yahweh's command, it is clear that he believed God would return Isaac to him alive even if he sacrificed him on an altar. Genesis 22: 5 tells us that when Abraham, Isaac, and the men who accompanied them on the trip reached their destination, Mount Moriah, Abraham said that he and Isaac would climb the mountain, worship, and return together.[266] Obviously, they could not return together unless Isaac was still alive, and to fulfill Yahweh's covenant and His promises, Isaac had to live and have children of his own.

Genesis 22: 5 is the first verse in the Bible that mentions worship. The Hebrew word translated in this verse as "worship" is "shachah" (shaw-khaw'), and it means to prostrate one's self before God or to fall down before Him in humility. In this situation, Abraham's "act of worship" was to willingly surrender to God the one he loved most—his son Isaac. Additionally, by telling Abraham to sacrifice Isaac, Yahweh was actually showing him what He would do later to atone for our sins.

It is clear from Genesis 22: 5 that worship involves action on our part coupled with faith in God. In other words, simply believing in the existence of God is not enough. We must be willing to do what Yahweh requires. If we fail to act when we know what God expects, then we are showing Him that we do not have the kind of faith He demands. Abraham had a choice to make, and he made the right decision. Each one of us has a choice to make as well. Please make the right choice.

As they climbed Mount Moriah, Isaac told Abraham that they did not have an animal for the sacrifice, and Abraham said, "God will provide for Himself the lamb for the burnt offering...."[267] In the ancient eastern text of the Bible, Genesis 22: 8 reads this way: "God will provide Himself the lamb for a burnt offering,"[268] and a literal translation of the Hebrew is consistent with this translation. Therefore, prophetically Abraham was telling Isaac that Yahweh would provide Himself as the sacrifice at an unspecified future date. Yahweh provided the sacrifice that day as well, and Abraham called the place Yahweh Yireh, or Yahweh will (future tense) provide[269] a sacrifice "on this mountain."[270] Abraham was prophesying that at some future date unknown to him Yahweh would provide a sacrifice on Mount Moriah and save His people. When they nailed the Messiah to the tree, this prophecy was fulfilled.

A literal interpretation of the Name "Yahweh Yireh" is "Yahweh will (future tense) see to it."[271] This is the same message

God gave Moses and the Children of Israel when He instituted Passover and led them out of Egypt. Yahweh had to make the atoning sacrifice personally. No other sacrifice would do.

When Abraham raised the knife to kill Isaac, Yahweh stopped him and said,

> "By Myself I have sworn, declares Yahweh, because you have done this thing and have not withheld your son, your only son, indeed I will greatly bless you, and I will greatly multiply your seed as the stars of heaven and as the sand which is on the seashore; and your seed shall possess the gate of their enemies. In your seed all the nations of the earth shall be blessed, because you have obeyed My Voice."[272]

Yahweh referred to Isaac as Abraham's "only son." We know Ishmael was Abraham's son as well and that Ishmael was born before Isaac, but Isaac was Abraham's only son by Sarah and the only son of the covenant. Yahweh was telling Abraham that He would sacrifice His only Son on Mount Moriah to atone for our sins. Additionally, Yahweh told Abraham that through his seed all the nations of the earth "shall be blessed." The Hebrew word translated in this verse as "seed" (singular) is "zra,"[273] and it means posterity, offspring, or descendant. Thus, Yahweh was telling Abraham that One, not many, of his descendants would be a special blessing to the whole world. That Person is the Messiah, and as you will see shortly, He is Yahweh.

Yahweh Promises to Bless Us When He Causes Us to Remember His Name

When Yahweh gave the Ten Commandments, He tied them closely to His Name, and He promised to bless us when He causes us to remember His Name. In Exodus 20: 24, He said,

> "In every place where I cause My Name to be remembered, I will come to you and bless you."[274]

This is an unconditional promise, and it is not a new revelation. But we have lost sight of the importance Yahweh places on His Name. Yahweh never intended for us to "forget" His Name. People did that on their own initiative, even though they were influenced by Satan.

Yahweh Promises a Prophet Like Moses

While the Children of Israel wandered in the wilderness, Yahweh promised that He would raise up a prophet like Moses to shepherd His people:

> "I will raise up a prophet from among their countrymen like you (Moses), and I will put My words in His mouth, and He shall speak to them all that I command Him. It shall come about that whoever will not listen to My words which He shall speak in My Name, I Myself will require it of him."[275]

The Prophet to whom Yahweh referred in these verses is the Messiah, and He made it clear that the Messiah is a very special

Person. He speaks Yahweh's words, and everyone must pay attention to Him and obey Him. Failure in this regard will provoke Yahweh's wrath.

Yahweh Promises the Messiah through David's Line

Yahweh said that David was a man after His own heart.[276] Even though he was a sinner, David understood that Yahweh is his Redeemer and Savior, and Yahweh blessed David for having faith in Him. The greatest blessing Yahweh bestowed on David was the promise that the Messiah would come through his line. In 2 Samuel 7: 12-13, Yahweh said,

> "When your days are complete and you lie down with your fathers, I will raise up your Descendant after you, who will come forth from you, and I will establish His kingdom. He shall build a house for My Name, and I will establish the throne of His kingdom forever."[277]

Yahweh was not referring to David's son Solomon in these verses because Solomon died. There is little or no dispute about the fact that these verses pertain to the Messiah, and Yahweh repeats this promise in 1 Chronicles 17: 14:

> "But I will settle Him in My house and in My kingdom forever, and His throne shall be established forever."[278]

After David learned about this promise, he visited the Tabernacle and sat down in front of the Holy of Holies to pray.

David's prayer is found in 2 Samuel 7: 18-29. Several verses in his prayer have a direct bearing on the message of this book:

> "Is there another people on earth like your people, like Israel, whom a god proceeded to redeem, to make them his people and to make a name for himself by performing great and terrible things on their behalf, by driving out nations and their gods before his people?"[279]

The answer to this question is NO. There is no god on earth who has redeemed his people and performed mighty acts on their behalf. But Yahweh did, and His promise to David makes it clear that in the future He will perform an even greater act for His people. David understood all of this, and he said,

> "Now, Yahweh God, may the promise which You have made for Your servant and for his family stand firm forever as You have said, so that Your Name will be exalted for ever and people will say, 'Israel's God is Yahweh Sabaoth.'"[280]

David knew that Yahweh would bring forth One of his descendants and exalt Him and His Name. One day, people everywhere will know that His Name is Yahweh, that He alone is God, and that He is our One and only Redeemer and Savior. The Person about whom David is speaking is the Messiah.

Yahweh Promises a New Covenant

As I said at the beginning of this chapter, the institution of a New Covenant is Yahweh's most important promise. The use of the word "new" suggests two things. First, it indicates that there is an Old Covenant. Second, it implies that the old one has been fulfilled or completed. By definition, the Old Covenant must have been completed, or the New Covenant could not take effect.

Yahweh explained the New Covenant to Jeremiah in Jeremiah 31: 31-33:

> "'Behold, days are coming,' declares Yahweh, 'when I will make a new covenant with the house of Israel and with the house of Judah, not like the covenant which I made with their fathers in the day I took them by the hand to bring them out of the land of Egypt, My covenant which they broke, although I was a husband to them,' declares Yahweh. 'But this is the covenant which I will make with the house of Israel after those days,' declares Yahweh, 'I will put my Law within them and on their heart I will write it; and I will be their God, and they shall be My people.'"[281]

This is the same covenant Yahweh referred to when He spoke these words about the Messiah through the prophet Isaiah:

> "'Behold, My Servant, whom I uphold; My chosen One in whom My soul delights, I have put My Spirit upon Him; He will bring forth justice to the nations. He will not cry out or raise His Voice, nor make His Voice heard in the street. A bruised reed He will not break and a dimly burning wick He will not extinguish; He will faithfully bring forth justice. He will not be disheartened or crushed until He has established

justice on the earth; and the coastlands will wait expectantly for His Law.'

Thus says Yahweh God, who created the heavens and stretched them out, who spread out the earth and its offspring, who gives breath to the people on it and spirit to those who walk in it, 'I am Yahweh, I have called You in righteousness, I will also hold You by the hand and watch over You, and I will appoint You as a covenant to the people, as a light to the nations, to open blind eyes, to bring out prisoners from the dungeon and those who dwell in darkness from the prison. I am Yahweh, that is My Name; I will not give My glory to another, nor My praise to graven images. Behold, the former things have come to pass, now I declare new things; before they spring forth I proclaim them to You.'"[282]

Moreover, as I said before, this is the covenant Yahweh talked about in Ezekiel chapters 34 and 36.[283] In Ezekiel, He called it a "covenant of peace." In effect, the New Covenant is a "covenant of peace" between Yahweh and His people because the price for our sins was paid by the Messiah when He was hung on a tree. The sin that prevented us from having intimacy with Yahweh was covered by His blood, and the conditions for peace were satisfied once and for all.

The covenant Yahweh made with His people is explained in Genesis chapter 15, and the laws associated with it are spelled out in the Torah. In the next chapter, you will see that faith in Yahweh is the common thread tying the Old and New Covenants together.

Chapter 7

Without Faith We Are Dead

Yahweh's creation changed dramatically when Satan deceived Eve and she and Adam ate fruit from the tree of the knowledge of good and evil against Yahweh's explicit instructions. Their sin forged a gulf between God and man that remains mankind's most pressing problem and it was not simply eating forbidden fruit. They attempted to usurp Yahweh's sovereignty and impose their own authority over God's creation. This is something Yahweh will not allow. He will not relinquish sovereignty over His creation to anyone.

The Relationship between Yahweh and Satan

The relationship between Yahweh and Satan is very difficult to understand, but we know from God's Word that Satan is mankind's Adversary and Accuser. He is referred to in the Bible by many names. Each one of them describes him as a spirit bent on subverting Yahweh's plan for mankind and preventing man from having intimacy with the Creator. Why God allows, and has allowed, Satan to exercise authority in His universe is a mystery, but from the third chapter of Genesis through the remainder of the Bible he is seen as the enemy of mankind and God's opponent in a spiritual war that rages to this day.

Satan led a rebellion in heaven against Yahweh, and eventually he and his angels were defeated and thrown out. Ezekiel 28: 12-15 describes him before he rebelled:

"You had the seal of perfection, full of wisdom and perfect in beauty. You were in Eden, the garden of God; every precious stone was your covering: the ruby, the topaz, and the diamond; the beryl, the onyx and the jasper; the lapis lazuli, the turquoise and the emerald; and the gold, the workmanship of your settings and sockets, was in you. On the day that you were created they were prepared. You were the anointed cherub who covers, and I placed you there. You were on the holy mountain of God; you walked in the midst of the stones of fire. You were blameless in your ways from the day you were created until unrighteousness was found in you."[284]

Isaiah 14: 12-14 describes Satan's sin that initiated the war in heaven between Yahweh and Satan and his angelic followers:

"How you have fallen from heaven, O star of the morning, son of the dawn! You have been cut down to the earth, you who have weakened the nations! But you said in your heart, I will ascend to heaven; I will raise my throne above the stars of God, and I will sit on the mount of assembly in the recesses of the north. I will ascend above the heights of the clouds; I will make myself like the Most High."[285]

Satan's sin was pride. Take a close look at the "I will" statements in these verses from Isaiah. Satan wanted to take God's place and for that he was thrown down to earth. He has been very active in the terrestrial realm since then, but Satan's first attack on mankind occurred in the Garden of Eden.

Satan's Deception and the Loss of Intimacy with Yahweh

Satan came to Eve in the Garden of Eden in the guise of a serpent and said, "Indeed, has God said, 'You shall not eat from any tree of the garden'?"[286] Eve quickly told him that they were free to eat from any tree in the Garden except the tree in the middle of the Garden—the tree of the knowledge of good and evil. Then she explained that God told them, "You shall not eat from it or touch it, or you will die."[287]

Clearly, Eve misunderstood Yahweh's command. In Genesis 2: 17, He told Adam, not Eve, that if he disobeyed Him by eating from the tree of the knowledge of good and evil, He would impose a death sentence on him. Stated another way, he would be "doomed to die" or he would "surely die," but Yahweh did not say he would die immediately.[288] Adam must have told Eve about Yahweh's warning, and it is obvious that her understanding was flawed because God said absolutely nothing about touching the tree of the knowledge of good and evil.[289] Also, Yahweh gave Adam this command before He created Eve[290] so it is reasonable to assume that Adam told her about it.

Satan knew exactly what Yahweh told Adam, and Eve's misunderstanding of God's command enabled him to deceive her and to perpetuate the lie that death is not the penalty for sin. Even today, when people disobey God and nothing happens to them immediately they think they are safe, but they are not safe. They are doomed to die unless they are redeemed. Someone must pay the price for our sins. Either we pay, or our Redeemer pays for us. It is just that simple.

Knowing that Eve misunderstood Yahweh's explicit command, Satan said,

"You surely shall not die! For God knows that in the day you eat from it your eyes will be opened, and you will be like God, knowing good and evil."[291]

Eve thought the fruit looked very appealing, and the notion that she could be as wise as God was more than she could resist. She picked fruit from the tree, ate it, and offered Adam a bite. Their rebellion in the Garden of Eden set in motion a spiritual war between Yahweh and Satan for the souls of men and women and created a sin problem for mankind that only Yahweh can solve.

As I have said before, Yahweh would visit Adam in the Garden to walk and talk. Adam must have looked forward to God's visits. He probably felt like a small child awaiting the arrival of his favorite grandparents. It is possible, even likely, that Adam would run up to Yahweh, hug Him tightly, and kiss Him. But after they ate the forbidden fruit, Adam and Eve hid from God instead.

What a contrast. Before Adam sinned, he could hardly wait for Yahweh's visits, but afterwards he could not bear the thought of seeing Him. Why? Because he knew he had made a mistake—a big one. He had sinned against God, and he knew it. He was ashamed of himself, and he must have thought that by hiding from Yahweh his guilt and shame would simply disappear—the way a child thinks.

Adam's sin destroyed the intimacy he had with Yahweh, and only he was responsible. Yes, Eve took the first bite, but Adam was responsible. According to Genesis 3: 6, he was right there beside Eve while she was talking with Satan. His inaction at that critical moment made him responsible for the problem mankind has been dealing with since that day—rebellion against Yahweh.

Take a look at this exchange between God and Adam and Eve and see if it does not remind you of a father talking with his children. Yahweh knew what Adam had done, and He knew that Adam was hiding, but He asked, "Where are you?"[292]

Adam replied,

"I heard the sound of You in the garden, and I was afraid because I was naked; so I hid myself."[293]

Then God asked,

"Who told you that you were naked? Have you eaten from the tree of which I commanded you not to eat?"[294]

Since God knew what Adam had done, He was simply trying to get him to admit his mistake and accept responsibility, but as a child does, Adam made excuses instead. He said,

"The woman whom you gave to be with me, she gave me from the tree, and I ate."[295]

In other words, Adam was telling Yahweh that He was ultimately responsible for the problem because He gave the woman to him, and she offered him the fruit. The fact that he disobeyed God and ate the fruit was beside the point. Is this not exactly the way a child thinks?

Then God turned to Eve and asked, "What is this you have done?"[296]

She replied, "The serpent deceived me, and I ate."[297]

Eve behaved like a child as well. In her mind, she was not responsible because the serpent told her the fruit was good. It did not matter to her at that moment that she ate the fruit so she could be as wise as Yahweh.

Adam and Eve denied responsibility for destroying the intimacy they had with Yahweh, and both of them were wrong. They were responsible for creating the gulf between God and mankind, even though Satan tempted them, and Adam was ultimately responsible, as I explained earlier. Although Adam and Eve created the problem, only Yahweh can repair the damage they did.

God Acts to Restore the Lost Intimacy

Yahweh desires to have an intimate, personal relationship with each and every one of us. That is why He created us in the first place. God did not create man to obey rules. He gave us the Law to teach and guide us, but obeying His Law is not our end goal. Our objective is to have intimacy with Yahweh. He loves us and yearns to enjoy the same kind of relationship with us today that He had with Adam before he sinned. If you are not experiencing close, personal fellowship with God, then you need to examine yourself carefully to find out what the problem is.

Our lack of intimacy with Yahweh is not His problem, so resist the temptation to lay the blame on Him the way Adam did. Blaming Him only hurts you because you cannot find God by blaming Him for something He did not do. He stands ready right now to enter into an intimate relationship with you, but you must come to God the way He directs or you will not find Him. In the truest sense of the word, He is as close to you as He can possibly be—literally right at your door, but if you do not approach Him the way He intends you will never find Him.

Earlier, I said that Yahweh is holy and that for us to enter into a personal relationship with Him we must be holy too. You will recall that Moses was ready to approach God directly when the Children of Israel reached Mount Sinai, but everyone else had to prepare to meet Him. They had to wash their clothes and spend two days getting ready. Exactly what did God count on them doing during those two days? He expected them to do what He wants us to do today—turn their hearts toward Him and seek Him with all their hearts.

Deuteronomy 4: 29 says,

"Seek Yahweh your God, and you will find Him if you search for Him with all your heart and all your soul."[298]

We must seek Yahweh, but we must do it with all our heart and all our soul. Regrettably, that is not the way many people seek Yahweh. God wants us to have a burning desire to know Him, and then He reveals Himself to us in a close, personal way.

Be honest with yourself and think for a moment about the way many people seek God. For many of them, it is a once a week activity at best. On Sunday Christians head for church and on Saturday Jewish people head for synagogue, and religiously they take their seats. Someone (a preacher, a rabbi, a song leader, or maybe an elder) stands in front of the congregation and reads from a script, and they dutifully follow along by doing whatever they are told to do. Some congregates are prepared before they arrive, and they are actually seeking Yahweh. But others are not ready, and they are simply going through the motions.

They stand up. They sit down. They read a verse from the Bible. They sing a song. They go through a well-rehearsed routine, and they call it worship—seeking Yahweh. But they are not seeking Yahweh with all their heart and all their soul, and Yahweh is under no obligation to reveal Himself to them.

Many congregates are simply engaging in religious activity, and God never once promised that He would honor religious activity. In fact, He said just the opposite in Isaiah 29: 13-14:

"Because this people draw near with their words and honor Me with their lip service, but they remove their hearts far from Me, and their reverence for me consists of tradition learned by rote, therefore behold, I will once again deal marvelously with this people, wondrously marvelous; and the wisdom of their wise men shall perish, and the discernment of their discerning men shall be concealed."[299]

These verses make it clear that Yahweh hated their religious activity because it was not what He desired, and He punished them for it. He aimed His remarks primarily at the religious leaders, the priests, since they should have known better. They were leading the people astray, and in effect they were mocking Yahweh seeing as they must have thought that He did not know, or worse, that He knew and did not care. Through Isaiah, Yahweh was telling them to wake up and do right or suffer the consequences.

God will not honor our religious activity unless we are worshipping Him with all our heart and all our soul. In fact, it offends God when we simply go through the motions and call it worship. Yahweh wants our hearts and souls, and He knows that if we give them to Him our attitudes and actions will come into proper alignment with His will.

I used the word "obligation" earlier, and that is exactly what I intended to say. God made a promise. If we seek Him with all our heart and all our soul, then He will reveal Himself to us. In a literal sense, God is obligated to reveal Himself to us if we seek Him the way He directs because He said He would, and Yahweh cannot lie. But He does not do it out of duty or obligation. He does it because He loves us and because He wants to have an intimate relationship with us. Try Him and see for yourself.

The Bible says a great deal about seeking God in a way that will glorify His Name and be rewarded. Below are a few examples:

- "Oh give thanks to Yahweh, call upon His Name; make known His deeds among the peoples. Sing to Him, sing praises to Him; speak of all His wonders. Glory in His holy Name; let the heart of those who seek Yahweh be glad. Seek Yahweh and His strength; seek His face continually."[300]

- "...for Yahweh searches all hearts, and understands every intent of the thoughts. If you seek Him, He will let you find Him; but if you forsake Him, He will reject you forever."[301]

- "If...My people who are called by My Name humble themselves and pray and seek My face and turn from their wicked ways, then I will hear from heaven, will forgive their sin and will heal their land."[302]

- "Yahweh is with you when you are with Him. And if you seek Him, He will let you find Him; but if you forsake Him, He will forsake you."[303]

- "And those who know Your Name will put their trust (faith) in You, for You, O Yahweh, have not forsaken those who seek you."[304]

- "Let all those who seek You rejoice and be glad in You; let those who love Your salvation say continually, 'Yahweh be magnified!'"[305]

- "How blessed are those who observe His testimonies, who seek Him with all their heart."[306]

From these verses, it is clear that seeking Yahweh the way He desires is not a once-in-a-while thing, and it is not something we are supposed to do only in church or in synagogue. Yahweh instructed us to seek Him continually with all our heart and all our soul. Continually means all the time—literally all day every day. Yahweh should always be on our minds and never far from the front of our minds. That is what seeking Yahweh means, and when we seek Him that way He will let us find Him. If you catch yourself constantly thinking about Yahweh, rejoice. He will honor you for it because that is exactly what He desires.

Yahweh is speaking today, and we can hear His Voice if we will just seek Him and listen. Listening begins when we read His Word and obey Him. Prayer is also a form of listening because God talks with us while we pray. Over time, if you read God's Word and pray earnestly seeking Him, you will learn to recognize His Voice. When you obey His Voice, His blessings will flow.

It has been said, and it is absolutely true, that faith is a gift from Yahweh. Similarly, seeking Yahweh is a gift from Him because the desire to seek and know Him comes from Him. If you feel Yahweh tugging at your heart and drawing you to Him, then you should do what Moses did when he met Yahweh at the burning bush. You should respond by coming close to Him and allowing Him to reveal Himself to you.

Righteousness is Yahweh's Gift to Us

It is quite natural for us to think we should earn righteousness, and it is tempting and appealing to think we can earn it by doing good works, performing acts of kindness, and obeying all the Laws in the Bible. This makes perfect sense from a human perspective because most of us have been brought up to think this way.

For instance, what employer would pay you for simply having faith in him? That does not make any sense, and few if any would do it. In our world, we know we must actually do something tangible, something people can see with their eyes and touch with their hands to earn any reward at all. Using our common (natural) wisdom, we know there is no such thing as a free lunch and that no one gives us anything without expecting something in return, even if it is just a simple "thank you."

But Yahweh does not think the way we think. He said,

"'For My thoughts are not your thoughts, neither are your ways My ways,' declares Yahweh. 'For as the heavens are higher than the earth, so are My ways higher than your ways and My thoughts than your thoughts.'"[307]

Although God understands common (natural) wisdom, He does not use it, and He does not want us to use it either. Consider this. We know God expects us to forgive people who hurt us and that we should forgive them again and again if they ask for forgiveness. Does this sound like common (natural) wisdom? No, but it is God's wisdom.

Why does God want and expect us to forgive people time after time even when we think they will never change? Because that is the way He forgives us. He wants and expects us to apply His logic and behave the way He behaves. This wisdom is not common wisdom. It is God's wisdom, and learning about God means patterning our lives and our thoughts after His. If we pay attention to God's Word, listen to His Voice, and obey Him, then He uses all circumstances, even unpleasant ones, to teach us His ways and His thoughts and to make us holy.

If we apply only human logic we will never understand righteousness. It is a gift from Yahweh that we cannot earn. He set it up that way for a reason. If righteousness were payment from God for our good works, then He would be our debtor simply paying us what He owes us. But Yahweh is not our debtor. He is the Sovereign Creator, the God of the universe, and He owes us nothing. We are

His creation, and He loves us dearly, but He does not owe us a thing. God will not allow Himself to be put into the position of owing us anything, and this is especially true when it comes to righteousness. Thus, our good works could never earn righteousness for us.

Yahweh is a wonderful Father. All He has done, is doing, and will do for us is based on His love for us. He enjoys blessing us and giving us gifts, but He does not do it because He has to. He does it because He wants to. Yahweh wants us to be righteous, and He wants to give us righteousness that leads to salvation. But we must understand that it is a gift from Him that we cannot earn.

Yahweh's plan for making us righteous and saving us is based on His redemptive work alone. In effect, He covers us with His righteousness, a standard we cannot attain on our own. Isaiah explained it this way:

> "For all of us have become like one who is unclean, and all our righteous deeds are like a filthy garment; and all of us wither like a leaf, and our iniquities, like the wind, take us away."[308]

Since we cannot earn righteousness, God gives us His righteousness and salvation freely if we have faith in Him. This may sound strange, but from God's perspective it makes perfect sense. You should recall that one of God's Names is Yahweh Tsidkenu — Yahweh our Righteousness. His Names tell us about Him, and this Name for God declares that He is our righteousness. But even more, it proclaims that we have no righteousness apart from Him. Take a look at the context in which the Name "Yahweh Tsidkenu" is used, and it will help you to understand a mystery:

> "Behold, the days are coming, declares Yahweh, when I shall raise up for David a righteous Branch; and He will reign as king and act wisely and do justice and righteousness in the land. In His days Judah will be saved, and Israel will dwell securely; and this is His Name by which He will be called, Yahweh our Righteousness."[309]

These verses are about the Messiah (David's righteous Branch or an offspring of David), and they reveal one of His Names—Yahweh Tsidkenu or Yahweh our Righteousness.[310] I hope you understand the significance of these verses because Jeremiah told us the Messiah's Name in such plain language that you need help to misinterpret what he said. The Messiah's Name is Yahweh our Righteousness. It just doesn't get any clearer than that.

The fact that our righteousness comes from Yahweh makes sense from a human perspective if you think about it this way. Consider a married couple for a moment. The relationship between man and wife is not good if either one of them conditions their love on the other one doing something for them. If they feel as though they must earn the love of their spouse by doing something, then they are miserable.

They may accept a bad relationship and learn to live with it, but it is not a healthy, happy relationship because they never know where they stand with one another. They wake up each morning uncertain, wondering if their relationship will fall apart and knowing that if they make a mistake it could come to an end at any moment. In the backs of their minds, they are constantly thinking that maybe he or she will meet another person, someone who can do more than I can or do things better than I can. Doubt and uncertainty take their toll over time and make life miserable.

Healthy marriage relationships are built on love that is unconditional. Each spouse loves the other no matter what happens, and both of them know it. Unconditional love is the hallmark of a good marriage relationship, and it is the kind of love God has for us. He wants us to wake up each morning confident and certain that we cannot lose His love. God wants us to have faith in Him to love us and to take care of us forever.

By declaring that our righteousness is not based on our own effort and initiative but on Yahweh's righteousness instead, He opens the door for us to have the kind of permanent relationship with Him that He and we desire. Yahweh's righteousness never changes. He is righteousness.

God does not want us to wake up every morning thinking we might sin today and destroy our relationship with Him. God absolutely does not want us to go through life wondering what will happen when we die and meet Him face-to-face for the final judgment. The truth is that all of us sin every day. If God's love for us were conditioned on our being sinless, then He simply could not love any of us. Therefore, Yahweh bases His love for us on His steadfast righteousness instead of our righteousness, which as Isaiah said, is "like a filthy garment."[311] That is true love.

Yahweh is a wonderful Father, and He knows how to give wonderful gifts. He wants us to know that we have been forgiven already and that we are safe with Him. God wants us to understand that He paid the price for our sins, all the sins we will ever commit, and cloaked us with His perfect righteousness. Doubt and uncertainty are removed, and we are truly free to love Him.

In Isaiah 45: 21-24, Yahweh explained it this way:

"There is no other God besides Me, a righteous God and a Savior; there is none except Me. Turn to Me and be saved, all the ends of the earth; for I am God, and there is no other. I have sworn by Myself, the Word has gone forth from My mouth in righteousness and will not turn back, that to Me every knee will bow, every tongue will swear allegiance. They will say of Me, 'Only in Yahweh are righteousness and strength.' Men will come to Him, and all who are angry at Him shall be put to shame."[312]

Now look at Isaiah 61: 10:

"I will rejoice greatly in Yahweh, my soul will exult in my God; for He has clothed me with garments of salvation, He has wrapped me with a robe of righteousness, as a bridegroom decks himself with a garland, and as a bride adorns herself with her jewels."[313]

Clearly, righteousness is Yahweh's gift to us. We could never earn it. In his letter to Titus, the apostle Paul explained it this way:

"There was a time when we too were ignorant, disobedient and misled and enslaved by different passions and dissipations; we lived then in wickedness and malice, hating each other and hateful ourselves.

But when the kindness and love of God our Saviour for humanity were revealed, it was not because of any upright actions we had done ourselves; it was for no reason except His own faithful love that he saved us....so that, justified by His grace (unmerited favor), we should become heirs in hope of eternal life. This is doctrine that you can rely on."[314]

In his letter to the Galatians, Paul went even further:

"Behold I, Paul, say to you that if you receive circumcision, the Messiah will be of no benefit to you. And I testify again to every man who receives circumcision, that he is under obligation to keep the whole Law. You have been severed from the Messiah, you who are seeking to be justified by law; you have fallen from grace. For we through the Spirit, by faith, are waiting for the hope of righteousness. For in Messiah Jesus neither circumcision nor uncircumcision means anything, but faith working through love."[315]

In other words, if you believe you can earn justification and righteousness by obeying the Law, you are doomed. This does not mean that the Law is unimportant or that we can disobey the Law without fear of consequences—far from it. It simply means that obeying the Law is no substitute for faith in Yahweh. God expects us to obey the Law as He commanded, but faith in Him is the only thing that leads to salvation, justification, and righteousness. This subtle distinction is very important, and it has been the source of much controversy since the creation of the human race.

Yahweh Honors His Desires

Although God's love for us is unconditional, He is holy, and He cannot abide sin. We should be thankful that God does not require us to earn salvation by doing "good works" because if He did no one would be saved, ever. Why? Because God's standard for righteousness is not like ours.

We need to keep this fact in mind at all times. His thoughts are not our thoughts, and His ways are not our ways. His standard for righteousness is beyond our reach. Yahweh requires perfect holiness, flawless purity, and absolute sinlessness. In other words, He will accept no blemishes at all, and we are incapable of attaining His standard for righteousness no matter how good we are. What we call "good" simply does not pass Yahweh's test.

In His infinite mercy, God planned things so that we do not have to earn righteousness. All He requires from us is faith in Him — faith that He will do for us what we cannot do for ourselves. He is our Redeemer. He willingly and lovingly died in our place and paid the price demanded by His Law for our sins so we would not have to die. Yahweh, the Almighty God, is our absolutely perfect, unblemished, Sacrificial Lamb.

Does this sound farfetched to you? If it does, then ask yourself this question. Would good parents take a deadly disease on themselves if it threatened the life of their child? Of course they would, if they could, but they could not do it even if they wanted to. Thankfully, nothing is impossible for God. He could take our sins on Himself, and He gladly did. If good parents would die for their children, why would anyone believe that Yahweh, who is a perfect Parent, would not die for His? The only difference is that He can actually do it, and He did it. Do we really believe we are better parents than God is? I certainly hope not.

If we believe Yahweh died to atone for our sins, we are forgiven. Faith in Him alone leads to righteousness and salvation. It is a gift from God, and all we have to do is decide if we want to accept His gift because it cannot be earned. However, if we stubbornly refuse to obey God, we are demonstrating that we do not have saving faith. As the apostle James said, and I am paraphrasing, "Without faith we are dead, but faith without works, or obedience, is dead as well."[316] Just as a good tree produces good fruit, so must saving faith produce works that Yahweh calls "good." In a nutshell, obedience that flows from faith in Yahweh pleases Him, and obedience without faith cannot save us.

You may still be thinking that all of this sounds fantastic, but it does not make any sense from a human perspective. No one would do that for me, and it cannot be that easy. Surely God expects me to do more than simply accept His gift. Well, if you apply only human logic, it is impossible to understand what God is doing. So do not use human logic. Read God's Word and apply His logic.

Yahweh does expect us to do good works, but the good works He wants from us have absolutely nothing to do with our redemption and salvation. These issues have to be settled before we can even think about doing works that God calls "good." He gives us His righteousness and salvation freely, and all we need to do to secure them is have faith in Him. When we have faith in Yahweh, He does something else for us that is very special. It is discussed in Psalm 37: 4-5:

> "Delight yourself in Yahweh; and He will give you the desires of your heart. Commit your way to Yahweh, trust also in Him, and He will do it."[317]

Yahweh gives us the desires of our heart because we have faith in Him. He actually gives us His desires so that our works become works that He calls "good." Clearly, this is a very special gift from Him.

When we have faith in Yahweh and He gives us the desires of our hearts, we will actually want to obey Him and do good things for Him because we love Him, truly love Him. For example, He loves us, and He wants us to love others the way He loves us. He forgives us, and He wants us to forgive others the way He forgives us. He shares with us, and he wants us to share with others the way he shares with us.

These are the good works Yahweh wants and expects from us, but they are not sufficient to earn our redemption and salvation, and they cannot make us righteous before Him. Only faith in Him does that. Psalm 49: 7-8 and 15 make this point clearly:

"No man can by any means redeem his brother or give to God a ransom for him—for the redemption of his soul is costly, and he should cease trying forever[318]....But God will redeem my soul from the power of Sheol, for He will receive me."[319]

As the psalm says, our redemption is costly. The price for our redemption is the blood of Yahweh. Only He could pay the price for our sins, and He gladly did. Now think for a moment about how God feels when we decide to reject His gift, and we strive instead to earn righteousness as if His sacrifice were meaningless. He suffered and died for us, and if we reject His gift, then He will reject us. It is just that simple. As the psalm says, we should "cease trying forever." Simply accept His gift. Yahweh has done His part already, and our response must be to have faith in Him and to obey His Word.

If we insist on believing that our good works can earn our redemption and salvation and make us righteous before Yahweh, then we have stumbled over the stumbling stone. That's exactly what Isaiah was talking about when he said,

"Then He (the Messiah) shall become a sanctuary; but to both the houses of Israel, a stone to strike and a rock to stumble over, and a snare and a trap for the inhabitants of Jerusalem. Many will stumble over them, then they will fall and be broken; they will even be snared and caught."[320]

A little later Isaiah said,

"Therefore thus says Adonai Yahweh, behold, I am laying in Zion a stone, a tested stone, a costly cornerstone for the foundation, firmly placed. He who believes in it will not be disturbed."[321]

A literal translation of the Hebrew in this verse reads as follows:

"Thus says Adonai Yahweh, 'See! I am laying a stone in Zion, a stone of testing, a precious cornerstone for a strong foundation. The one who trusts in it will never be dismayed.'"

Finally, Isaiah laid it on the line so everyone could understand, or at least he thought everyone could understand:

"Listen to me, you who pursue righteousness, who seek Yahweh: Look to the rock from which you were hewn and to the quarry from which you were dug. Look to Abraham your father and to Sarah who gave birth to you in pain."[322]

Isaiah was telling them, and he is telling us, to have faith in Yahweh and to look to Him for salvation the way Abraham did. And look to Sarah who believed God when He told her she would have a child after she had passed the normal childbearing years. Look to their faith in Yahweh.

Without Faith It Is Impossible to Please Yahweh

Habakkuk 2: 3-4 says,

"For the vision is yet for the appointed time; it hastens toward the goal and it will not fail. Though it tarries, wait for it; for it will certainly come, it will not delay. Behold, as for the proud one, his soul is not right within him; but the righteous will live by his faith."[323]

Paul said it as clearly and succinctly as I can be said in Hebrews 11: 6:

"And without faith it is impossible to please Him, for he who comes to God must believe that He is and that He is a rewarder of those who seek Him."[324]

In other words, without faith we are dead.

Faith in Yahweh leads to righteousness and salvation, and righteous people live by faith. While it makes sense to us that God should require good works from us as the price for our salvation, in reality our good works are not good enough. As the proverb says, "There is a way which seems right to a man, but its end is the way of death."[325] What seems right to us is actually wrong. If we persist in pursuing a course that seems right, but is not, we will miss out on righteousness and salvation altogether.

Having made these points, we need to consider what Abraham did that made him righteous before God since Isaiah used him as the example we should follow. Genesis 15: 6 says,

"Then he (Abraham) believed in Yahweh; and He (Yahweh) reckoned it to him as righteousness."[326]

A literal translation of the Hebrew in this verse reads as follows:

"Then he (Abraham) believed in Yahweh, and He (Yahweh) credited it to him as righteousness."[327]

If you search the Bible thoroughly, you will find nothing that even suggests Abraham's righteousness was dependent on anything except his faith in Yahweh. If you doubt this, then look for yourself or ask someone you trust to show you. Notice that I did not say ask them to tell you. Make them show you because it does not exist.

Why is this important? Because God made promises to Abraham that all of us depend on for our salvation, and all of God's promises, every single one of them, were and are dependent on our having faith in Him just as Abraham did.

Yahweh declared Abraham righteous because he had faith in Him. Today God declares anyone righteous who has faith in Him, but faith in Him to do what? We must have faith in Yahweh to redeem and save us, to take care of us, to protect us, and to provide for us as we carry out the work He gives us to do.

In Romans 4: 19-22, the apostle Paul said Abraham drew strength from his faith. He was about 100 years old and Sarah was about 90, but he remained convinced that Yahweh was able to do exactly what He promised—i.e., that He would give him a son by Sarah through whom the covenant would pass to future generations. Even though Yahweh's promise seemed impossible to fulfill from a human perspective, Abraham remained steadfast in faith and gave glory to God.

Abraham's righteousness was not dependent on circumcision. We know this because circumcision is only an outward, visible sign of the covenant and nothing more.[328] It was important as a sign, but Abraham's righteousness was NOT dependent on it. Also, God declared Abraham righteous before He required circumcision as the sign of the covenant. Thus, his righteousness could not have been dependent on it. Furthermore, we know that circumcision of the flesh is symbolic of the inward condition Yahweh truly desires— circumcision of the heart.

Deuteronomy 30: 6 says,

"Moreover, Yahweh your God will circumcise your heart and the heart of your descendants, to love Yahweh your God with all your heart and with all your soul, in order that you may live."[329]

As Isaiah would say, "See!" Yahweh wants our hearts and souls.

What's more, we know from Yahweh's Word that Abraham's righteousness could not have been dependent on obeying the Law (the Torah) since Yahweh did not give the Law until hundreds of years after He declared Abraham righteous. Genesis 15: 6 says that Yahweh declared Abraham righteous because he had faith, and His requirement has never changed. However, Yahweh tested Abraham's faith by telling him to sacrifice Isaac,[330] and Abraham's willingness to obey God demonstrated that he had the kind of faith that pleases Him.

Yahweh never intended for the Torah to impart life to His people. In fact, the Torah brought us death because it showed us how pure and holy God is and how filthy and dirty we are when compared to Him. The Torah is perfect and good, and it shows us how much we need a Redeemer and Savior. But it cannot impart life. In fact, it exposes us as sinners who are guilty and shows us that we deserve God's punishment.

Paul explained it this way in his letter to the Romans:

"So then, no human being can be found upright at the tribunal of God by keeping the Law; all that the Law does is to tell us what is sinful....Are we saying that the Law has been made

158

pointless by faith? Out of the question; we are placing the Law on its true footing."[331]

Yahweh neither says nor implies that the Torah can impart salvation or life, but He does say we should live by the Laws in the Torah and that not obeying His Laws will bring us death. Yet, again and again Yahweh declares that faith in Him is the requirement for salvation. He could not have made it any clearer.

Our Decision

There are about 7 billion people living on the earth right now, and there may be twice that many opinions about what God requires from us for salvation. However, Yahweh is sovereign, and He has exclusive jurisdiction in this matter. Any attempt we make to substitute our personal views for His unambiguous command is the same as the sin Adam committed in the Garden of Eden.

From God's perspective, Adam's sin was an act of moral independence. It was a direct assault on His sovereignty and a sin of the highest magnitude. Only God has the authority to determine right and wrong, good and evil, and He alone has the privilege of determining how He redeems and saves mankind.

It would be foolish to ignore these facts because the consequences for doing so are catastrophic. Search the Scriptures and find out what Yahweh said He would do to people who reject His gift and choose to follow their own instincts instead. He said that He would reject them and send them to the lake of fire where there will be perpetual burning and eternal punishment, and forever is a long, long time.

God laid out His plan for our redemption and salvation very clearly in the Bible. He did not give us a list of options and tell us to select the one that is most consistent with our personal preferences and traditions. He told us to accept or reject His plan, and each one of us must do just that.

At the end of the day, God requires us to decide if we have faith in Him. Abraham made his choice, and Yahweh declared him righteous. Since God never changes, He will declare us righteous as well if we have faith in Him, but if we do not have faith in Him we are doomed to die an eternal death. It is very frightening and just that simple.

Saving faith is alive and active and it produces works that Yahweh calls "good," but it does not have to be perfect. Abraham did not have perfect faith, but Yahweh used him to bless the whole world. Noah did not have flawless faith either, but Yahweh preserved life on earth through him. Samson and Gideon did not display unswerving faith, but Yahweh delivered Israel from her adversaries through them. These people were ordinary human beings who God used to do extraordinary things because they had saving faith. Yahweh still uses ordinary human beings to change the world. Are you one of these people?

Jesus' comments on the importance of faith are revealing. Following the transfiguration (see Matthew 17: 1-13), Jesus encountered the father of a demon-possessed boy. His disciples had tried unsuccessfully to exorcise the demon, and when the man saw Jesus coming down off the mountain, he pleaded with Him to heal his son. Jesus healed him instantly, and His disciples asked Him why they were unable to drive the demon out of the boy. Jesus said,

> "Because of the littleness of your faith; for truly I say to you, if you have faith the size of a mustard seed, you will say to this mountain (the Mount of Transfiguration or Mount Tabor), 'Move from here to there,' and it will move; and nothing will be impossible to you."[332]

The people who heard Him say these words must have been shocked. Using human logic, it did not make any sense, but Jesus was telling them not to rely on human logic. He was admonishing them to have faith in Yahweh, to be firm in their convictions, and to go forward without fear, relying on God.

Yahweh uses small measures of faith (i.e., faith as small as a tiny mustard seed) to accomplish colossal things, or things that seem impossible using human logic. Put your faith to work and trust Yahweh to accomplish His objectives, and you can actually experience what I'm talking about. Yahweh is ready right now to do what He said He will do. Are you willing to let Him?

Chapter 8

The Messiah in the Old Testament

Messiah means "Anointed One," and Genesis 3: 15 is the first verse in the Bible that mentions Him:

> "And I will put enmity between you and the woman, and between your seed and her seed; He shall bruise you on the head, and you shall bruise Him on the heel."[333]

The seed of the woman is the Messiah, and Satan is the one He will bruise on the head. In this verse, Yahweh says Satan will wound the Messiah, but He will achieve victory in the end, redeem His people, and destroy His archenemy. Christians are not the only ones who have interpreted this verse as a Messianic prophecy. Midrash Rabbah, an ancient rabbinic commentary, says this about Genesis 3: 15:

> "R. (Rabbi) Tanhuma said in the name of Samuel Kozith: [She hinted at] that seed which would arise from another source, viz. the king Messiah."[334]

17 Prophecies of the Messiah's First-Coming

The Messiah is the central figure in the Old Testament from Genesis to Malachi. Prophecies about Him deal with every facet of his life—His birth, His ministry on earth, His death, and His ultimate victory. Grant Jeffrey, a Bible scholar and author, has estimated the probability of anyone fulfilling just 17 prophecies about the Messiah's first-coming, and his results are astonishing.[335] Jeffrey's probability estimates are presented below,[336] and they are extremely conservative:

1. He will be born in Bethlehem and descended from Judah—Micah 5: 2 and Genesis 49: 10—Probability: 1 in 2,400.
2. A messenger will precede the Messiah—Isaiah 40: 3 and Malachi 3: 1—Probability: 1 in 20.
3. He will enter Jerusalem on a colt—Zechariah 9: 9—Probability: 1 in 50.
4. He will be betrayed by a friend—Psalm 41: 9—Probability: 1 in 10.
5. His hands and feet will be pierced—Psalm 22: 16—Probability: 1 in 100.
6. His enemies will wound Him—Isaiah: 54: 5—Probability: 1 in 10.
7. His betrayer will receive 30 pieces of silver for betraying Him—Zechariah 11: 12—Probability: 1 in 50.
8. He will be spit upon and beaten—Isaiah 50: 6—Probability: 1 in 10.
9. The money for His betrayal will be thrown into the Temple and used to buy a potter's field—Zechariah 11: 13—Probability: 1 in 200.
10. He will be silent before His accusers—Isaiah 53: 7—Probability: 1 in 100.
11. He will die with thieves—Isaiah 53: 9—Probability: 1 in 100.
12. People will gamble for His garments—Psalm 22: 18—Probability: 1 in 100.
13. His side will be pierced—Zechariah 12: 10—Probability: 1 in 100.

14. None of His bones will be broken—Psalm 34: 20—Probability: 1 in 20.
15. His body will not decay—Psalm 16: 10—Probability: 1 in 10,000.
16. He will be buried in a rich man's tomb—Isaiah 53: 9—Probability: 1 in 100.
17. Darkness will cover the earth at His death—Amos 8: 9—Probability: 1 in 1000.

The odds of anyone in earth's history fulfilling these 17 prophecies are 1 in 480,000,000,000,000,000,000,000,000,000,000.[337] We can state this number another way: 1 in 5 trillion multiplied by 96 trillion. The denominator in this fraction is so large that it boggles the mind.

Here is a way to think about these odds. In 2001, The United States' national debt was about 5 trillion dollars. Imagine you have in front of you 5 trillion times 96 trillion $1 bills. It would take an area the size of Texas to pile them up. We mark one of the $1 bills, hide it somewhere in the pile, blindfold you, and tell you to pick the marked bill out of the pile in one try. In 2011, the United States' national debt is about $15 trillion. I used the 2001 figure because the math was easier to do and because I wanted you to see how rapidly our nation's debt has grown.

The probability of you picking the correct $1 bill in this example is the same as the likelihood of anyone fulfilling these 17 prophecies about the Messiah by chance, but there are hundreds of Messianic prophecies in the Bible—not 17. Thus, logic and probability indicate that anyone who fulfills these prophecies must be the Messiah.

There is (and Can Be) Only One Messiah

As you think about Jeffrey's estimates, remember that most of them require God's direct intervention. For instance, no one decides where to be born. Neither can anyone choose the family into which he or she will be born. Obviously, these decisions are Yahweh's alone. Therefore, we must conclude that the Messiah's birth was a gift from God that no man could copy or manufacture under any set of circumstances.

To his credit, Jeffrey's estimates are conservative in every instance. For example, his 5th prophecy deals with the Messiah's crucifixion. Somewhere between 1010 B.C. and 970 B.C., King David prophesied that the Messiah would be crucified. In Psalm 22: 16 he wrote,

> "For dogs have surrounded me; a band of evildoers has encompassed me; they pierced my hands and my feet."[338]

Crucifixion is a form of capital punishment that was invented by the Romans in the 1st century B.C. In David's day, stoning was the prescribed method for capital punishment so his prophecy that the Messiah would be crucified at least 800 years before crucifixion was invented is remarkable. Jeffrey estimates the probability of this happening as 1 in 100, but I believe it is closer to zero. David simply could not have foretold the Messiah's crucifixion unless God explained it to him.

Many Jewish people believe Christians have misinterpreted the Hebrew word in Psalm 22: 16 that is translated as "pierced." The Hebrew word appearing in this verse is "ariy" (ar-ee'). Its present-day meaning suggests violence, and it seems to involve a lion or a young lion. Based on this fact Samuel Levine, author of You Take Jesus, I'll Take God, has said,

> "That verse of 'they pierced my hands and feet,' which seems to point to Jesus, is a mistranslation, according to all the classical Jewish scholars, who knew Hebrew perfectly. In fact, the Christians have invented a new word in the process, which is still not in the Hebrew dictionary."[339]

Even though the contemporary definition of "ariy" seems to indicate something other than "piercing," I believe Mr. Levine is mistaken, and this is why. The Jewish authorized Greek Septuagint[340] Tanach (the version of the Tanach I mentioned earlier that was translated by 70 rabbis in 285 B.C.—i.e., almost 285 years before Jesus' birth) and Targums[341] written at that time interpret "ariy" as "pierced" exactly the way Christians have translated the word.[342] No one alive today has a better understanding of the Hebrew used in the Tanach than that group of rabbis, so I defer to them and rely on their translation of "ariy" to support my conclusion.

Furthermore, Zechariah 12: 10 refers to the "piercing" of the Messiah. The Hebrew word translated as "pierced" in this verse is "daqar" (daw-kar'), and it means "to stab" or "to thrust through."

166

This is what the Babylonian Talmud (Sukkah 52a) says about Zechariah 12: 10:

> "What is the cause of the mourning? It is well according to him who explains that the cause is the slaying of Messiah, the son of Joseph, since that well agrees with the Scriptural verse, 'And they shall look upon me because they have thrust Him through, and they shall mourn for Him as one mourneth for his only son.'"[343]

I will not go into much detail about this issue, but many Jewish sages[344] and rabbis over the millennia have had difficulty with the notion that the Messiah Son of David had to suffer for His people. They understood that the Bible describes a suffering Messiah, but they could not accept the fact that He was the Messiah referred to as the Son of David. Therefore, they called Him by another name—the Messiah son of Joseph—even though the only Messiah referred to in the Bible by Name is the Messiah Son of David.

According to Raphael Patai, a Jewish Bible scholar,

> "When the death of the Messiah became an established tenet in Talmudic times,[345] this was felt to be irreconcilable with the belief in the Messiah as the Redeemer who would usher in the blissful millennium of the Messianic age. The dilemma was solved by splitting the person of the Messiah in two: one of them, called Messiah ben Joseph...would fall victim....The other, Messiah ben David, will come after him...and will lead

Israel to ultimate victory, the triumph, and the Messianic era of bliss."[346]

It is perfectly clear that all classical Jewish scholars do not agree with Mr. Levine, and neither do I. Obviously, the 70 rabbis who translated the Greek Septuagint Tanach in 285 B.C. do not agree with him, and I would be foolish to accept his interpretation over theirs. It is also perfectly clear from the weight of evidence and from the Word of God that there is (and can be) only One Messiah. He is the Messiah Son of David; He is the suffering Messiah described in Isaiah 53; and He is the victorious King Messiah described throughout the Old Testament and the Tanach.

Now, take a look at Jeffrey's 17th prophecy. It deals with darkness covering the entire earth at the time of the Messiah's death, and it is almost impossible to predict. Amos 8: 9 says,

> "'It will come about in that day,' declares Adonai Yahweh, 'That I will make the sun go down at noon and make the earth dark in broad daylight.'"[347]

Amos was a sheep breeder from Tekoa, a town about 10 miles south of Jerusalem, and he wrote this prophecy in about 755 B.C.[348] He was not a scientist, and he did not possess sophisticated instruments to calculate the movements of heavenly bodies. Furthermore, this event could not have been a total eclipse of the sun because an eclipse would not affect the entire earth all at once. According to Jeffrey, two ancient historians, Thallus and Phlegon, confirmed that an unusual darkness did blot out the sun for 3 hours during Passover in the year the Messiah was crucified.[349]

Jeffrey estimates the probability of Amos predicting this event more than 700 years before it happened as 1 in 1000. In my opinion, it is almost zero for the same reason I stated before. There is only one rational explanation for this event. It was an act of Yahweh, and Amos was simply declaring it hundreds of years in advance.

A Virgin Will Bear This Child

Jeffrey did not mention the most unlikely prophecy about the Messiah. It is found in Isaiah 7: 14—"a virgin will be with Child."[350] I can only guess the reasons why he decided not to include this prophecy, but it adds great weight to his argument. The probability of a virgin having a child in Isaiah's day was almost zero (if not zero), and it could not have happened at all until the late 20th century except under very rare circumstances. Even today virgins cannot bear children without the aid of sophisticated medical technology, and at great cost, unless they have an incredibly unusual medical condition. Including this prophecy in his list would have provided convincing proof that the Messiah's birth was a miracle from Yahweh that will never be repeated.

Some Bible scholars argue that the Hebrew word translated as "virgin" in Isaiah 7: 14 can also mean "a young girl or a young, recently married woman."[351] Therefore, they believe God was simply saying that a "maiden"[352] would have a child. However, the Hebrew word translated as virgin, "almah," is used seven times[353] in the Old Testament, and in every instance it speaks of a virgin as we understand the meaning of the word. Also, the 70 rabbis who translated the Greek Septuagint Tanach in the third century B.C. used the Greek word "parthenos" which means "virgin" as we use the term today.

If we look at the context in which this prophecy was made, we can see that logic does not support this conclusion either. At the time, King Ahaz of Judah was afraid that his kingdom would be attacked and conquered by two allied kings from the north—Razon King of Aram and Pekah King of Israel. Yahweh assured him that they would not be successful, and He instructed Isaiah to tell Ahaz to ask Him for a sign—any sign—to prove the truth of His Word:

"Ask a sign for yourself from Yahweh your God; make it deep as Sheol or high as heaven."[354]

Ahaz responded by saying,

"I will not ask, nor will I test Yahweh."[355]

The king's reply infuriated Isaiah, and he said,

"Is it too slight a thing for you to try the patience of men, that you will try the patience of my God as well?"[356]

Then he told Ahaz,

"Therefore Yahweh Himself will give you a sign: Behold, a virgin will be with Child and bear a Son, and she will call His Name Immanuel."[357]

If a young girl or a young, recently married woman has a child, would anyone consider it to be a sign from God that is "deep as Sheol or high as heaven?" Absolutely not. That would be an ordinary childbirth, and no one would interpret it as a great sign. But if a virgin had a Child, everyone would believe it was a sign from God.

Furthermore, this Child's Name would be Immanuel—literally "God who is with us." Isaiah 9: 1-6 tells about Him:

- He will come out of Galilee.[358]
- He is a light blazing forth in a dark land.[359]
- He will remove His people's yoke or burden.[360]
- He will be called Wonderful, Counselor, Mighty God, Eternal Father, and Prince of Peace.[361]

Isaiah 11: 1-9 provides more details about this Child:

- He will come from the stock of Jessie (David's father).[362]
- The Spirit of Yahweh will rest on Him.[363]
- He will be the Righteous Judge.[364]
- "He will strike the earth with the rod of His mouth, and with the breath of His lips He will slay the wicked."[365]

In other words, this Child speaks, and it is done. This is reminiscent of Yahweh at the creation. Obviously, this Child is no ordinary child, and it would be preposterous to conclude that He would come into the world in the usual way. Isaiah was telling Ahaz that this would be the sign of signs from Yahweh. A virgin would bear this Child, and He is God who is with us.

Ironically, rabbis have known for thousands of years that the names of Isaiah's children are "divinely ordained signs for events that will befall the people of Israel,"[366] and the Bible says as much explicitly.[367] Below are the names of Isaiah's children and the meanings of their names:

- Maher-Shalal-Hash-Baz — Plunder hastens and spoil quickens.
- Shear-Jashub — A remainder will return.
- Immanuel — God who is with us.

The names of Isaiah's children reveal that Israel will be plundered and exiled. A remnant will return to the Promised Land. Then God will be with us. These things have happened already. We are not awaiting the fulfillment of this prophecy. Yahweh has done it already.

Other Messianic Prophecies

There are hundreds of Messianic prophecies in the Old Testament that Jeffrey did not mention. A few of them are presented below:

Psalm 2: 7-9 — "I will surely tell of the decree of Yahweh: He said to Me, 'You are My Son, today I have begotten You. Ask of Me, and I will give the nations as Your inheritance, and the very ends of the earth as Your possession. You shall break them with a rod of iron, You shall shatter them like earthenware."[368]

This is what Midrash Tehelim says about Psalm 2: 7:

"When the time of the advent of Messiah will be near, then the blessed God will say to him: 'With him I will make a new covenant.' And this is the time when he will acknowledge him as his Son, saying, 'This day I have begotten thee.'"[369]

As you can see, the Messiah's role in establishing the New Covenant was not lost on the ancient rabbis. At least some of them understood perfectly that the Messiah would institute the New Covenant with His people, and the use of the word "new" unquestionably means the Messiah had to complete, or to fulfill, the Old Covenant.

Psalm 8: 4-5—"What is man that You take thought of him, and the Son of Man that You care for Him? Yet You have made Him a little lower than God, and You crown Him with glory and majesty."[370]

Because of Psalm 2: 7-9 and Psalm 8: 4-5, the Messiah is referred to as the Son of Man. He is also known as the Son of David because He came into the world through the line of David. Jewish people call Him Ha Mashiach ben David (the Messiah Son of David). To complete His mission, the Messiah had to become a Man and live His life in perfect obedience to the Torah. Only then could He become the flawless sacrifice for the sins of mankind—the unblemished Lamb of Yahweh. As I said before, the Bible points toward the fact that obeying the Torah by saying Yahweh's Name led to His crucifixion.

Psalm 69: 3—While He was dying on the tree, He said, "I am thirsty."[371]

Psalm 69: 21—To mock and ridicule Him, they gave Him vinegar to drink while He was nailed to the tree dying for their sins.

Jeremiah 31: 31-33—"'Behold, days are coming,' declares Yahweh, 'when I will make a new covenant with the house of Israel and with the house of Judah, not like the covenant which I made with their fathers in the day I took them by the hand to bring them out of the land of Egypt, My covenant which they broke, although I was a husband to them,' declares Yahweh. 'But this is the covenant which I will make with the house of Israel after those days,' declares Yahweh, 'I will put my Law within them and on their heart I will write it; and I will be their God, and they shall be My people.'"[372]

Daniel 9: 26—"Then after the sixty-two weeks the Messiah will be cut off and have nothing, and the people of the prince who is to come will destroy the city and the sanctuary. And its end will come with a flood; even to the end there will be war; desolations are determined."[373]

The Messiah died on the tree (i.e., He was "cut off") 40 years before the Romans destroyed the Temple of Yahweh in 70 A.D. The "desolations" Daniel mentioned refer to End of Days judgments that are yet to occur. At the End of Days, the anti-Messiah will take his seat in the rebuilt Temple of Yahweh and declare his divinity. Jesus refers to this as "the abomination of desolation."[374]

Hosea 2: 16—The Messiah will be referred to as our Husband (Ishi), not as our owner (Baali).

This verse says the Messiah will join Himself with us, and we will be united with Him the way a husband becomes one flesh with his wife. This is a description of the New Covenant in its purest and simplest sense, and in John chapter 17, Jesus uses analogous symbolism to describe His role in uniting Yahweh the Father with His people.

Hosea 11: 1—Yahweh called Him "out of Egypt."[375]

After the Messiah's birth, His parents took Him to Egypt to flee Herod the Great's persecution. Herod wanted to kill Him because he understood that the King Messiah had been born. This verse makes reference to the Messiah's return to Israel following Herod's death.

Micah 5: 2— He will be born in Bethlehem and descended from Judah.

Jeffrey includes this verse as one of his 17 prophecies because it says the Messiah will be born in Bethlehem, but it does much more than that. Micah 5: 2 reads as follows:

"But as for you Bethlehem Ephrathah, too little to be among the clans of Judah, from you One will go forth for Me to be ruler in Israel. His goings forth are from long ago, from the days of eternity."[376]

This verse says the Messiah will be born in Bethlehem, and it also says He was in the beginning. In other words, He existed before anything or anyone else. Only One Person has existed from the beginning—Yahweh. This is what Targum Jonathan says about Micah 5: 2:

"And you, O Bethlehem Ephrath, you who were too small to be numbered among the thousands of the House of Judah, from you shall come forth before Me the Messiah, to exercise dominion over Israel, he whose name was mentioned before, from the days of creation."[377]

And the Jerusalem Talmud says this about Micah 5: 2:

"Son of Judah, Judaean! Tie your ox and tie your plow, for the King Messiah has been born!....He asked him: 'From where is he?' He answered: 'From the royal fort of Bethlehem in Judah.'"[378]

Obviously, this interpretation is not a Christian misunderstanding of the Hebrew Scriptures. It falls in line perfectly with the teachings of the ancient rabbis.

Micah 2: 12-13—He will lead His children the way a shepherd leads his flock.

Repeatedly in the Scriptures, the Messiah is referred to as the Shepherd of His people. For instance, Ezekiel chapter 34 explains Yahweh's role as Shepherd, as does Psalm 23. It begins with these words: "Yahweh is my Shepherd..." Later in this chapter, you will see that the Messiah and Yahweh are One, and in the next chapter you will see that Jesus claimed to be the fulfillment of this prophecy.

Zephaniah 1: 14-18—He will return at the End of Days as the Righteous Judge and the Mighty God.

This prophecy deals with Yahweh returning to earth at the End of Days to redeem the Children of Israel and to liberate the Promised Land.

Isaiah 52: 14—He was brutally treated and disfigured to the point that He did not even resemble a man.

Isaiah 53: 4-6—He is our sin offering.

Isaiah 53: 7—He is the Lamb of Yahweh.

Zechariah 13: 7-9 and Isaiah 53: 10—Yahweh struck, or crushed, Him for our sins.

In fact, human beings killed the Messiah (i.e., they "struck" or "crushed" Him), but Yahweh allowed it to happen for our redemption and salvation. Thus, in essence Yahweh struck, or crushed, Him because of His deep and abiding love for us and because He promised that He would when He ratified the covenant. The Messiah's death for our sins initiated the New Covenant.

Isaiah 53: 12—He is our intercessor before Yahweh the Father.

Isaiah 8: 14-15—He is a stumbling stone for both houses of Israel.

This prophecy was fulfilled following the Messiah's crucifixion, and to this day the Messiah remains a "stumbling stone" for most Jewish people. At the End of Days, Yahweh will solve this problem.

Isaiah 11: 10—Gentiles followed Him.

Isaiah 53: 3—He was rejected by His own people.

Overwhelming evidence presented in the Scriptures compels us to conclude that the Messiah's birth, life, and death were divinely inspired. How could I believe otherwise? The probability of anyone fulfilling all the Messianic prophecies in the Bible by chance is so small that Yahweh had to make it happen. There is no other rational explanation. Furthermore, we must conclude that there is, and can be, only One Messiah. Now we need to search the Bible and find out more about Him.

The Messiah in the Old Testament

Many references to the Messiah in the Old Testament are obscure by God's design. Once you learn to recognize Him, it will be relatively simple to identify verses and passages telling about Him. Until you do, it may not be that easy.

For instance, identifying Bethlehem as the birthplace of the Messiah requires virtually no effort because it is presented in such a straightforward manner. The same is true about the fact that He came from the tribe of Judah. However, other Old Testament verses and passages about Him are vague, and a trained eye, or better yet an eye focused by Yahweh, is required to understand them. I hope and pray that Yahweh will open your heart and your mind as you read the presentation below and that you will see Him in these verses.

The Messiah is the Word of Yahweh

Genesis 1: 1-26 tells about the creation. Eight times in these verses, we see the phrase "God said."[379] This expression is revealing because Yahweh spoke the universe into existence. By the "Word of Yahweh," everything we see, and even things we cannot see, came into being. Psalm 33: 4, 6, and 9 make this point:

"For the Word of Yahweh is upright, and all His work is done in faithfulness...By the Word of Yahweh the heavens were made, and by the breath of His mouth all their host...For He spoke, and it was done; He commanded, and it stood fast."[380]

The "Word of Yahweh" mentioned in these verses is not a sound we hear or words written on paper. The "Word of Yahweh" is a Person who has all the power of Yahweh. In fact, He is the Messiah. Psalm 103: 20 points to this truth:

"Bless Yahweh, you His angels, mighty in strength, who perform His Word, obeying the Voice of His Word!"[381]

Stated another way, Yahweh's Word has a Voice, and He can speak. Sometimes the "Word of Yahweh" is called the "Voice of Yahweh." The 70 rabbis who translated the Septuagint Tanach in 285 B.C. suggested this when they rendered Genesis 3: 8 in the following way: Adam and Eve "heard the Voice of the LORD God (i.e., Yahweh Elohim) walking in the garden in the afternoon."[382] The King James Version interprets Genesis 3: 8 the same way.

Psalm 29: 3-9 makes this point beautifully:

"The Voice of Yahweh is upon the waters; the God of glory thunders, Yahweh is over many waters. The Voice of Yahweh is powerful, the Voice of Yahweh is majestic. The Voice of Yahweh breaks the cedars; yes, Yahweh breaks in pieces the cedars of Lebanon. He makes Lebanon skip like a calf, and Sirion like a young wild ox. The Voice of Yahweh hews out flames of fire. The Voice of Yahweh shakes the wilderness; Yahweh shakes the wilderness of Kadesh. The Voice of

Yahweh makes the deer to calve and strips the forests bare; and in His temple everything says, 'Glory!'"[383]

Psalm 29 uses the Name "Yahweh" and the "Voice of Yahweh" interchangeably and hints at the fact that they are One and the same Person.

In the King James Version of the Old Testament, the exact phrase the "Word of Yahweh" appears 255 times, and it appears 58 times in the book of Ezekiel.[384] Most of the time, it is used this way: "The Word of Yahweh came to me..." If we read quickly, we will inevitably interpret this phrase to mean that someone, Ezekiel as a case in point, simply heard words, but this is not always the case. In fact, when this phrase appears many times it refers to the Messiah appearing in Person and speaking to someone.

For example, Jeremiah 1: 4 begins this way: "Now the Word of Yahweh came to me...."[385] Then in Jeremiah 1: 9, Yahweh stretched out His hand, touched Jeremiah's mouth, and said, "I have put My Words into your mouth."[386] Therefore, the "Word of Yahweh" referred to in Jeremiah 1: 4 must be Yahweh Himself. A few verses later Yahweh said, "I am watching over my Word to perform it."[387] In other words, the Person called the "Word of Yahweh" is watching over Yahweh's literal words to make sure all of them come to pass. Understanding this fact will be essential in chapter 9 when I discuss the Messiah.

Psalm 18: 30 hints at this truth as well:

"As for God, His way is blameless; the Word of Yahweh is tried; He is a shield to all who take refuge in Him."[388]

Does the phrase the "Word of Yahweh" in this verse make reference to Yahweh or His literal words? Since this verse is about Yahweh, it is reasonable to conclude that the "Word of Yahweh" refers to the Person Yahweh.

Earlier, I said the "Word of Yahweh" referred to in Genesis chapter 15 is actually the Messiah. Take a look at Genesis 15: 1 and you will see what I mean:

"After these things the Word of Yahweh came to Abram in a vision, saying, 'Do not fear, Abram, I am a shield to you; Your reward shall be very great.'"[389]

The "Word of Yahweh" came to Abraham and told him that He is a shield to him. That is exactly what Psalm 18: 30 says, and in Genesis 15: 4 we learn that the "Word of Yahweh" told Abraham he would have a son. Then in Genesis 15: 5 the Bible says,

"And He (Yahweh or the "Word of Yahweh"?) took him (Abraham) outside and said, 'Now look toward the heavens, and count the stars, if you are able to count them.' And then He said to him, 'So shall your descendants be.'"[390]

Obviously, literal words did not take Abraham outside. Someone took Abraham outside and that Someone was the Person called the "Word of Yahweh," and He is the Messiah. Then in

Genesis 15: 6, Yahweh declares Abraham righteous because he had faith in Him, and later in the chapter He ratified the covenant. This fact is essential because it means the Messiah ratified the Old Covenant and the New Covenant.

Psalm 107: 19-20 tells us that the "Word of Yahweh" performs the Messiah's work:

"Then they cried out to Yahweh in their trouble; He saved them out of their distresses. He sent His Word and healed them, and delivered them from their destructions."[391]

According to these verses, Yahweh sent His Word and healed them. We know from Genesis 1: 1-26 that He easily could have spoken His Word and healed them. Psalm 107: 19-20 makes perfect sense when you understand that the "Word of Yahweh" is the Messiah and that He came to heal us, among other things. Isaiah 53: 5 explains it this way: "by His (the Messiah's) scourging we are healed."[392] Literally, He took the penalty for our sins on Himself, redeemed us, reconciled us to God, and healed us completely.

Now take a look at Psalm 40: 6-7:

"Sacrifice and meal offering You have not desired; My ears You have opened; burnt offering and sin offering You have not required. Then I said, 'Behold, I come; in the scroll of the book it is written of Me.'"[393]

These verses spell out the Messiah's mission, although not in great detail. They begin by explaining that Yahweh does not desire sacrifice and meal offerings or burnt offerings and sin offerings. What, then, does He require?

The next verse provides the answer: "Behold, I come; in the scroll of the book it is written of Me."[394] Yahweh requires an unblemished sacrifice, and He is the only One in all of creation capable of being the perfect sacrifice He demands. Therefore, He came to redeem us and to atone for our sins. The book mentioned in Psalm 40: 7 is the Torah and the Messiah—the "Word of Yahweh"—is the focal point of the Torah, Yahweh's written Word.

Psalm 138: 2 illustrates how much Yahweh honors His Word:

"I will bow down toward Your holy temple and give thanks to Your Name for Your lovingkindness and Your truth; for You have magnified Your Word according to all Your Name."[395]

A literal translation of this verse from the Hebrew reads as follows: "...for You have exalted Your Word above Your Name."[396] Yahweh is the Name that is above every name, and Yahweh has exalted "His Word"—the Messiah—above His Name. Be sure of this fact. Yahweh does not honor words written on paper above His Name. The only Person or thing exalted above Yahweh's Name is Yahweh Himself.

A Jewish sage named Jonathon ben Uziel wrote the Jerusalem Targum before the Messiah's birth. In it, he refers to Yahweh as the

"Word of the Lord" in keeping with the Jewish tradition that prohibits saying or writing God's Name except on special occasions. Below are two examples that prove my point. First you will read a verse from the Torah and then the Jerusalem Targum's explanation of that verse:

- Genesis 19: 24—"Then Yahweh rained on Sodom and Gomorrah brimstone and fire from Yahweh out of heaven."

- The Jerusalem Targum—"And the Word of the Lord caused to descend upon the people of Sodom and Gomorrah, brimstone and fire from the Lord from heaven."[397]

- Exodus 3: 14—"God said to Moses, 'I AM WHO I AM'; and He said, 'Thus you shall say to the sons of Israel, I AM has sent me to you."

- The Jerusalem Targum—"And the Word of the Lord said unto Moses: I am He who said unto the world, Be! and it was: and who in the future shall say to it Be! and it shall be. And He said Thus thou shalt say to the Children of Israel: I am hath sent me unto you."[398]

Before the Messiah's birth, at least one prominent Jewish thinker understood that the "Word of Yahweh" and Yahweh are One. The writers of the New Testament corroborate this perspective. For example, in his letter to the Hebrews, the apostle Paul said,

"The Word of God is something alive and active: it cuts more incisively than any two-edged sword: it can seek out the place where soul is divided from spirit, or joints from marrow; it can pass judgment on secret emotions and thoughts. No created thing is hidden from Him; everything is uncovered and stretched fully open to the eyes of the One to whom we must give account of ourselves."[399]

Paul refers to the "Word of God" as "Him"—meaning a Person. He is the One to whom we must give account for everything we have done and said and thought. Additionally, the apostle John opens his Gospel with these words: "In the beginning was the Word, and the Word was with God, and the Word was God."[400]

It is an empirical fact that New Testament manuscripts, both ancient and contemporary, routinely substitute the titles "God" and "Lord" for the Name "Yahweh." Thus, it is logical to conclude that Paul is referring to Jesus as the "Word of Yahweh" in his letter to the Hebrews, and we know for certain that John is writing about Jesus.

Yahweh Has Physical and Spiritual Characteristics

Genesis 1: 26 says,

"Then God said, 'Let Us make man in Our image, according to Our likeness.'"[401]

This verse suggests that God is talking with a manifestation of His Divine Being, an interpretation that is consistent with the meaning of the Hebrew word for God, "Elohim." As I said in chapter

2, "Elohim" is a plural word that "expresses the majesty and fullness of God's being."[402] Also, the Hebrew word translated as "image" in Genesis 1: 26 is "tselem" (tseh'-lem). This is a "concrete term implying a physical resemblance"[403] between God and man that is similar to the physical likeness between Adam and his son. Moreover, Genesis 2: 7 says that Adam became "a living being"[404] when Yahweh breathed His Spirit into him. Thus, Genesis 1: 26 suggests that Yahweh has physical and spiritual characteristics and that He gave both traits to mankind through Adam.

Targum Yonasan and the Midrash suggest another interpretation of Genesis 1: 26. Targum Yonasan says,

"And God said to the ministering angels who had been created on the second day of Creation of the world, 'Let us make man.'"[405]

The Midrash expands on this notion:

"When Moses wrote the Torah and came to this verse (let us make), which is in the plural and implies that there is more than one Creator, he said: 'Sovereign of the Universe! Why do you thus furnish a pretext for heretics to maintain that there is a plurality of divinities?' 'Write!' God replied. 'Whoever wishes to err will err...Instead, let them learn from their Creator Who created all, yet when He came to create Man He took counsel with the ministering angels."[406]

187

It is obvious that Genesis 1: 26 says one thing and that Targum Yonasan and the Midrash say something entirely different. Thankfully, the Bible provides information that sheds light on this controversial issue.

Yahweh is One — Yahweh Echad

Jewish people refer to Deuteronomy 6: 4-5 as "The Shema" and many Jews read and recite it daily. "Shema" (shem-ah') is a Hebrew word that means to hear and to obey what you hear. It should be interpreted as a command.

Deuteronomy 6: 4-5 says,

"Hear, O Israel! Yahweh is our God, Yahweh is One! You shall love Yahweh your God with all your heart and with all your soul and with all your might."[407]

"Echad" (ekh-awd') is the Hebrew word translated as "One" in The Shema, and the Bible uses "echad" in other ways that make its meaning clear. For example, "echad" appears in Genesis 2: 24 where God explains the relationship between a man and a woman when they marry: "They shall become one (echad) flesh."[408] And in Numbers 13: 23, "echad" is used to describe one cluster of grapes:

"Then they came to the valley of Eshcol and from there they cut down a branch with a single (echad) cluster of grapes."[409]

These two verses make clear that "echad" can be used to describe a compound unity — a single entity with multiple manifestations, and they shed light on the true meaning of Deuteronomy 6: 4-5. Yahweh our God is One (Echad), but He is a compound unity, just as the meaning of "Elohim" indicates.

Yahweh's compound nature is revealed clearly in Isaiah 48: 16:

"Come near to Me, listen to this: from the first I have not spoken in secret, from the time it took place, I was there. And now Adonai Yahweh has sent Me, and His Spirit."[410]

In this verse, Yahweh refers to Himself as three distinct Beings. First, we are told to come near and listen. Then the Speaker (i.e., the Messiah) explains that He was in the beginning with God and that God sent Him and His Holy Spirit to earth. These three manifestations of God were together in the beginning, and the Father sent the Messiah and His Spirit to earth for a purpose.

Now, take a look at Proverbs 30: 2-6:

"Surely I am more stupid than any man, and I do not have the understanding of a man. Neither have I learned wisdom, nor do I have the knowledge of the Holy One. Who has ascended into heaven and descended? Who has gathered the wind in His fists? Who has wrapped the waters in His garment? Who has established all the ends of the earth? What is His Name or His Son's Name? Surely you know! Every Word of God is tested; He is a shield to those who take refuge in Him. Do not add to His Words or He will reprove you, and you will be proved a liar."[411]

This proverb asks the Name of the Holy One, and the answer is "Yahweh." It also asks His Son's Name and suggests that the answer is apparent by saying, "Surely you know!" The Son's Name is obvious—it is "Yahweh." God's Name is Yahweh; Yahweh has a Son; He is the Messiah; His Name is Yahweh; and They are One.

By the way, "Surely you know!" could have been transliterated this way: "Can't you see this? Surely you can!"

Do Not Add to His Words or....You Will be Proved a Liar [412]

In chapter 2, I deviated from my rule by criticizing Rabbi Scherman's translation of the Tanach, and I said that I would depart from it one more time. Now is the time. As I said, translating from one language to another is difficult, but in this instance we do not have a translation problem. Here we have a much more grievous error—a rewriting of Yahweh's Word. This He expressly forbids.

In *The Stone Edition Tanach, The ArtScroll Series®*, Rabbi Scherman inserts "[but Moses]" in Proverbs 30: 4:

"Who [but Moses] ascended to heaven and descended? Who else gathered the wind in his palm? Who else tied the waters in a cloak? Who established all the ends of the earth? What is his name, and what is his son's name, if you know?[413]

Rabbi Scherman's insertion of "[but Moses]" in this verse violates a fundamental principle of God—i.e., that we must present His Word accurately. Since Moses' name does not appear in Hebrew manuscripts of this passage of Scripture, Rabbi Scherman has rewritten Yahweh's Word. As I said earlier, he argues that his translation relies on "Talmudic and Rabbinic sources," and in this instance he is relying on Rashi's interpretation that is presented in the Talmud (Megillah 31a).[414]

Obviously, these verses contradict Jewish tradition and support Christian doctrine. Therefore, it is logical to assume that Rabbi Scherman was attempting to deal with this perceived "problem" in his translation of the Tanach by inserting Moses' name in Proverbs 30: 4. Ironically, Proverbs 30: 6 explains how Yahweh looks upon people who distort the meaning of this particular passage of Scripture:

> "Do not add to His Words, lest He test you and find that you deceived."[415]

The Bible is crystal-clear about this fact. Yahweh and the Messiah are two distinct Beings yet They are One, and They have One Name. God's admonition not to tamper with His Word suggests that He knew some people would attempt to add their own meanings and interpretations to these specific verses, and He warned us not to do it.

The importance of Proverbs 30: 4 should not be underestimated because Jesus used this verse in His explanation to Nicodemus about the meaning of salvation, or being born again.[416] Nicodemus was a Jewish religious leader and a member of the Sanhedrin, and he asked Jesus this question:

"How can a man be born when he is old? He cannot enter a second time into his mother's womb and be born, can he?"[417]

Below is part of Jesus' response:

"Are you a teacher of Israel and do not understand these things? Truly, truly, I say to you, we speak of what we know and testify of what we have seen, and you do not accept our testimony. If I told you earthly things and you do not believe, how will you believe if I tell you heavenly things?

No one has ascended into heaven, but He who descended from heaven: the Son of Man. As Moses lifted up the serpent in the wilderness, even so must the Son of Man be lifted up; so that whoever believes will in Him have eternal life. For God so loved the world, that He gave His only begotten Son, that whoever believes in Him shall not perish, but have eternal life. For God did not send the Son into the world to judge the world, but that the world might be saved through Him."[418]

Nicodemus was an intelligent and well-educated man. Therefore, we can assume that he was familiar with Proverbs 30: 4 and that he must have known Jesus was claiming to be Yahweh. Nicodemus would have been familiar with Isaiah 43: 11 as well, and it says Yahweh is the only Savior. Eventually, Nicodemus became a believer in Jesus and was saved, as were many other Jewish religious leaders who lived at that time. The fact that a significant number of well-educated, religious Jews accepted Jesus as the Messiah (i.e.,

Yahweh) has been a major "problem" for non-believing religious Jews since that time and the "problem" persists to this day.

Be that as it may, Rabbi Scherman has no right to alter Yahweh's Word to make it comply with his or with Rashi's beliefs. No one has that right, and no one ever will. Rabbi Scherman must know this.

The Messiah is Called "Mighty God" and "Eternal Father"

Before we leave this topic, consider two additional passages of Scripture to support the argument that the Messiah and Yahweh are One. First, take another look at Isaiah 9: 6-7:

> "For a Child will be born to us, a Son will be given to us; and the government will rest on His shoulders; and His Name will be called Wonderful, Counselor, Mighty God, Eternal Father, Prince of Peace. There will be no end to the increase of His government or of peace, on the throne of David and over his kingdom, to establish it and to uphold it with justice and righteousness from then on and forevermore. The zeal of Yahweh Sabaoth will accomplish this."[419]

The Child referred to in this passage is the Messiah, and two of His Names are "Mighty God" and "Eternal Father." Now ask yourself this question. What Person mentioned in the Bible did Yahweh ever refer to as "Mighty God" or "Eternal Father?" The answer is only One Person—Himself. Therefore, the Messiah is Yahweh.

Second, look at Jeremiah 23: 5-6. I referred to this passage of Scripture before, but I need to do it again here:

"Behold, the days are coming, declares Yahweh, when I shall raise up for David a righteous Branch; and He will reign as king and act wisely and do justice and righteousness in the land. In His days Judah will be saved, and Israel will dwell securely; and this is His Name by which He will be called, Yahweh our Righteousness."[420]

David's righteous Branch is the Messiah, and His Name is Yahweh Tsidkenu—or Yahweh our Righteousness. The Midrash accepts this fact without reservation or qualification:

"What is the name of the King Messiah? Rabbi Abba, son of Kahana, said: Jehovah (Yahweh); for it is written, 'This is his name whereby he shall be called, the Lord our Righteousness.'"[421]

If you still have doubts about whether the Messiah is Yahweh, you need to remember what God's Word says about Abraham:

"Then he (Abraham) believed in Yahweh; and He reckoned it to him as righteousness."[422]

God's ways are not our ways, and His thoughts are not our thoughts. As high as the heavens are above the earth, so are His ways higher than our ways and His thoughts higher than our thoughts. We must simply have faith in Yahweh and believe His

Word. His Word is incredibly clear. The Messiah is Yahweh. They are One.

The Messiah is the Redeemer and the Savior

Isaiah 59: 1-2 says,

"Behold, Yahweh's hand is not so short that it cannot save; neither is His ear so dull that it cannot hear. But your iniquities have made a separation between you and your God, and your sins have hidden His face from you so that He does not hear."[423]

The Messiah came into the world to die for our sins as our Sacrificial Lamb, to redeem us, and to reconcile us with the Father. He is the One referred to in Isaiah 59: 1 as Yahweh's Hand and Ear, but in Isaiah 42: 1-9 He is called Yahweh's Servant:

"Behold, My Servant, whom I uphold; My chosen One in whom my soul delights. I have put My Spirit upon Him; He will bring forth justice to the nations. He will not cry out or raise His Voice, nor make His Voice heard in the street. A bruised reed He will not break and a dimly burning wick He will not extinguish; He will faithfully bring forth justice. He will not be disheartened or crushed until He has established justice in the earth; and the coastlands will wait expectantly for His Law.

Thus says God, Yahweh, who created the heavens and stretched them out, who spread out the earth and its offspring, who gives breath to the people on it and spirit to those who walk in it, I am Yahweh, I have called You in righteousness, I will also hold You by the hand and watch over You, and I will appoint You as a covenant to the people, as a light to the nations, to open blind eyes, to bring out prisoners from the dungeon and those who dwell in darkness from the prison. I am Yahweh, that is my Name; I will not give my glory to another, nor my praise to graven images. Behold, the former things have come to pass, now I declare new things; before they spring forth I proclaim them to You."[424]

Isaiah 52: 3-53: 12 describes the Messiah as the Suffering Servant and the ultimate victor in the battle Yahweh fights with Satan to redeem and save His people. Commenting on this passage of Scripture, Rabbi Elijah DeVidas, a 16th century A.D. Jewish sage, said,

"The meaning of 'He was wounded for our transgressions, bruised for our iniquities,' is that since the Messiah bears our iniquities, which produce the effect of His being bruised, it follows that who will not admit that the Messiah thus suffers for our iniquities must endure and suffer them for himself."[425]

I have included Isaiah 52: 3-53: 12 verbatim below, with one exception. I put Yahweh's Name where it belongs. The Messiah came and died for us, and Rabbi DeVidas was absolutely correct. Unless we have faith in Him to redeem and save us, we will suffer the consequence for our sin—eternal punishment. This is what Yahweh told Isaiah about Him:

"For thus says Yahweh, 'You were sold for nothing and you will be redeemed without money.' For thus says Adonai Yahweh, 'My people went down at the first into Egypt to reside there; then the Assyrian oppressed them without cause. Now therefore, what do I have here,' declares Yahweh, 'seeing that My people have been taken away without cause?'

Again Yahweh declares, 'Those who rule over them howl, and My Name is continually blasphemed all day long. Therefore My people shall know My Name; therefore in that day I am the One who is speaking, 'Here I am.' How lovely on the mountains are the feet of Him who brings good news, who announces peace and brings good news of happiness, who announces salvation, and says to Zion, 'Your God reigns!'

Listen! Your watchmen lift up their voices, they shout joyfully together; for they will see with their own eyes when Yahweh restores Zion. Break forth, shout joyfully together, you waste places of Jerusalem; for Yahweh has bared His holy arm in the sight of all the nations, that all the ends of the earth may see the salvation of our God.

Depart, depart, go out from there, touch nothing unclean; go out of the midst of her, purify yourselves, you who carry the vessels of Yahweh. But you will not go out in haste, nor will you go as fugitives; for Yahweh will go before you, and the God of Israel will be your rear guard.

Behold, My Servant will prosper, He will be high and lifted up and greatly exalted. Just as many were astonished at you, My people, so His appearance was marred more than any man and His form more than the sons of men. Thus He will sprinkle many nations, kings will shut their mouths on account of Him; for what had not been told them they will see, and what they had not heard they will understand.

Who has believed our message? And to whom has the arm of Yahweh been revealed? For He grew up before Him like a tender shoot, and like a root out of parched ground; He has no stately form or majesty that we should look upon Him, nor appearance that we should be attracted to Him. He was despised and forsaken of men, a man of sorrows and acquainted with grief; and like one from whom men hide their face He was despised, and we did not esteem Him.

Surely our griefs He Himself bore, and our sorrows He carried; yet we ourselves esteemed Him stricken, smitten of God, and afflicted. But He was pierced through for our transgressions, He was crushed for our iniquities; the chastening for our well-being fell upon Him, and by His scourging we are healed. All of us like sheep have gone astray, each of us has turned to his own way; but Yahweh has caused the iniquity of us all to fall on Him.

He was oppressed and He was afflicted, yet He did not open His mouth; like a lamb that is led to slaughter, and like a sheep that is silent before its shearers, so He did not open His mouth.

By oppression and judgment He was taken away; and as for His generation, who considered that he was cut off out of the land of the living for the transgression of My people, to whom the stroke was due? His grave was assigned with wicked men, yet He was with a rich man in His death, because He had done no violence, nor was there any deceit in His mouth.

But Yahweh was pleased to crush Him, putting Him to grief; if He would render Himself as a guilt offering, He will see His offspring, He will prolong His days, and the good pleasure of Yahweh will prosper in His hand. As a result of the anguish of His soul, He will see it and be satisfied; by His knowledge the Righteous One, My Servant, will justify the many, as He will bear their iniquities. Therefore, I will allot Him a portion with the great, and He will divide the booty with the strong; because He poured out Himself to death, and was numbered with the transgressors; yet He Himself bore the sin of many, and interceded for the transgressors."[426]

Are You Ready to Accept the Truth?

As I said at the beginning of this chapter, the Messiah is the central figure in the Old Testament from Genesis to Malachi. The prophet Nathan promised Israel's King David a permanent, royal dynasty,[427] and throughout the Scriptures his Descendant—the Anointed One, the Messiah, Ha Mashiach ben David—is referred to as the Suffering Servant and the Eternal King.

Isaiah refers to the Messiah as Immanuel, God who is with us, and Jeremiah calls Him Yahweh Tsidkenu, Yahweh our righteousness. These two Names sum up the Messiah's mission in its purest and simplest sense.[428] Ezekiel presents Him as a Prince, and he describes the Messiah as the Mediator and as the Shepherd of His people.[429] Zechariah portrays Him as a humble King who returns to rule His dominion.[430]

The Messiah appears in many ways in the Scriptures. For instance, He is Yahweh's Servant, His Strong Right Arm, an Offshoot of Jessie's root, the Branch of David, the Son of Man, the Teacher of His people, and the Light to the nations. He was despised and rejected by His own people, yet He laid down His life for our redemption and salvation.

Chapter 9
Jesus is Yahweh

"In the beginning was the Word, and the Word was with God, and the Word was God. He (Jesus) was in the beginning with God. All things came into being through Him, and apart from Him nothing came into being that has come into being. In Him was life, and the life was the Light of men. The Light shines in the darkness, and the darkness did not comprehend it."[431]

So begins the Gospel[432] of John. In this beautiful introduction, John declares that the Word of God is God. We know from the last chapter that the Word of God is Yahweh and that John is talking about Jesus. Therefore, John is saying that Jesus is Yahweh.

John 1: 3 says that Jesus created everything, and Genesis 1: 1 says that in the beginning God created the heavens and the earth. Therefore, John is saying that Jesus is the Creator. By the way, John 1: 3 is the precise definition of the Hebrew word for created (bara) that is used in Genesis 1: 1.[433] Bara means to create something out of nothing.

"He (Jesus) was in the world, and the world was made through Him, and the world did not know Him. He came to His own, and those who were His own did not receive Him. But as many as received Him, to them He gave the right to become the children of God, even to those who believe in His Name, who were born, not of blood nor of the will of the flesh nor of the will of man, but of God. And the Word became flesh, and dwelt among us, and we saw His glory, glory as of the only begotten from the Father, full of grace and truth.[434]

For the Law was given through Moses; grace and truth were realized through Jesus the Messiah. No one has seen God at any time; the only begotten God who is in the bosom of the Father, He has explained Him."[435]

John 1: 12 says that we become the children of God when we "believe in His Name." The Name to which this verse refers must be Yahweh. A study of the Scriptures shows that it cannot be another name. Then John tells us that the Word of God became flesh and dwelt among us. Yahweh, the God of all creation, came to earth in the form of Jesus the Messiah to teach us and to fulfill His promise to redeem and save us. The meaning of the Name He was actually given at birth, Yeshua, is "Yahweh saves" or "Yahweh is salvation." Thus, Jesus' Name tells us who He is and what He came to do.

The Greek word translated as "dwelt" in John's introduction is "skenoo," and it means "to tabernacle," or literally "to pitch your tent." In other words, Yahweh, in the form of Jesus, pitched His tent and tabernacled among us the way He did in the wilderness with the Children of Israel. However, when Jesus came, Yahweh revealed Himself to us completely. In the wilderness, the Children of Israel could see only His Shekinah, but John and many others saw His bodily form, and before He returned to heaven they saw His glorified form. Isaiah foretold all of this, and he called Him Immanuel — "God who is with us." Jesus is God who is with us.

Jesus Fulfilled the Messianic Prophecies in the Old Testament

As I said in chapter 8, no one could fulfill the Messianic prophecies in the Old Testament by chance, and Jesus fulfilled all of them. The Appendix presents information about Jesus' life that proves this fact. Therefore, Jesus must be the Messiah.

Also, Jesus said He is Yahweh, and in chapter 8, I showed that the Old Testament makes it clear the Messiah is Yahweh. By their reactions, we know the Jewish priests understood what Jesus said, but instead of believing Him they had Him crucified for committing "blasphemy." Thus, Yahweh's Name played an important part in all the events surrounding Jesus' life — including His crucifixion.

Jesus Explained the Law and the Prophets

Most of the Jewish religious leaders in Jesus' day saw Him as a renegade and as a vagabond preacher. To them His teaching seemed peculiar because it focused on faith in Yahweh, obedience to His Word, and love for our fellowman. But Jesus did not minimize the importance of the Law and the prophets. He clarified both by explaining precisely what Yahweh meant. For example, He said,

> "You have heard that it was said (in the Law), 'You shall not commit adultery'; but I say to you that everyone who looks at a woman with lust for her has already committed adultery with her in his heart.'"[436]

Jesus made it clear that Yahweh expects far more from us than most of us realize. In His Sermon on the Mount,[437] He explained why He came into the world:

"Do not think that I came to abolish the Law or the Prophets; I did not come to abolish but to fulfill. For truly I say to you, until heaven and earth pass away, not the smallest letter or stroke shall pass from the Law until all is fulfilled."[438]

And in another place, He said,

"But it is easier for heaven and earth to pass away than for one stroke of a letter of the Law to fail."[439]

This fact is irrefutable. Jesus elevated the Law and the prophets by saying they are error free. His death for our sins was part of Yahweh's plan all along. It was spelled out clearly in the Law and foretold by the prophets. In reality, Jesus' atoning sacrifice fulfilled the Law and ratified the New Covenant.

Jesus' Teaching Threatened the Priests

Jesus' teachings exposed the flaws in many Jewish religious traditions. That is why the priests wanted to kill Him. According to John, the priests also believed the Jewish people's enthusiastic response to Jesus' message might compel the Romans to abolish their coveted positions.[440] Thus, it is reasonable to conclude that the priests' reactions to Jesus were normal human responses to perceived threats.

Even more threatening from the priests' perspective, convincing miracles accompanied Jesus' teaching. He healed the sick, raised the dead, cleansed the lepers, gave sight to the blind, caused the lame to walk, and cast out demons. These supernatural miracles caused many people to believe in Jesus, and they turned to Him in ever increasing numbers.

By comparison, the message of the priests was embarrassingly weak. It focused on ritualistic adherence to doctrines, laws, and traditions, many of which were man-made. It must have been obvious to them and to the people that Jesus' words had supernatural power, and their own message did not. The priests were well-educated, intelligent men. They must have known that their religious, social, and political standing were in jeopardy if Jesus continued teaching.

On top of everything else, Jesus empowered His disciples to perform healing miracles in His Name prior to and after His resurrection. The Talmud speaks about this fact and offers insights into the priests' attitudes toward Jesus and His disciples:

- Abodah Zarah 27b: "A man shall have no dealings with the heretics [Christians], nor be cured by them, even for the sake of an hour of life. There was the case of Ben Dama nephew of R. [Rabbi] Ishmael, whom a serpent bit. There came Jacob [the apostle of Jesus referred to as James who wrote the book of James in the New Testament] the heretic of the village of Sechanya to cure him (in the name of Yeshu ben Pandera var. leg.); but R. Ishmael would not allow him. Ben Dama said to him, R. Ishmael, my brother, do allow him, that I may be cured, and I will produce a text from the Law to prove that this is permitted. But hardly had he finished his discourse when his soul departed, and he died."[441]

In this passage from the Talmud, the name "Yeshu" was used instead of Yeshua, the Name He was actually given at birth. The name "Yeshu" is a curse because it means "may his name and memory be blotted out."[442] Leading rabbis of Jesus' day hated Him so much that they used a curse in lieu of His Name, and they refused to allow healing in His Name even in cases where the life of the person being healed was at stake. In this passage, the "text" Ben Dama referred to is Exodus 15: 26:

> "If you will give earnest heed to the Voice of Yahweh your God, and do what is right in His sight, and give ear to His commandments, and keep all His statutes, I will put none of these diseases on you which I have put on the Egyptians; for I, Yahweh, am your healer (Yahweh Raphah or Yahweh your doctor)."[443]

Ben Dama knew about Yahweh's promise, and he must have been anxious to claim it for his own healing. But Rabbi Ishmael would not allow James to heal him using the Name of Jesus so Ben Dama died.

- Shabbath 14b: "The grandson of R. Joshua ben Levi had something stuck in his throat. There came a man and whispered to him in the name of Jesus and he recovered. When the healer came out, R. Joshua said to him, What was it you whispered to him? He said to him, A certain word. He said to him, It had been better for him that he had died rather than that."[444]

Yahweh was the "Word" whispered to Rabbi Joshua's grandson, and it is "the Name of Jesus." Rabbi Joshua was so incensed that the disciple equated Jesus and Yahweh that he would have preferred his grandson's death to his healing under that condition. The Talmud says Rabbi Joshua's grandson recovered after the disciple prayed for him in "the Name of Jesus." This passage from the Talmud gives you a glimpse of the rabbis' intense hatred of Jesus.

- Sanhedrin X, 1: "R. Akiba said, He who reads in external books (the New Testament Gospels telling about Jesus), and he who whispers over a wound, and says, 'None of the diseases which I sent on Egypt will I lay on thee, I am the Lord thy healer' has any share in the world to come."[445]

In this passage from the Talmud, Rabbi Akiba is quoting Exodus 15: 26, and as I said before, it refers to Jesus as Yahweh Raphah. The people who were seeking healing understood that it makes specific reference to Jesus and refers to Him as Yahweh. They permitted His disciples to pray for them if they used this verse instead of His Name, thinking that they could obtain healing without offending the rabbis, but Rabbi Akiba would have none of that. He said that people who committed this "offense" were destined to spend eternity in hell because it meant they believed Jesus is Yahweh.

Jesus Confronted the Priests—on the Sabbath

Jesus performed many miracles on the Sabbath to send a strong message to the priests. God wanted the Sabbath to be a day of rest and an opportunity for His people to fellowship with Him. The priests had turned it into a ritualistic, tradition-bound event by creating a vast array of laws that people were forced to obey, and it did not even resemble what Yahweh had in mind when He said, "Remember the Sabbath day and keep it holy."[446] Jesus told them that their traditions were way off base, and He revealed Yahweh's enormous power as proof that He was right and they were wrong.

Although the Bible includes many examples of Jesus challenging the priests on the Sabbath, I will mention only one. It is discussed in Luke 13: 10-17. Jesus was teaching in a synagogue on the Sabbath, and a woman who had been crippled by an evil spirit for 18 years was in the congregation. When Jesus saw her, He called her over, laid His hands on her, and said, "Woman, you are freed from your sickness."[447]

Her healing was instantaneous. She stood erect for the first time in almost two decades and immediately began praising God. But the "president of the synagogue"[448] was indignant because Jesus healed her on the Sabbath. He said,

"There are six days in which work should be done; therefore come during them and get healed, and not on the Sabbath day."[449]

Jesus was furious. He looked directly at the priests and said,

"You hypocrites, does not each of you on the Sabbath untie his ox or his donkey from the stall, and lead him away to water him? And this woman, a daughter of Abraham as she is, whom Satan has bound for eighteen long years, should she not have been released from this bond on the Sabbath day?"[450]

Everyone in the synagogue, except the priests, rejoiced. Luke 13: 17 refers to them as Jesus' opponents, or His adversaries, and the Bible describes Satan as Yahweh's adversary. In this case, the priests were following Satan's lead. Although the "president of the synagogue" aimed his remark at the healed woman, Jesus was his real target because He had violated their tradition by "working on the Sabbath."

With a simple demonstration of Yahweh's healing power, Jesus showed everyone, including the priests, that their traditions were contrary to Yahweh's desires. He had much more to tell them, and in Matthew chapter 23, He held nothing back. Matthew chapter 23 is the best example in the New Testament of Yahweh's attitude toward the priests because of what they had done to misrepresent His Law.

The Corruption of the Priesthood and Jesus' Response

According to Josephus[451] and the Talmud, the corruption of the priesthood occurred long before Jesus' birth. Herod the Great started the practice of selling the office of high priest to the family willing to pay the most money for it. According to Dr. Phillip Moore, a Bible scholar and writer,

> "For nearly a century a detestable abuse prevailed, which consisted in the arbitrary nomination and deposition of the high priest. The high priesthood, which for fifteen centuries had been preserved in the same family, being hereditary according to the divine command,[452] had at the time of Christ's advent become an object of commercial speculation. Herod commenced these arbitrary changes,[453] and after Judea became one of the Roman conquests the election of the high priest took place almost every year at Jerusalem, the procurators appointing and deposing them in the same manner as the praetorians later on made and unmade emperors.[454] The Talmud speaks sorrowfully of this venality and the yearly changes of the high priest.
>
> This sacred office was given to the one that offered the most money for it, and mothers were particularly anxious that their sons should be nominated to this dignity[455]....M. Derembourg, a modern Jewish savant, has remarked: 'A few priestly, aristocratic, powerful, and vain families, who cared for neither the dignity nor the interests of the altar, quarreled with each other respecting appointments, influence, and wealth.'"[456]

The priests had turned Judaism into repetitious ceremonies that lacked the kind of reverence for and faith in Yahweh that He requires. In their minds, their traditions were the heart and soul of their faith. They could not have been more mistaken, and Jesus told them in no uncertain terms that they were dead wrong. In Matthew chapter 23, He said,

> "The scribes and the Pharisees have seated themselves in the chair of Moses; therefore all that they tell you, do and observe, but do not do according to their deeds; for they say things and do not do them. They tie up heavy burdens and lay them on men's shoulders, but they themselves are unwilling to move them with so much as a finger.
>
> But they do all their deeds to be noticed by men; for they broaden their phylacteries and lengthen the tassels of their garments. They love the place of honor at banquets and the chief seats in the synagogues, and respectful greetings in the market places, and being called Rabbi by men.
>
> But do not be called Rabbi; for One is your Teacher, and you are all brothers. Do not call anyone on earth your father; for One is your Father, He who is in heaven. Do not be called leaders; for One is your Leader, that is, the Messiah. But the greatest among you shall be your servant. Whoever exalts himself shall be humbled; and whoever humbles himself shall be exalted.

But woe to you scribes and Pharisees, hypocrites, because you shut off the kingdom of heaven from people; for you do not enter yourselves, nor do you allow those who are entering to go in.

Woe to you scribes and Pharisees, hypocrites, because you devour widow's houses, and for a pretense you make long prayers; therefore you will receive greater condemnation.

Woe to you scribes and Pharisees, hypocrites, because you travel around on sea and land to make one proselyte; and when he becomes one, you make him twice as much a son of hell as yourselves.

Woe to you blind guides who say, 'Whoever swears by the temple, that is nothing; but whoever swears by the gold of the temple is obligated.' You fools and blind men! Which is more important, the gold or the temple that sanctified the gold? And, 'Whoever swears by the altar, that is nothing, but whoever swears by the offering on it, he is obligated.' You blind men, which is more important, the offering, or the altar that sanctifies the offering. Therefore, whoever swears by the altar, swears both by the altar and by everything on it. And whoever swears by the temple, swears both by the temple and by Him who dwells within it. And whoever swears by heaven, swears both by the throne of God and by Him who sits upon it.

Woe to you, scribes and Pharisees, hypocrites! For you tithe mint and dill and cummin, and have neglected the weightier provisions of the Law: justice and mercy and faithfulness; but these are the things you should have done without neglecting the others. You blind guides, who strain out a gnat and swallow a camel!

Woe to you, scribes and Pharisees, hypocrites! For you clean the outside of the cup and of the dish, but inside they are full of robbery and self-indulgence. You blind Pharisee, first clean the inside of the cup and of the dish, so that the outside of it may become clean also.

Woe to you, scribes and Pharisees, hypocrites! For you are like whitewashed tombs which on the outside appear beautiful, but inside they are full of dead men's bones and all uncleanness. So you, too, outwardly appear righteous to men, but inwardly you are full of hypocrisy and lawlessness.

Woe to you, scribes and Pharisees, hypocrites! For you build the tombs of the prophets and adorn the monuments of the righteous, and say, 'If we had been living in the days of our fathers, we would not have been partners with them in shedding the blood of the prophets.' So you testify against yourself, that you are sons of those who murdered the prophets. Fill up, then, the measure of the guilt of your fathers.

You serpents, you brood of vipers, how will you escape the sentence of hell? Therefore, behold, I am sending you prophets and wise men and scribes; some of them you will kill and crucify, and some of them you will scourge in your synagogues, and persecute from city to city, so that upon you may fall the guilt of all the righteous blood shed on earth, from the blood of righteous Abel to the blood of Zechariah, the son of Berechiah, whom you murdered between the temple and the Altar. Truly I say to you, all these things will come upon this generation.

Jerusalem, Jerusalem, who kills the prophets and stones those who are sent to her! How many times I wanted to gather your children together, the way a hen gathers her chicks under her wings, and you were unwilling. Behold, your house is being left to you desolate! For I say to you, from now on you will not see Me until you say 'Blessed is He Who comes in the Name of Yahweh!'"[457]

Jesus condemned the priests and their traditions. They were supposed to represent Him before His people. Instead, they were leading His children astray. If you think Jesus' words in Matthew chapter 23 were harsh, take a look at His description of the penalty for this offense:

"But whoever causes one of these little ones who believe in Me to stumble, it would be better for him to have a heavy millstone hung around his neck, and to be drowned in the depth of the sea."[458]

This penalty is very severe, even inhumane, but Jesus said the punishment for leading His children astray is much worse. It is eternal damnation and perpetual burning. This is a deadly serious matter, and the priests should have known better. Through His prophets, Yahweh had told the priests many times not to substitute religious ritual and tradition for faith and obedience—but to no avail. For example, He said,

- "I hate, I reject your festivals, nor do I delight in your solemn assemblies. Even though you offer up to Me burnt offerings and your grain offerings, I will not accept them; and I will not even look at the peace offerings of your fatlings. Take away from Me the noise of your songs; I will not even listen to the sound of your harps. But let justice roll down like waters and righteousness like an ever-flowing stream."[459]

- "Because this people draw near with their words and honor Me with their lip service, but they remove their hearts far from Me, and their reverence for Me consists of tradition learned by rote, therefore behold, I will once again deal marvelously with this people, wondrously marvelous; and the wisdom of their wise men shall perish, and the discernment of their discerning men shall be concealed."[460]

- "How can you say, 'We are wise, since we have Yahweh's Law?' Look how it has been falsified by the lying pen of the scribes! The wise men are put to shame, alarmed, caught out because they have rejected Yahweh's Word. What price their wisdom now?"[461]

- "'But as for you, you have turned aside from the way; you have caused many to stumble by the instruction; you have corrupted the covenant of Levi,' says Yahweh Sabaoth. 'So I also have made you despised and abased before all the people, just as you are not keeping My ways but are showing partiality in the instruction.'"[462]

Jeremiah went so far as to blame the priests as a group for all the hardships inflicted on the Jewish people:

"The shepherds (i.e., the priests) are the ones who have been stupid: they have not searched for Yahweh. This is why they have not prospered and why their whole flock has been dispersed."[463]

In response to Jesus' rebuke, the priests plotted to kill Him. How ironic. They conspired to kill the One who came to redeem and save them, and their sin opened the door for the whole world to be saved by the shedding of His innocent blood.

The Priests Look for a Way to Accuse Jesus

One day the priests brought a woman to Jesus who had been caught in the act of adultery and told Him that the Law of Moses said she should be stoned. Then they asked Him what He thought.[464] Obviously, this was a trap because they brought the woman to Him, but not the man. If she was caught in the act of adultery, then he must have been caught too. When Jesus said, "He who is without sin among you, let him be the first to throw a stone at her,"[465] they lowered their heads and walked away one-by-one.

This incident set in motion a series of discussions between Jesus and the priests.[466] Eventually, the priests told Jesus that He was demon-possessed, and He said, "I do not have a demon; but I honor My Father, and you dishonor Me."[467] Then He told them that anyone who believes in Him will never die. In response, the priests said,

"Now we know you have a demon. Abraham died, and the prophets also; and You say, 'If anyone keeps My word, he will never taste death.' Surely You are not greater than our father Abraham, who died?"[468]

Jesus' reply left no room for doubt in their minds about who He claimed to be:

"If I glorify Myself, My glory is nothing; it is My Father who glorifies Me, of whom you say, 'He is our God'; and you have not come to know Him, but I know Him; and if I say that I do not know Him, I will be a liar like you, but I do know Him and keep His Word. Your father Abraham rejoiced to see My day, and he saw it and was glad….Truly, truly, I say to you, before Abraham was born, I Am."[469]

The New Jerusalem Bible's translation of John 8: 58 is better:

"In all truth I tell you, before Abraham ever was, I am."[470]

The priests understood perfectly that Jesus was claiming to be Yahweh. Take a look at John 8: 59 and see what I mean. They picked up stones to throw at Him, and they would have killed Jesus on the spot if they could have done it legally. He had claimed to be Yahweh without saying the Name "Yahweh." It is obvious that Jesus wanted to be tried for claiming to be Yahweh, and eventually He was, but in fact, the priests convicted Him and sentenced Him to death for committing "blasphemy," or for simply saying the Name "Yahweh." I will discuss this issue shortly.

When Jesus raised Lazarus from the dead, it was the last straw as far as the priests were concerned.[471] They were convinced that if He continued preaching and performing miracles everyone would believe in Him,[472] so they convened the Sanhedrin and decided it was time to do away with Jesus.

Jesus Said Plainly That He is Yahweh

During Jesus' earthly ministry, He said clearly that He is I Am—Yahweh, the One and only God. He also said we must accept Him as God and put our faith in Him. Once He told a group of priests,

> "You search the Scriptures because you think that in them you have eternal life; it is these that bear witness of Me; and you are unwilling to come to Me so that you may have life[473]....I have come in My Father's Name, and you do not receive Me; if another shall come in his own name, you will receive him[474]....Do not think that I will accuse you before the Father; the one who accuses you is Moses, in whom you have set your hope. For if you believed Moses, you would believe Me, for he wrote about Me. But if you do not believe his writings, how will you believe My words?"[475]

Jesus said the Torah tells about Him, but the religious leaders of His day did not believe Him. Supposedly, they put their hope for redemption and salvation in the Torah, but Jesus made it clear that they did not believe Moses either because He was the One about whom Moses was writing.

Jesus' I AM Statements

The Bible, the Talmud, and other rabbinic sources tell us that a large and growing number of people in Israel believed in Jesus as they witnessed His many miracles. According to Raymond Fischer, a Messianic Jew[476] from Israel and author of The Children of God, about one-quarter of the people in Jerusalem at the time of Jesus' death believed in Him.[477] To understand exactly what they believed about Him, we need to look at what He said about Himself. Below are Jesus' I AM statements, and in each one of them Jesus declares that He is Yahweh:

- "I AM the bread of life; he who comes to Me will not hunger, and he who believes in Me will never thirst[478]....I AM the bread that came down out of heaven[479]....I AM the bread of life. Your fathers ate the manna in the wilderness, and they died. This is the bread which comes down out of heaven, so that one may eat of it and not die[480]....I AM the living bread that came down out of heaven; if anyone eats of this bread, he will live forever; and the bread also which I will give for the life of the world is My flesh."[481]

In these verses, Jesus likens Himself to the manna Yahweh provided for the Children of Israel in the wilderness. He said that people who eat His bread will never die the way they did. His "living bread" symbolizes His body, or His flesh, that was sacrificed for us. When we consume His "living bread," we are uniting with Him and the sacrifice He made to atone for our sins, and since He is eternal we will live with Him forever. The Passover in Egypt and The Last Supper use this same symbolism.

- "I AM the Light of the world; he who follows Me will not walk in darkness, but will have the Light of life....For unless you believe that I am He, you will die in your sins."[482]

Jesus said He is the Light of the world that exposes the darkness. Just as light from the sun is the source of physical life, so is Jesus the source of spiritual life. He likens darkness to death, and in Him there is no darkness.

According to the editors of The New Jerusalem Bible, in John 8: 24 when Jesus said, "...unless you believe that I am He....," He was claiming to be Yahweh:

"'I Am' or 'I Am He' is the Divine Name revealed to Moses (Yahweh) ....When Jesus appropriates this Name, He is claiming to be the One incomparable Saviour, the goal of Israel's faith and hope."[483]

In John 8: 28, Jesus said "I am He" again:

"When you lift up the Son of Man, then you will know that I am He...."[484]

The Bible says that many people who heard Jesus make these claims "came to believe in Him."[485] Since He had told them that He is Yahweh, that is what they must have believed. Even more, they must have believed that they would die in their sins unless they believed Jesus is Yahweh because that's what He said in John 8: 24. Jesus addressed this remark specifically to the people who believed He is Yahweh:

> "If you abide in My Word, then you are truly disciples of Mine; and you will know the truth, and the truth will make you free."[486]

In John 8: 31, "My Word" must refer to the Old Testament because there was no New Testament at that time. Besides, the people to whom Jesus was speaking already believed He is Yahweh, so it makes perfect sense that they would have understood that He was referring to the Old Testament. When Jesus said "you will know the truth," they would have understood that He was referring to the Scriptures again because Yahweh's Word is truth.[487] Don't miss the significance of these points. By calling the Old Testament "My Word," Jesus was claiming to be Yahweh.

In a nutshell, John 8: 31-32 is a warning to distinguish between Yahweh's Word, or the Old Testament, and the traditions taught by the priests, many of which contradicted the Scriptures. Every one of Jesus' followers would have been familiar with this line of reasoning since He had told them on several occasions that every Word in the Law and the prophets is perfect.

When He finished speaking to His followers, Jesus addressed these remarks to the priests:

"I know that you are Abraham's descendants; yet you seek to kill Me, because My Word has no place in you. I speak the things which I have seen with My Father; therefore you also do the things which you heard from your father....You are of your father the devil, and you want to do the desires of your father...."[488]

Jesus made it crystal clear that the source of the priests' traditions was Satan himself, and His contempt for their traditions defies description. As I said before, eventually He would die for violating their tradition prohibiting saying the Name "Yahweh."

- "I AM the door of the sheep. All who came before Me are thieves and robbers, but the sheep did not hear them. I AM the door; if anyone enters through Me, he will be saved..."[489]

Jesus said He is "the door" to eternal life. There is no other way to salvation. Any other way to God that may seem right to us is actually wrong no matter what we may think.

- "I AM the good shepherd, and I know My own and My own know Me, even as the Father knows Me and I know the Father; and I lay down My life for the sheep. I have other sheep, which are not from this fold; I must bring them also, and they will hear My Voice; and they will become one flock with One Shepherd. For this reason the Father loves Me, because I lay down My life so that I may take it up again. No one has taken it away from Me, but I lay it down on My own initiative. I have authority to lay it down, and I have authority to take it up again."[490]

In Ezekiel, Yahweh referred to Himself as the Shepherd of His people, and Jesus' claim to be the Good Shepherd is a declaration that He is Yahweh. This passage from Ezekiel explains exactly what Jesus meant:

"Therefore, you shepherds, hear the Word of Yahweh: 'As I live,' declares Adonai Yahweh, 'surely because My flock has become a prey, My flock has even become food for all the beasts of the field for lack of a shepherd, and My shepherds did not search for My flock, but rather the shepherds fed themselves and did not feed My flock.' Therefore, you shepherds, hear the Word of Yahweh: Thus says Adonai Yahweh, 'Behold, I am against the shepherds, and I shall demand My sheep from them and make them cease from feeding my sheep. So the shepherds will not feed themselves anymore, but I will deliver My flock from their mouth, that they may not be food for them.'

For thus says Adonai Yahweh, 'Behold, I Myself will search for My sheep and seek them out. As a shepherd cares for his herd in the day when he is among his scattered sheep, so I will care for My sheep and will deliver them from all the places to which they were scattered on a cloudy and gloomy day. I will bring them out from the peoples and gather them from the countries and bring them to their own land; and I will feed them on the mountains of Israel, by the streams, and in all the inhabited places of the land. I will feed them in a good pasture, and their grazing ground will be on the mountain heights of Israel. There they will lie down on good grazing ground and feed in rich pasture on the mountains of Israel. I will feed My flock and I will lead them to rest,' declares Adonai Yahweh. 'I will seek the lost, bring back the scattered, bind up the broken and strengthen the sick; but the fat and the strong I will destroy. I will feed them with judgment.'"[491]

Yahweh said that the priests had failed to do their jobs. Instead of feeding the flock, they fed off of them. Yahweh also told the priests that He would assume the role of shepherd Himself and do the job they should have done. In this I AM statement, Jesus is saying He fulfilled that promise. In Ezekiel 34: 25 Yahweh said He would make a "covenant of peace" with His people when He came to shepherd them. In this I AM statement, Jesus is saying He is the fulfillment of that promise as well. The "covenant of peace" is the New Covenant that Jesus ratified with His own blood.

- "I AM the resurrection and the life; he who believes in Me will live even if he dies, and everyone who lives and believes in Me will never die."[492]

Jesus offers eternal life to anyone who believes in Him. He protects us no matter what happens to our physical bodies. Thus, we can be bold and confident as we go about doing the work He gives us to do with the full assurance that He is our Rock and our Refuge.

- "I AM the way, and the truth, and the life; no one comes to the Father but through Me. If you had known Me, you would have known My Father also; from now on you know Him, and have seen Him."[493]

In response to this I AM statement, Philip asked Jesus to show them the Father, and He said,

"Have I been so long with you, and yet you have not come to know Me, Philip? He who has seen Me has seen the Father; how can you say, 'Show us the Father'?"[494]

Without a doubt, Jesus claimed to be Yahweh. Despite the clarity of this statement, some people cannot believe that a loving God would provide only one way to salvation. In their minds, there must be many ways to come to Him. The only problem with their thinking is that He said there is only one way, and He is sovereign. Jesus said, "I AM the way, and the truth, and the life; no one comes to the Father but through Me"[495] and that is exactly what He meant.

- "I AM the vine, and My Father is the vine-dresser....I AM the vine, you are the branches; he who abides in Me and I in him, he bears much fruit, for apart from Me you can do nothing."[496]

The vineyard Jesus refers to in these verses is the Kingdom of Yahweh. The Father is the vinedresser, and Jesus is the vine. We are the branches on His vine, and we get all our nutrients from Him. The Father expects us to bear fruit. In John 15: 2-3, Jesus said the Father removes the branches that bear no fruit and prunes the productive branches so they bear even more fruit. But we are not left alone to do our work. He said, "...apart from Me you can do nothing." The corollary to this statement is "with Him we can do anything."

The Message is Clear

In his book *Jesus Among Other Gods*, Ravi Zacharias summarizes the meaning of Jesus' I AM statements perfectly:

> "He (Jesus) was identical with His message. 'In Him,' say the Scriptures, 'dwelt the fullness of the Godhead bodily.' He did not just proclaim the truth. He said, 'I am the truth.' He did not just show a way. He said, 'I am the Way.' He did not just open up vistas. He said, 'I am the door.' 'I am the Good Shepherd.' 'I am the resurrection and the life.' 'I am the I Am.'"[497]

At this point, there should be no doubt in your mind that Jesus claimed to be Yahweh. In fact, in John 8: 24 Jesus said that unless we believe He is Yahweh we will die in our sins. It's almost impossible to misinterpret that verse, and as far as I am concerned, that's as serious as it gets. And one more thing, it should be obvious that this is Jesus' message—not mine, and it is all over the Scriptures. This is the only relevant question. Do you believe the Bible? If you do, then it's time to recognize Jesus for who He is and tell the world about Him by Name—His Divine Name, Yahweh.

Chapter 10

Everyone Who Calls on the Name of Yahweh Will be Saved

John chapter 12 tells about Jesus' return to Jerusalem for Passover the year He was crucified. When the time for His death drew near, He said,

> "Now My soul has become troubled; and what shall I say, 'Father, save Me from this hour? But for this purpose I came to this hour. Father, glorify Your Name.' There came a Voice out of heaven: 'I have both glorified it, and will glorify it again.'"[498]

In these verses, Jesus is referring to His own Name—Yahweh, and the Father is alluding to the glorification of His Name brought about by Jesus' redemptive work. He is the Son, and He is the One and only personification and manifestation of the Father. That is exactly what Jesus meant when He said,

> "He who believes in Me, does not believe in Me but in Him who sent Me. He who sees Me sees the One who sent Me."[499]

John chapter 17 is the prayer Jesus prayed just before His trial and crucifixion. It is especially revealing given our discussion in the last chapter:

- "I have manifested Your Name to the men whom You gave Me out of the world."[500]   (In other words, Jesus is the manifestation of Yahweh.)

- "....Holy Father, keep them in Your Name, the Name which You have given Me, that they may be one even as We are. While I was with them, I was keeping them in Your Name which you have given Me."[501]   (In other words, Yahweh the Father gave the Name "Yahweh" to His Son—Jesus.)

- "....I have made Your Name known to them, and will make it known, so that the love wherewith You loved Me may be in them, and I in them."[502]   (In other words, Jesus is the personification of Yahweh.)

Jesus came to fulfill the Law, to inaugurate the New Covenant, and to make Yahweh's Name known again.[503]   Look closely at John 17: 22-23.   These two verses, which are part of the same prayer, capture the essence of Jesus' mission on earth:

> "The glory which you have given Me I have given to them, that they may be one, just as We are One; I in them and You in Me, that they may be perfected in unity, so that the world may know that You sent Me, and loved them, even as You have loved Me."[504]

Jesus' blood sacrifice atoned for our sins, reconciled us with the Father, and restored the intimacy with Him that was lost when Adam sinned. This is the heart and soul of the New Covenant.

Why Was Jesus Crucified?

Most Christians believe Jesus was crucified for claiming to be the Messiah, but that is not correct. Many so-called "messiahs" came before and after Him, but none of them were abused the way He was.[505] Jesus was crucified for saying the Name "Yahweh."

As I said before, violating the ban against saying the Name "Yahweh" was considered a capital offense—i.e., it was punishable by death, and the prescribed manner of death for people committing "blasphemy" was a combination of stoning and being hung on a tree.[506] Also, you will recall that according to the Mishnah, "The blasphemer is not considered culpable unless he exactly pronounces the Name."[507] That is why Jesus' claim to be Yahweh was not enough to execute Him. He had to say the Name "Yahweh" precisely in the presence of witnesses who were willing to testify against Him to be convicted for committing "blasphemy."

This information sheds a revealing light on Jesus' trial before the high priest, Caiaphas. In Matthew chapter 26, the priests were seeking "false testimony"[508] against Him, but they were unable to find the corroborating witnesses required by the Law. Eventually, they questioned a man who had heard Jesus say, "I am able to destroy the Temple of God and to rebuild it in three days."[509]

As you are about to see, Jesus could not have said "the Temple of God." He must have said "the Temple of Yahweh," and that set in motion the series of events that led to His crucifixion. Caiaphas stood up immediately when he heard the man's testimony and demanded an explanation from Jesus, but He offered none.[510] Then

Caiaphas ordered Jesus to tell them plainly if He was "the Messiah, the Son of God."[511]

According to Matthew, Jesus said,

"You have said it yourself; nevertheless I tell you, hereafter you will see the Son of Man sitting at the right hand of Power, and coming on the clouds of heaven."[512]

According to Luke, Jesus said,

"But from now on the Son of Man will be seated at the right hand of the power of God."[513]

Luke goes on to say that the priests continued to press Jesus for an answer and that eventually He responded by saying, "Yes, I am."[514] All of them understood His point, but according to the Mishnah Jesus still had not committed a capital offense.

Ancient New Testament manuscripts indicate that Jesus actually told Caiaphas that he would see Him "at the right hand of the Power of God."[515] Furthermore, we know for a fact that those ancient manuscripts routinely substitute the title "God" for the Name "Yahweh."[516] You can still see examples of this in almost every modern English Bible translation on the market today including the KJV, the NIV, and the NAS. When Old Testament quotes containing the Name "Yahweh" appear in the New Testament, the titles "God," "the Lord," "the LORD," or "the Lord GOD" are substituted for the Name "Yahweh."

From Caiaphas' response to Jesus' statement, it is obvious that He told the priests they would see Him "at the right hand of the Power of Yahweh." Look at your Bible and see for yourself. Caiaphas lunged out of his chair, tore his robes, and said,

"He has blasphemed! What further need do we have of witnesses? Behold, you have now heard the blasphemy."[517]

The Mishnah's definition of blasphemy was very precise, and according to Jewish religious law, it was the only definition of blasphemy in effect at that time. Therefore, the only logical explanation for Caiaphas' response to Jesus' statement is that He said the Name "Yahweh." There is no other explanation that makes any sense, and all those present at the trial said He deserved to die.[518]

The irony should be obvious. Obeying Yahweh's Law by declaring His Name made Jesus guilty of a capital offense according to Jewish religious law which was nothing more than tradition. Since Jewish religious law called for stoning Him, the people who lined the streets probably threw rocks at Jesus as He struggled to carry His crossbar to the crucifixion site. That helps to explain why He needed assistance carrying it.

The Mishnah states unequivocally that Jesus was hung on a tree and stoned[519] because "he had practiced magic and deceived and led astray Israel."[520] "Practicing magic" was not a problem for the priests. They claimed to have the ability to perform magic as well, and according to Bible scholar R. Travers Herford,

"Miracles, whether done by Jews or Christians, were ascribed to magic, and were not on that account despised."[521]

The priests were irate because Jesus used Yahweh's Name when He healed people—i.e., "practiced magic." They used Yahweh's Name as well when they prayed for healing, but they believed they were authorized to use it and that Jesus was not.[522] Since the priests had not given Jesus permission to use Yahweh's Name, His so-called "magic" was considered "blasphemy."

In John 10: 25, Jesus actually said that He used Yahweh's Name when He healed people. At the time, He was engaged in a discussion with the priests in the Temple, and they asked Him to tell them plainly if He was the Messiah. Jesus said,

"I told you, and you do not believe; the works that I do (i.e., the miracles He performed) in My Father's Name, these testify of Me."[523]

Clearly, restoring the use of Yahweh's Name was a critical part of Jesus' mission on earth. It was no coincidence that the Romans had invented a form of capital punishment (i.e., crucifixion) that fit perfectly with Yahweh's Law, and they hung Him on a tree. As you will see, Jesus and His disciples used the Name "Yahweh" frequently.

Jesus Left an Empty Tomb

The priests were very concerned about Jesus' disciples' activities, and the Acts of the Apostles tells about their many attempts to prevent His disciples from spreading the good news about Him. But no matter how hard they tried, every day more and more Jewish people accepted Jesus as their Messiah. Therefore, it is reasonable to conclude that the priests who conspired with the Roman authorities to kill Jesus felt even more threatened after His death than before.

The priests knew that Jesus foretold His death and resurrection,[524] so they asked the Roman governor to guard His tomb:

> "Sir, we remember that when He was still alive that deceiver said, 'After three days, I am to rise again.' Therefore, give orders for the grave to be made secure until the third day, otherwise His disciples may come and steal Him away and say to the people, 'He has risen from the dead,' and the last deception will be worse than the first.'"[525]

They did secure the tomb, and He did rise from the dead in three days just as He said. You may be wondering, "How can he know Jesus rose from the dead?" The answer is simple. If He had not risen from the dead, the priests needed only to produce His corpse to silence His followers. The fact that they did not produce His dead body for people to see is powerful evidence that they could not produce it.

But there is more. After Jesus' resurrection, He appeared many times. He appeared to Mary Magdalene[526] and other women;[527] His disciples saw Him several times after His resurrection;[528] and on one occasion, He appeared to a group of about 500 men and women.[529] All the eyewitness testimony about the resurrected Messiah was, and is, impossible to refute without producing His remains.

At Mount Vernon, Virginia, you can visit the gravesite of George and Martha Washington and see their caskets. Underneath those casket lids, you will find their remains. In Charlottesville, Virginia, you will find the grave of Thomas Jefferson. If you wanted to see his body, all you would need to do is dig it up. In Seville, Spain, the casket holding the remains of Christopher Columbus is on display, and in Jerusalem you can see and touch the casket holding David's corpse. None of these people have been resurrected. We know this because we have their remains with us today. Jesus left no remains. All we have is an empty tomb.

The Rules of Evidence Confirm Jesus' Resurrection

Some brilliant jurists have studied the resurrection of Jesus and concluded that His resurrection is a fact. For example, a gifted lawyer named Frank Morison set out to prove the fallacy of the resurrection, and he intended to write a book about it titled Disproving the Resurrection of Jesus. When he completed his research, he did write a book, but it had a different title: *Who Moved the Stone?*[530] In this book, Morison showed that the rules of evidence confirm Jesus' resurrection.

Additionally, Simon Greenleaf, a Harvard law professor in the 1800s whose work is still considered to be among the best in the world in terms of the rules of evidence, wrote *The Testimony of the Evangelists: The Gospels Examined by the Rules of Evidence in Courts of Justice*.[531] In this book, Greenleaf concluded that the resurrection of Jesus is the most verifiable fact in history.

A highly regarded Jewish scholar named Pinchas Lapide wrote *The Resurrection of Jesus: A Jewish Perspective* in which he concluded:

> "...according to my opinion, the resurrection belongs to the category of the truly real and effective occurrences...a fact of history...."[532]

Lapide drew this conclusion despite what he must have known would be the reaction to his findings by many, if not most, Jewish people. Josh McDowell, a lawyer and a best-selling author, reached the same conclusion and wrote *Evidence That Demands a Verdict*.[533] This book addresses several hypotheses pertaining to Jesus' death and resurrection, and McDowell concludes that no theory about what happened to Jesus after His crucifixion makes any sense except His resurrection.

Jesus and His Disciples Used the Name "Yahweh"

While I was writing this book and making presentations to various groups, this question arose many times: did Jesus and His disciples use the Name "Yahweh"? The answer is YES. Jesus and His disciples used the Name "Yahweh" regularly, and in fact, the disciples' message to the world was that we have salvation in the

Name Yahweh, but sometimes they used the phrase "the Name of Jesus" in lieu of the Name "Yahweh" to avoid being killed prematurely. After reading this chapter, reread the New Testament and pay attention to direct quotes and paraphrased passages from the Old Testament. When you do, you will discover that Yahweh's Name is all over the New Testament.

Jesus Used the Name "Yahweh"

I have shown already that Jesus used the Name "Yahweh" when He performed healing miracles and that He was crucified for saying "Yahweh." But there are many other examples in the Bible of Jesus saying the Name "Yahweh." For example,

- Matthew 4: 7 and Luke 4: 12: Jesus responding to Satan by quoting Deuteronomy 6: 16—"On the other hand, it is written, 'You shall not put Yahweh your God to the test.'"[534]

- Matthew 4: 10 and Luke 4: 8: Jesus responding to Satan by quoting Deuteronomy 6: 13—"Go Satan! For it is written, 'You shall worship Yahweh your God, and serve Him only.'"[535]

- Matthew 22: 43-44: Jesus responding to a group of Pharisees by quoting Psalm 110: 1—"Then how does David in the Spirit call Him Lord, saying, 'Yahweh said to my Lord, sit at my right hand, until I put Your enemies beneath Your feet?'"[536]

- Matthew 23: 37-39: Jesus quoting Psalm 118: 26 after condemning the Jewish religious leaders—"Jerusalem, Jerusalem, who kills the prophets and stones those who are sent to her! How many times I wanted to gather your children together, the way a hen gathers her chicks under her wings, and you were unwilling. Behold, your house is being left to you desolate! For I say to you, from now on you will not see Me until you say 'Blessed is He Who comes in the Name of Yahweh.'"[537]

- Mark 12: 29-30 and Luke 10: 27: Jesus responding to a scribe in the presence of many witnesses by quoting Deuteronomy 6: 4-5 (the Shema)—"The foremost is, 'Hear, O Israel! Yahweh our God is One; and you shall love Yahweh your God with all your heart, and with all your soul, and with all your mind, and with all your strength.'"[538]

- Luke: 4: 18-19 and 21: Jesus announcing His earthly ministry and His identity to His neighbors in Nazareth by quoting Isaiah 61: 1-2—"The Spirit of Yahweh is upon Me, because He has appointed Me to preach the gospel to the poor. He has sent Me to proclaim release to the captives, and recovery of sight to the blind, to set free those who are downtrodden, to proclaim the favorable year of Yahweh....Today this Scripture has been fulfilled in your hearing."[539]

When Jesus told His neighbors in Nazareth who He is, they tried to kill Him, but miraculously He escaped.[540] The only justification for their action was the fact that He said the Name

238

"Yahweh." Simply put, there is no other rational explanation for their response to Jesus' comment.

The Apostles' Message to the World: We Have Salvation in the Name "Yahweh"

After His resurrection, Jesus told His disciples to wait in Jerusalem until they received the outpouring of the Holy Spirit. Acts chapter 2 talks about the outpouring of the Holy Spirit[541] and the salvation of about 3000 people in Jerusalem in one day.[542]

When Yahweh's Spirit descended on Peter and his companions, God gave them the gift of tongues. This extraordinary incident attracted the attention of a group of devout Jews and proselytes from many nations who lived in Jerusalem.[543] Peter and his companions were known to be Galileans,[544] but everyone in the crowd heard his native language.[545] Some of the on-lookers believed Peter and his friends were intoxicated,[546] but Peter assured them that they were not drunk.[547] In Acts 2: 16, Peter told them that they were witnessing the fulfillment of Joel's prophecy recorded in Joel 2: 28-32.

Acts 2: 15-21 sets the stage for everything discussed in Acts chapters 3, 4, 5 and 9, and this short passage of Scripture lays out the foundation for the message the apostles preached to the world. In Acts 2: 21, Peter concludes by quoting Joel 2: 32:

"And it will come about that whoever calls on the Name of Yahweh will be delivered."[548]

According to the NAS, NIV, KJV, and The New Jerusalem Bible, Peter used the word "saved" in Acts 2: 21 instead of the word "delivered." The Greek word translated as "saved" in Acts 2: 21 is "sozo" (sode'-zo), and it means "to save, deliver, or protect." The Hebrew word translated as "delivered" in Joel is "malat" (maw-lat'), and it means "to release, rescue, or deliver." Thus, "sozo" and "malat" are synonymous.

Furthermore, Joel said that deliverance (or salvation) is granted to people who call on "the Name of Yahweh." However, Acts 2: 21 in the NAS, NIV, KJV, and The New Jerusalem Bible tells us that Peter used the phrase "the LORD" or "the Lord" instead of the Name "Yahweh." Since Peter was explaining salvation, it is illogical to believe that he misquoted Joel on this essential subject at this critical moment. He did say the Name "Yahweh;" the people who heard his message understood that Peter was referring to Jesus as Yahweh; and 3000 of them believed what he said and were saved. This is an incredibly important point, and it is ludicrous to think that the Holy Spirit would have permitted Peter to veer from Yahweh's explicit message one iota at this juncture.

Even so, we do know that the apostles used the phrase "the Name of Jesus" in lieu of the Name "Yahweh" many times to avoid being killed prematurely. For example, as I pointed out before, Paul was referring to the Name "Yahweh" when he said,

"God...bestowed on Him (Jesus) the Name which is above every name, so that at the Name of Jesus every knee shall bow, of those who are in heaven and on earth and under the earth, and every tongue will confess that Jesus the Messiah is Lord, to the glory of God the Father."[549]

As I said, Paul is actually paraphrasing Yahweh speaking to Isaiah:

"And there is no other God besides Me, a righteous God and a Savior; there is none except Me. Turn to Me, and be saved, all the ends of the earth; for I am God, and there is no other. I have sworn by Myself, the Word has gone forth from My mouth in righteousness and will not turn back, that to Me every knee will bow, every tongue will swear allegiance, they will say of Me, 'Only in Yahweh are righteousness and strength.' Men will come to Him and all who were angry with Him shall be put to shame."[550]

Acts chapters 3 and 4 provide another example of the apostles substituting the phrase "the Name of Jesus" for the Name "Yahweh." In this instance, Peter and John were walking to the Temple to pray, and a crippled beggar asked them for money.[551] Peter told the beggar that he had no money and then said,

"...I will give you what I have: in the Name of Jesus the Messiah the Nazarene, walk!"[552]

The crippled man was 40 years old at the time,[553] and he earned a living by begging from people who were on their way to the Temple. People who went to the Temple regularly knew him, and they knew he was lame. When Peter told the beggar to walk in "the

241

Name of Jesus," he stood up immediately and walked. The onlookers were amazed, and they rushed over to take a closer look. Then Peter said,

> "...it is the Name of Jesus which, through faith in Him, has brought back the strength of this man whom you see here and who is well known to you. It is faith in Him that has restored this man to health, as you can see."[554]

While Peter and John were talking, the Temple guards arrested them and took them to jail. The next day Caiaphas and other religious leaders interrogated them, and someone asked this question:

> "By what power, and by whose Name have you men done this?"[555]

Peter was filled with the power of the Holy Spirit,[556] and he said,

> "Rulers and elders of the people, if we are on trial today for a benefit done to a sick man, as to how this man has been made well, let it be known to all of you, and to all the people of Israel, that by the Name of Jesus the Messiah the Nazarene, whom you crucified, whom God raised from the dead—by this Name this man stands here before you in good health. He is the stone which was rejected by you, the builders, but which became the very corner stone. And there is salvation in no one else; for

there is no other name under heaven that has been given among men, by which we must be saved."[557]

Although the Bible does not tell us who asked the question that prompted Peter's reply, it is reasonable to assume it was Caiaphas. He had used a similar question to elicit the answer from Jesus that resulted in His crucifixion, and he probably thought he could eliminate Peter and John the same way. However, the Holy Spirit led Peter to use the phrase "the Name of Jesus" instead of the Name "Yahweh" in his answer, thus denying Caiaphas the opportunity to murder two more innocent people.

We know Peter meant the crippled beggar had been healed in Yahweh's Name because of his conclusion:

> "And there is salvation in no one else; for there is no other name under heaven that has been given among men, by which we must be saved."[558]

The only Name under heaven that has been given among men by which we must be saved is Yahweh, and we know this because that is exactly what Yahweh told Isaiah:

> "I, even I, am Yahweh, and there is no Savior besides Me."[559]

Acts chapter 5 talks about a similar incident. Peter and the other apostles were performing miracles and healing large numbers of people, and Caiaphas became jealous and had them arrested.[560] In their hearing before the Sanhedrin, Caiaphas said,

"We gave you a strong warning not to preach in this Name, and what have you done? You have filled Jerusalem with your teaching and seem determined to fix the guilt for this Man's death on us."[561]

In response, Peter said,

"Obedience to God comes before obedience to men; it was the God of our ancestors who raised up Jesus, whom you executed by hanging Him on a tree. By His own right hand God has now raised Him up to be leader and Saviour, to give repentance and forgiveness of sins through Him to Israel. We are witnesses to this, we and the Holy Spirit whom God has given to those who obey Him."[562]

Since Yahweh is our only Savior and because He alone can forgive sins, Peter was telling Caiaphas that Jesus is Yahweh. It is clear that Caiaphas understood Peter perfectly because he wanted to execute him on the spot,[563] and he would have if he could have done it legally. But according to the Mishnah, Peter had not committed a capital offense. He had told them that Jesus is Yahweh without saying the Name "Yahweh."

The hearing before the Sanhedrin came to an end when Gamaliel,[564] Paul's mentor, prudently suggested releasing them. He reasoned that if God were with the apostles no human being could stop them. If, on the other hand, Yahweh were not with them, they would fail miserably. Caiaphas accepted Gamaliel's advice, had the disciples flogged, and sent them away.[565] The apostles left that day badly beaten physically, but the Bible tells us that they were "glad to have had the honour of suffering humiliation for the sake of the Name."[566]

Acts chapter 9 tells about Saul, whose name Jesus changed to Paul, hunting down and bringing to trial anyone calling on "the Name of Jesus." While he was traveling to Damascus to arrest the Jewish believers in that town, Saul had a personal encounter with Jesus. A "light from heaven flashed"[567] that temporarily blinded Saul and Jesus spoke to him:

> "Saul, Saul, why are you persecuting Me?....I am Jesus whom you are persecuting, but get up and enter the city (Damascus), and it will be told you what you must do."[568]

At about the same time, Jesus told a man in Damascus named Ananias to go to a particular place where he would find Saul and to lay his hands on Saul so he could regain his sight. Ananias said,

> "Lord, I have heard from many about this man, how much harm he did to Your saints at Jerusalem; and here he has authority from the chief priests to bind all who call on Your Name."[569]

Jesus' response is revealing:

"Go, for he is a chosen instrument of Mine, to bear My Name before the Gentiles and kings and the sons of Israel; for I will show him how much he must suffer for My Name's sake."[570]

Paul went on to become the greatest evangelist of all time, and he spent the rest of his life proclaiming "the Name of Jesus" which is "Yahweh." In Romans 10: 13, Paul presents the essence of his message to the church:

"Whoever will call on the Name of the LORD will be saved."[571]

We Have Salvation in the Name "Yahweh"

Paul and Peter summed up their testimony by quoting Joel: "Whoever calls on the Name of Yahweh will be saved."[572] It just doesn't get any clearer than that. So these facts are irrefutable. We have One God—Yahweh; we have One Redeemer—Yahweh; we have One Savior—Yahweh; there is only One Name that has been given among men by which we must be saved—Yahweh; and Jesus is Yahweh.

This message is so clear and it's repeated so often in the Scriptures that you need help to be confused. That's why I said in the first chapter that I don't understand why Bible scholars and preachers have failed to pick up on the importance of God's Name and to tell people about it forcefully. By now you must know that this is not a new message because it is all over the Bible, but regrettably it has not been delivered to the Church. I know I'm repeating myself, but it's time for Christians to obey Yahweh and tell the world about Him by Name. That's exactly what He commanded us to do.

Chapter 11

Conclusion

The Romans Destroy the Temple of Yahweh

In 70 A.D., forty years after Jesus' death on the tree, the Romans destroyed Jerusalem and the Temple of Yahweh just as He said, and the Temple has never been rebuilt. The Temple's destruction is significant as this quote from The End of Days: Fundamentalism and the Struggle for the Temple Mount by Gershom Gorenberg points out:

> "Until 70 C.E., Judaism centered on the Temple and burnt offerings. Strikingly, the two Jews most responsible for post-Temple religion are remembered as predicting the sanctuary's destruction. 'There shall not be left here one stone upon another, that shall not be thrown down,' the Gospels quote Jesus as declaring. That was about 40 years before Titus. 'Forty years before the Temple's destruction,' says the Talmud, a crimson ribbon that miraculously turned white each Yom Kippur ceased doing so—that is, the ritual inside Herod's edifice had gone hollow—and the doors of the sanctuary opened by themselves, as if to allow enemies to enter. 'Sanctuary, Sanctuary,' said Yohanan ben Zakkai, a leading rabbi of the time, interpreting the signs, 'I know that your destiny is to be destroyed.'"[573]

The exact quote from the Talmud referred to by Gorenberg says,

"During the last forty years before the destruction of the Temple the lot did not come up in the right hand; nor did the crimson-coloured strap become white; nor did the westernmost light shine; and the doors of the Hekal (the Temple) would open by themselves...."[574]

This was a critical moment in the history of the world. In 30 A.D., the year Jesus died, God sent a powerful message to the Children of Israel. Every year on Yom Kippur until 30 A.D., the high priest would tie a crimson ribbon around the neck of the scapegoat, and miraculously it turned white after the sacrifice of the goat whose lot was to die. This event symbolized Yahweh forgiving the sins of His people, and it is not a folktale. It really happened every year on Yom Kippur until Jesus died on the tree. Leading rabbis and Jewish sages who lived during that time confirm this fact.

The sacrifices required by the Law, which were only symbols of the ultimate sacrifice Yahweh would make Himself, were no longer acceptable to Him. Jesus' death on the tree fulfilled the requirements of the Law for all time and completed the Old Covenant. His was the perfect sacrifice that will never be repeated. According to the apostle Paul, He "wiped out the record of our debt to the Law, which stood against us"[575] by nailing it to a tree.

In 30 A.D., at least one priest (Yohanan ben Zakkai, a leader among the priests) understood that their sacrifices were no longer pleasing to Yahweh, but they continued making sacrifices anyway until the Romans destroyed the Temple in 70 A.D. In that year, the Children of Israel eliminated the sacrificial system altogether, and it has not been reinstated to this day.

Jesus Told Us When He Will Return

The last paragraph in Matthew chapter 23 deserves another look:

"Jerusalem, Jerusalem, who kills the prophets and stones those who are sent to her! How many times I wanted to gather your children together, the way a hen gathers her chicks under her wings, and you were unwilling. Behold, your house is being left to you desolate! For I say to you, from now on you will not see Me until you say 'Blessed is He Who comes in the Name of Yahweh!'"[576]

When you read these words, you can almost feel Jesus' pain as He thinks back on what the priests and their forefathers had done. They had superimposed their traditions over Yahweh's Word and led His people astray. Additionally, they had portrayed Yahweh, the Almighty God and loving Father, as aloof and impersonal and had killed His prophets who came in His Name warning them to stop these practices.

Jesus concluded His condemnation of their practices by telling them that they will not see Him again until they say, "Blessed is He

Who comes in the Name of Yahweh!" I believe these are prophetic words and that Jesus is telling them He will not return until the Jewish people turn to Him in faith as a nation and call Him by His Name—Yahweh. We may be getting closer to that day than you realize.

In Luke 19: 42-44, Jesus said,

"If you, even you, had only known on this day what would bring you peace—but now it is hidden from your eyes. The days will come upon you when your enemies will build an embankment against you and encircle you and hem you in on every side. They will dash you to the ground, you and the children within your walls. They will not leave one stone on another, because you did not recognize the time of God's coming to you."[577]

Yahweh was with them in Person, and they missed Him completely. We are still waiting for the Jewish people to recognize that Jesus is the promised Messiah and that His Name is Yahweh. When they call on Him by Name, He will respond. This is how Isaiah explained it:

"Yes, people of Zion living in Jerusalem, you will weep no more. He will be gracious to you when your cry for help rings out; as soon as He hears it, He will answer you."[578]

Yahweh's Name Will Protect and Seal Believers at the End of Days

On the first Passover in Egypt, Yahweh protected and sealed the Children of Israel with the blood of the Passover lamb. At the End of Days, He will protect and seal believers with His Name by writing it on their foreheads. Revelation 3: 12, 14: 1, and 22: 4 deal with this issue:

- "He who overcomes, I will make him a pillar in the temple of My God, and he will not go out from it anymore; and I will write on him the Name of My God, and the name of the city of My God, the new Jerusalem, which comes down out of heaven from My God, and My new Name."[579]

- "Then I looked, and behold, the Lamb was standing on Mount Zion, and with Him one hundred and forty-four thousand, having His Name and the Name of His Father written on their foreheads."[580]

- "...they (believers) will see His (Yahweh's) face, and His Name will be on their foreheads."[581]

Jesus and the Father share the Name "Yahweh," and according to Jeremiah and Ezekiel Jerusalem will be called by Yahweh's Name at the End of Days.[582] Thus, Revelation 3: 12 and 14: 1 refer to only One Name—Yahweh, and the face of Yahweh referred to in Revelation 22: 4 is the face of Yahweh the Son.

Please do not underestimate the importance of these facts, because at the End of Days Yahweh will divide the world into two camps: those who have faith in Him and those who reject Him in favor of a global economic and religious system that is headed by Satan. Yahweh will write His Name on believers' foreheads and seal them, but those who reject Him will receive the "mark of the Beast." To understand what this means, read Revelation 13: 16-18 and 14: 9-11:

- "And he (the anti-Messiah's false prophet) causes all, the small and the great, and the rich and the poor, and the free men and the slaves, to be given a mark on their right hand or on their forehead, and he provides that no one will be able to buy or to sell, except the one who has the mark, either the name of the beast (the anti-Messiah) or the number of his name. Here is wisdom. Let him who has understanding calculate the number of the beast, for the number is that of a man; and his number is six hundred and sixty-six."[583]

- "...If anyone worships the beast and his image, and receives a mark on his forehead or on his hand, he also will drink of the wine of the wrath of God, which is mixed in full strength in the cup of His anger; and he will be tormented with fire and brimstone in the presence of the holy angels and in the presence of the Lamb. And the smoke of their torment goes up forever and ever; they have no rest day and night, those who worship the beast and his image, and whoever receives the mark of his name."[584]

The importance of Yahweh's Name should be obvious by now, and this is not a new idea. For example, take a look at Proverbs 18:10:

"The Name of Yahweh is a strong tower; the righteous runs into it and is safe."[585]

It is Time to Declare that Jesus is Yahweh

Today, most Christians have a firm grip on Jesus' role in our redemption and salvation, but somewhere down the line the importance of the Name "Yahweh" was lost. It is time for us to recognize that Jesus is Yahweh and that His Name has enormous significance. It is also time for us to realize that we must present Jesus accurately and completely. He is our Savior; He is our God; and His Name is Yahweh. Adjusting to this reality is not quick and easy for most of us. Here are some reasons why:

- Some Christian people, especially those who have attended church and read the Bible regularly for many years, have difficulty making the transition. Their resistance is understandable from a human perspective. Most of them read Bibles in which God's Name does not appear, and they have never heard a preacher mention the Name "Yahweh" from the pulpit. Using common human logic, they conclude that if this were true they would have heard it long ago.

- Other Christians already recognize that God's Name is important because the Bible makes this point repeatedly, but they wonder about the correct pronunciation of His Name.

Thus, they may dismiss the issue thinking it must not be all that significant. Using common human logic, they conclude that the Holy Spirit would have made certain to preserve His Name for us in whatever Bible translation we read if knowing His Name were important.

- Another group of Christians may be thinking, "I still don't understand why God's Name is important so why should I use it?"

I wish I could tell you all the reasons why Yahweh's Name is important, but I can't. However, I do know these facts. Joel, Peter, and Paul said everyone who calls on the Name of Yahweh will be saved. Yahweh told us that He is our One and only Savior, and Jesus said He is Yahweh. So this is my response to anyone who questions the importance of God's Name: the Name "Yahweh" is important because He said it is. I hope you don't require a better or more authoritative explanation than that. If you do, then you have a problem with Yahweh's Word.

How do you think Yahweh feels when people reject His Word? He died for us, and He commanded us to share His Name with the world. Refusing to obey God once you know the truth is analogous to the sin Adam committed in the Garden of Eden. It is an act of moral independence and a sin of the highest magnitude.

The fact that Yahweh has blessed us despite our not knowing His Name and our not obeying Him by declaring His Name to the world says a lot about Him:

- It tells us that He will allow us to make serious mistakes, even with something as essential as His Name, and still bless us if we are ignorant of the truth.

- It demonstrates that He will bless us even if we misunderstand the significance of something as crucial as His Name if we are seeking the truth.

- Its shows that Yahweh is merciful and kind to people who disobey Him in ignorance as long as they are attempting to obey Him.

Please do not confuse Yahweh's love, grace, mercy, patience, kindness, and forgiveness with His approval of our willful disobedience. He does not, and He will not, condone sin. Once we know what we are supposed to do, Yahweh expects us to obey Him, and not obeying Him is an act of moral independence. As I said, Yahweh reserves to Himself the exclusive right to determine right and wrong, and He alone has the privilege of deciding how He will save mankind. This is a fact, and we would be foolish to ignore it.

HalleluYah!

Four times in Revelation chapter 19 the word "HalleluYah" appears.[586] Sometimes it is spelled "Alleluia" or "Hallelujah," and sometimes the "Y" is not capitalized. "HalleluYah" is a combination of two Hebrew words: "hallelu" which means praise and "Yah" which is a short form of the Name "Yahweh" that is found in several psalms.

The word "HalleluYah" does not appear in any other place in the New Testament. This fact is interesting in itself, and the way the word is used in Revelation is revealing. Revelation chapter 18 talks about the destruction of the "harlot Babylon" at the End of Days, and chapter 19 talks about the second coming of the Messiah:

> "After these things I heard something like a loud voice of a great multitude in heaven saying, 'HalleluYah! Salvation and glory and power belong to our God; because His judgments are true and righteous; for He has judged the great harlot who was corrupting the earth with her immorality, and He has avenged the blood of His bond-servants on her.'
>
> And a second time they said, 'HalleluYah! Her smoke rises up forever and ever.' And the twenty-four elders and the four living creatures fell down and worshiped God who sits on the throne saying, 'Amen. HalleluYah!'
>
> And a voice came from the throne, saying, 'Give praise to our God, all you His bond-servants, you who fear Him, the small and the great.'
>
> Then I heard something like the voice of a great multitude and like the sound of many waters and like the sounds of mighty peals of thunder, saying, 'HalleluYah! For Yahweh our God, the Almighty, reigns. Let us rejoice and be glad and give the glory to Him, for the marriage of the Lamb has come and His bride has made herself ready.'"[587]

After this, Yahweh comes to earth in Person to complete His work and to claim His bride. HalleluYah. Those who know Him should praise His Name and rejoice because He is about to do wonderful and marvelous things that will surpass the things He did in Egypt at the time of the Exodus. We do not know the day or the hour, but He will not hold back forever. To believe otherwise is foolish.

Jesus' Return is an Absolute Certainty

Genesis 45: 3 tells about Joseph revealing himself to his brothers and saying, "I am Joseph."[588] Until he told them his true identity, they did not know Joseph had become viceroy (or prime minister) in Egypt. According to Chafetz Chaim, a Jewish sage,

> "When Joseph said, 'I am Joseph,' God's master plan became clear to the brothers; everything that had happened for the last twenty-two years fell into perspective. So, too, will it be in the time to come when God will reveal Himself and announce, 'I am HASHEM (Yahweh)!' The veil will be lifted from our eyes and we will comprehend everything that transpired throughout history."[589]

That day did come. Yahweh came to them in the Person of Jesus the Messiah, and He did say, "I am Yahweh." However, instead of receiving Him with great joy and honoring Him as God, the Jewish people were lead by their priests to reject and kill Him. The day is coming when He will return, and we call that day the End of Days. When He returns, those who know Him will rejoice. Those who do not know Him will regret it—deeply and sincerely regret it for all eternity.

C. S. Lewis explained Jesus' return this way:

"When that happens (when Jesus returns), it is the end of the world. When the author walks on to the stage the play is over. God is going to invade, all right: but what is the good of saying you are on His side then, when you see the whole natural universe melting away like a dream and something else— something it never entered your mind to conceive—comes crashing in; something so beautiful to some of us and so terrible to others that none of us will have any choice left? For this time it will be God without disguise; something so overwhelming that it will strike either irresistible love or irresistible horror into every creature. It will be too late then to choose your side. There is no use saying you choose to lie down when it has become impossible to stand up. That will not be the time for choosing: it will be the time when we discover which side we really have chosen, whether we realised it before or not. Now, to-day, this moment, is our chance to choose the right side. God is holding back to give us that chance. It will not last forever. We must take it or leave it."[590]

The day of Yahweh's burning anger is rapidly approaching. Although we do not know the exact day and hour Yahweh will pour out His wrath on a rebellious world, we do know we must be ready when He returns because that will not be the time for deciding. As C.S. Lewis said, that will be the day we learn what we have decided already. If you feel Yahweh tugging at your heart, do not delay. Turn to Him right now because tomorrow may be too late. Ask Him to forgive you and to save you, and then have faith in Him to do it.

What is Your Heart Condition?

Our willingness to obey God depends on the condition of our heart and our openness to the leading of His Spirit. Yahweh's message is not too complex for ordinary men and women to understand. He presented it in very simple terms so that in the end no one will have an excuse for disobeying Him. We do not need preachers, rabbis, and other learned individuals to tell us what God said, even though some of them may want us to believe we do. We need only Yahweh, His Word, and His Spirit to understand His message, and then our heart condition determines whether we get it. What is your heart condition?

Matthew 13: 1-23 is Jesus' parable about the sower of seeds. In the parable, He discusses four possible heart conditions, and He uses the fertility of the soil in which the seed is sown as a metaphor for the condition of our hearts in matters pertaining to God's Word and the leading of His Spirit. Below are the heart conditions and a brief summary of Jesus' comments about them:

- Soil beside a tightly packed roadway:[591] The soil beside the road is so tightly packed that birds eat the seed before it has a chance to sprout. This soil symbolizes a rock-hard human heart that God's Word cannot penetrate, and the birds represent Satan snatching away God's Word before it has a chance to grow and produce fruit.[592]

- Rocky soil just beyond the tightly packed dirt:[593] Seed planted in rocky soil sprouts immediately, but the soil has no depth so the young plants' roots cannot take a firm hold. Thus, they die quickly. This condition symbolizes people who hear the Word of God and immediately accept it with gladness, but when they experience hardship or any form of persecution for believing His Word they fall away without delay.[594]

- Soil infested with thorns:[595] This soil may be fertile, but it is incapable of sustaining young plants because the thorns choke them out. Jesus used this metaphor to symbolize people whose hearts are too preoccupied with worldly pursuits to produce fruit for Him. He specifically mentions people with an inordinate desire for creature comforts and financial security, and He calls this thorn the "deceitfulness of wealth."[596]   This may be the most difficult problem confronting United States citizens who claim to be Christians.

- Good soil:[597] Good soil symbolizes a heart that is open to God's Word and obedient to the leading of His Spirit. According to Jesus, people with this type of heart hear God's Word, understand it, apply it, and bear much fruit for Him.[598]

The message of this book is as uncomplicated as Yahweh's plan of salvation, and it comes directly from Him. Now you have the opportunity to make a decision to obey the only true God. Please do not test Yahweh. By this I mean, please do not require Yahweh to give you more evidence than He has made available in the Bible already to prove something that should be crystal clear. You have all the evidence you need, so decide. As for me and my house, we will trust Yahweh and obey Him. Any other choice makes no sense.

Appendix

Jesus Fulfilled the Messianic Prophecies

Below are facts about Jesus' life that prove He fulfilled the Messianic prophecies I discussed in chapter 8, and all of them are supported by an abundance of eyewitness testimony. Furthermore, His disciples devoted the remainder of their lives to His cause, and they were willing to die rather than abandon Him and His message about salvation. These, too, are compelling arguments that Jesus is the One He claimed to be.

- Jesus was born of a virgin named Mary (Miriam in Hebrew) in Bethlehem, a tiny village about 5 miles from Jerusalem, and He is from the tribe of Judah.[599]

- Before Jesus began His earthly ministry, John the Baptist prepared the way for Him by telling the people they needed to repent from their sins.[600]

John the Baptist fulfilled Malachi's prophecy about Elijah coming before the Messiah. Somewhere between 450 B.C. and 400 B.C., the prophet Malachi foretold that Elijah would return before the "great and terrible day of Yahweh...(to) restore the hearts of the fathers to their children and the hearts of the children to their fathers."[601] Because they knew about this prophecy, shortly after

Jesus' disciples understood clearly that He was the Messiah, they asked Him why the Jewish religious leaders said Elijah must return before the Messiah, and He told them,

> "Elijah is coming and will restore all things; but I say to you that Elijah already came, and they did not recognize him, but did to him whatever they wished. So also the Son of Man is going to suffer at their hands."[602]

John the Baptist's role in Jesus' ministry was to turn the hearts and minds of the Children of Israel back to Yahweh by declaring that they needed to repent. The Hebrew word translated as "repent" (or "relent") in the Old Testament and the Tanach is "nacham" (naw-kham'), and it means to sigh or to be sorry. The Greek word for repent that is used in the New Testament is "metanoeo" (met-an-o-eh'), and it means to think differently or to reconsider. Both of these words carry with them the connotation that people should change their behavior because they are sorry for what they have done and that they should begin immediately to think differently about sin. To repent, therefore, means to be sorry for sins already committed and to refrain from committing sins in the future. That is exactly what John the Baptist preached and that is exactly the role Malachi prophesied Elijah would play.

As you know, the Old Testament and the Tanach tell us that there is only one Messiah and that He plays two different roles at two different times. First, He had to come as Immanuel (God with us) to suffer and die for His people, to redeem us, and to atone for our sins.[603] Second, He will return as Wonderful, Counselor, Mighty

God, Everlasting Father, and Prince of Peace to rule the earth before the "great and terrible day of Yahweh."[604] A person with the spirit of Elijah (John the Baptist) heralded the Messiah's first coming, and many people believe another person with the spirit of Elijah will precede His second coming. That is exactly what Jesus meant when He said, "Elijah is coming and will restore all things."[605]

The second person with Elijah's spirit is discussed in Revelation chapter 11, and he is described as one of Yahweh's two witnesses. This witness will play a slightly different role than the one played by John the Baptist. While John preached a message of repentance from sin to avoid judgment, the witness depicted in Revelation chapter 11 will preach a message of repentance, but he will also initiate Yahweh's judgment before what Christians call the "Great Tribulation" and what the Old Testament and Tanach refer to as the "great and terrible day of Yahweh." This is what Malachi says about that day:

> "'For behold, the day is coming, burning like a furnace; and all the arrogant and every evildoer will be chaff; and the day that is coming will set them ablaze,' says Yahweh Sabaoth, 'so that it will leave them neither root nor branch. But for you who fear My Name, the sun of righteousness will rise with healing in its wings; and you will go forth and skip about like calves from the stall. You will tread down the wicked, for they shall be ashes under the soles of your feet on the day which I am preparing,' says Yahweh Sabaoth.'"[606]

- When He went to Jerusalem for Passover the year He died, He entered the city riding on a donkey, the colt of an ass.[607]

- Judas, one of Jesus' disciples, betrayed Him and collected 30 pieces of silver for turning Him over to the religious authorities.[608] When he realized what he had done, Judas returned the money to the priests. He entered the Temple and threw the silver coins at them. Since it was "blood money," the priests refused to accept it. Instead, they used the money to purchase the potter's field for use as a cemetery.[609]

- During His trials before the priests, the civil authorities, and the Roman Governor, Jesus' enemies treated Him brutally. They spit on Him and literally beat Him to a pulp. When they were through, He did not even look like a man.[610] Yet, He was silent before His accusers.[611]

- Jesus was crucified on Passover, and His followers refer to Him affectionately as the Lamb of God. He is our Sacrificial Lamb. He willingly and gladly sacrificed His own life and spilled His own blood to atone for our sins.[612] He, therefore, is the Passover Sacrifice and the Yom Kippur Sacrifice.

- Two thieves were crucified along with Him,[613] and the soldiers who nailed Him to the tree gambled for His clothing at the foot of the tree while He was dying to atone for their sins.[614]

As sundown approached, the priests asked the Roman Governor to kill the three men who had been crucified, including Jesus. Ironically, the priests shared responsibility for slaying Yahweh's Passover Lamb, but they were oblivious to the role they were playing in His divine plan to redeem and save mankind through the Messiah's shed blood. The Gentile rulers in Israel at the time (the Romans) also shared responsibility for the Messiah's death so it is correct to say that both Gentiles and Jews nailed Him to the tree. All of mankind, therefore, shares guilt for slaying the Messiah. The Jewish people are not more or less guilty than everyone else.

- Complying with the priests' request, the Roman governor sent his men to kill the three men. When they arrived at the crucifixion site, they could see that Jesus was already dead, but they pierced His side with a spear to make certain, and blood and water came pouring out of His body. They broke the legs of the other two men to hasten their deaths, but they did not need to break Jesus' legs since He was already dead.[615]

- When Jesus died and gave up His Spirit, a strange darkness covered the land.[616] There was an earthquake, and the veil in the Temple separating the Holy of Holies from the Outer Chamber of the sanctuary was torn in two. The people standing near the tree where He was crucified knew something strange was happening, but they had no idea what it was. Yahweh was taking on Himself all the sins we will ever commit to redeem us and to atone for our sins so He could declare us righteous, give us eternal life, and restore the intimacy He had with His people before Adam sinned.[617]

- As He was about to die, the Gospels tell us that Jesus said, "It is finished!"[618] However, this is not a good translation. He actually said, "Paid in full!"[619] The price for our sins had been paid; we were redeemed; and our sins were forgiven.

- With His death on the tree, Jesus took the curse of the Law[620] on Himself so we can receive the blessings promised to Abraham's descendants.

- Joseph of Arimathea, a wealthy friend of the Messiah, asked the Roman governor for permission to bury Him in a tomb he had dug for himself. It was located just a short distance from the crucifixion site in a beautiful garden.[621]

- Most of Jesus' own people, the Children of Israel, rejected Him,[622] and for most of them He has become a stumbling block.[623] However, Gentiles followed Him,[624] and today approximately 2 billion Gentile people living on earth, or about one third of the world's population, claim to be Christians.

All these facts about Jesus' life, death, and resurrection provide convincing proof that He is exactly who He claimed to be and that His death accomplished exactly what He said it would, and all of them have been confirmed. He lived His life in perfect obedience to the Law spelled out in the Torah, and His death sealed a New Covenant between Yahweh and all of mankind.

The New Covenant Sealed with Jesus' Blood

- Jesus paid the whole price for our sins. He suffered before His death, and after His death He went to hell for those who put their faith in Him. Yahweh's Law—the Torah—required it. But hell and the grave could not hold Him, and His body did not decay.[625]

- Jesus made the perfect sacrifice for our sins, and it will never be repeated. After His death, He became the chief Cornerstone[626] of the new Temple of Yahweh—a Temple not made with hands. The Temple of Yahweh is His body of believers who have put their faith in Him, and He is the Head of the body.

- When the Roman soldier pierced Jesus' side with his spear and blood and water came gushing out of His body, He sprinkled the Mercy Seat, fulfilled the Law's requirement, and sealed a New Covenant. This is the covenant referred to by Jeremiah,[627] Isaiah,[628] and Ezekiel.[629]

On the third day after His death, He arose from the grave and became our Intercessor before the Father. His death initiated a permanent priesthood that was not like the Levitical priesthood introduced by Moses. The Levitical priests were sinners themselves, and they had to make sacrifices for their own sins before they could offer sacrifices for the sins of the Children of Israel. Moreover, they

269

had to offer sacrifices yearly for atonement as a constant reminder that they needed a redeemer and savior. But Jesus' sacrifice was different. His offering was once and for all, and He became our permanent High Priest before the Father just as King David prophesied:

> "Yahweh has sworn and will not change His mind, You are a priest forever according to the order of Melchizedek."[630]

The Order of Melchizedek

Melchizedek symbolizes the Messiah uniting the roles of High Priest and King. According to Ramban, a Jewish sage, Melchizedek was actually Shem—Noah's son.[631] Charles Ryrie, the Bible scholar I mentioned before, says he "foreshadowed the crowning of Messiah, who at His second coming will build the (millennial) temple and unite the offices of King and Priest in one Person."[632] Others have said he is Seth (Adam's son), Job, or an angel, but many people believe Melchizedek is a preincarnate manifestation of the Messiah — in which case he would be Yahweh.

Melchizedek is mentioned in the Bible for the first time in Genesis chapter 14 where we are told about Abraham rescuing his nephew Lot after several allied kings had taken him and his family captive. When Abraham returned to Jerusalem after the rescue, Melchizedek came out to meet him. This is what the Bible says about their encounter:

> "And Melchizedek king of Salem brought out bread and wine; now he was a priest of God Most High (El Elyon).[633] He blessed

him and said, 'Blessed be Abram of God Most High, Possessor of heaven and earth; and blessed be God Most High, Who has delivered your enemies into your hand.' He (Abraham) gave him (Melchizedek) a tenth of all."[634]

About 1000 years later, King David said,

"Yahweh has sworn and will not change His mind, You are a priest forever according to the order of Melchizedek."[635]

Then David said,

"The Lord (the Messiah) is at Your (the Father's) right hand; He (the Messiah) will shatter kings in the day of His wrath. He will judge among the nations, He will fill them with corpses, He will shatter the chief men over a broad country. He will drink from the brook by the wayside; therefore He will lift up His head."[636]

In the book of Hebrews, the apostle Paul says this about Melchizedek:

"For this Melchizedek, king of Salem, priest of the Most High God, who met Abraham as he was returning from the slaughter of the kings and blessed him, to whom also Abraham apportioned a tenth part of all the spoils, was first of all, by the translation of his Name, king of righteousness, and then also king of Salem, which is king of peace. Without father, without mother, without genealogy, having neither beginning of days nor end of life, but made like the Son of God, he remains a priest perpetually."[637]

Paul goes on to say that Melchizedek was greater than Abraham, Levi, or Aaron[638] and that He prefigured the Messianic priesthood that is different from the Levitical order—a better priesthood that is both perfect and perpetual.[639] Paul says,

"For, on the one hand, there is a setting aside of the former commandment because of its weakness and uselessness (for the Law made nothing perfect), and on the other hand there is a bringing in of a better hope, through which we draw near to God[640] .... Jesus has become the guarantee of a better covenant[641] .... because He continues forever, holds His priesthood permanently. Therefore He is able to save forever those who draw near to God through Him, since He always lives to make intercession for them."[642]

This is the way Yahweh explained the Messiah's role to Zechariah:

"Take silver and gold, make an ornate crown and set it on the head of Joshua the son of Jehozadak, the high priest. Then say to him, Thus says Yahweh Sabaoth, 'Behold, a man whose Name is Branch, for He will branch out from where He is; and He will build the Temple of Yahweh. Yes, it is He who will build the Temple of Yahweh, and He will bear the honor and sit and rule on His throne. Thus, He will be a priest on His throne, and the counsel of peace will be between the two offices.'"[643]

We know from Jeremiah's[644] and Isaiah's[645] prophecies that the One whose Name is Branch is the Messiah, that He made the perfect sacrifice for our sins, and that He is called Wonderful, Counselor, Mighty God, Everlasting Father, and Price of Peace. Yahweh confirmed Jeremiah's and Isaiah's prophecies by telling Zechariah that One whose Name is Branch (the Messiah) is both King and Priest, and those are the offices Melchizedek held. Therefore, I believe Melchizedek is the preincarnate Messiah—Yahweh. He is King forever and perpetual High Priest, and He established a new and better covenant and became our permanent Intercessor before the Father.

Melchizedek's Messianic identity was not lost on the ancient rabbis. Many of them believed Melchizedek was the Messiah, and following Jesus' crucifixion this fact created quite a problem. After His resurrection, Jesus' disciples explained His priesthood by referring to Melchizedek, and the rabbis essentially abandoned any mention of Melchizedek from that time forward. For a complete discussion of this issue, read Jesus and Christian Origins Outside the New Testament by F.F. Bruce.[646]

Selected Bibliography

(A)

Aburish, Said K. *Saddam Hussein: The Politics of Revenge*, Bloomsbury Publishing, New York and London, 2000.

Aburish, Said K. *Arafat: From Defender to Dictator*, Bloomsbury Publishing, New York and London, 1998.

Aburish, Said K. *The Rise, Corruption and Coming Fall of the House of Saud*, St. Martin's Griffin, New York, NY, 1996.

Arens, Moshe. *Broken Covenant: American Foreign Policy and the Crisis Between the U.S. and Israel*, Simon & Schuster, New York, NY, 1995.

(B)

Bendiner, Elmer. *The Rise and Fall of Paradise: When Arabs and Jews Built a Kingdom in Spain*, Barnes & Noble Books, New York, NY, 1983.

Benvenisti, Meron. *City of Stone: The Hidden History of Jerusalem*, University of California Press, Berkeley and Los Angeles, CA, 1996.

Bevere, John. *A Heart Ablaze*, Thomas Nelson Publishers, Nashville, TN, 1999.

Brenton, Sir Lancelot C. L. *The Septuagint with Apocrypha: Greek and English*, 9th Printing, originally published by Samuel Bagster & Sons, Ltd., London, 1851. This version published by Hendrickson Publishers, 2001.

Brown, Michael L. *Answering Jewish Objections to Jesus*, Baker Books, Grand Rapids, MI, 2000.

Brown, Michael L. *Our Hands Are Stained with Blood*, Destiny Image Publishers, Shippensburg, PA, 1992.

Bruce, F.F. *Jesus and Christian Origins Outside the New Testament*, William B. Eerdmans Publishing Company, Grand Rapids, Michigan, 1984, pp. 64-65.

(C)

Cahill, Thomas. *The Gifts of the Jews: How a Tribe of Desert Nomads Changed the Way Everyone Thinks and Feels*, Nan A. Talese/Anchor Books, New York, NY, 1998.

Church, J. R. and Gary Stearman. *The Mystery of the Menorah*, Prophecy Publications, Oklahoma, OK, 1993.

Clover, R. *The Sacred Name Volume I Third Edition*, Qadesh La Yahweh Press, Garden Grove, California, 2002.

Cohen, Tim. *The AntiChrist and a Cup of Tea*, Prophecy House, Inc., Aurora, CA, 1998.

Collins, Larry and Dominique Lapierre, *O Jerusalem!*, Simon & Schuster, New York, NY, 1988.

(D)

Danby, Herbert, trans. *Mishnah*. Oxford University Press, 1974.

Dodd, C.H. *The Interpretation of the Fourth Gospel*, Cambridge University Press, 1958.

Drosnin, Michael, *The Bible Code*, Simon and Schuster, New York, 1997.

(E)

Eastman, Mark and Chuck Missler, *The Search for Messiah*, Fountain Valley: Joy Publishing, 1996.

Eisenman, Robert and Michael Wise. *The Dead Sea Scrolls Uncovered*, Barnes & Noble Books, New York, NY, 1994.

Encyclopedia Judaica, Volume 1 (corrected edition). Jerusalem: Keter Publishing House Jerusalem Ltd., (no date given).

Encyclopedia Judaica, Volume 11 (corrected edition). Jerusalem: Keter Publishing House Jerusalem Ltd., (no date given).

Encyclopedia Judaica, Volume 14 (corrected edition). Jerusalem: Keter Publishing House Jerusalem Ltd., (no date given).

Evans, Mike. *Jerusalem Betrayed: Ancient Prophecy and Modern Conspiracy Collide in the Holy City*, Word Publishing, Dallas, TX, 1997.

(F)

Faier, Zvi. Translator. *Malbim: Beginning and Upheaval*. Jerusalem: Hillel Press, 1978.

Fischer, Raymond Robert, *The Children of God: Messianic Jews and Gentile Christians Nourished by Common Jewish Roots*, Olim Publications, Tiberias, Israel, 2000.

Frankel, Ellen and Betty Platkin Teutsch, *The Encyclopedia of Jewish Symbols*. Northvale, NJ: Jason Aronson Inc., 1992.

(G)

Gilbert, Martin. *Jerusalem in the Twentieth Century,* John Wiley & Sons, Inc., New York, NY, 1996.

Gorenberg, Gershom. *The End of Days: Fundamentalism and the Struggle for the Temple Mount,* New York, The Free Press, 2000.

Greenleaf, Simon, *The Testimony of the Evangelists: The Gospels Examined by the Rules of Evidence in Courts of Justice,* Grand Rapids, MI: Kregel Publications, 1995.

Gruber, Dan. *The Church and the Jews,* Serenity Books, Hagerstown, MD, 1997.

(H)

HarperCollins Atlas of the Bible, London, England: HarperCollinsPublishers, 1987, 1989, 1994, and 1997.

Herford, R. Travers. *Christianity in Talmud and Midrash.* Reference Book Publishers, Inc., New Jersey, 1966.

Herzog, Chaim. *The Arab-Israeli Wars: War and Peace in the Middle East from the War of Independence Through Lebanon,* Vintage Books, New York, NY, 1984.

Holy Bible (The), *New International Version,* Zondervan Bible Publishers, Grand Rapids, Michigan, 1978.

Holy Bible, *King James Version,* Thomas Nelson, Inc., Nashville, Tennessee, 1976.

(J)

Jeffrey, Grant. *The Handwriting of God,* International Press, New York, 1996.

Jeffrey, Grant. *The Signature of God*, International Press, New York, 1996.

Jeffrey, Grant. *Jesus: The Great Debate*, Frontier Research Publications, Inc.: Toronto, 1999.

Jewish Encyclopedia (The), Volume 1. New York: Funk & Wagnell's Company, 1916.

Johnson, Nita. *Prepare for the Winds of Change II*, Eagle's Nest Publishing, Clovis, CA, 1991.

(K)

Kac, Arthur W. *The Messianic Hope*, Baker House, Grand Rapids, 1975.

Kaplan, Rabbi Aryeh, Translator. *The Torah Anthology, Volume 1*, Brooklyn, NY: Moznaim Publishing Corporation, 1977, 1978, 1979, 1981, and 1982.

Kaplan, Rabbi Aryeh, translator, *The Torah Anthology, Volume 2*, Brooklyn, NY: Moznaim Publishing Corporation, 1977, 1978, 1979, 1981, and 1982.

Kass, Robert. *"Equidistant Letter Sequences in the Book of Genesis,"* Statistical Science, August 1994.

Kirsch, Jonathan. *Moses: A Life*, Ballantine Books, New York, NY, 1998.

Kohlenberger, John III, *The Interlinear NIV Hebrew-English Old Testament*, Zondervan Publishing House, Grand Rapids, Michigan, 1987.

(L)

LaHaye, Tim and Jerry Jenkins, *The Mark: The Beast Rules the World*, Tyndale House Publishers, Inc., Illinois, 2000, dust cover material.

Landman, Isaac, ed. *Universal Jewish Encyclopedia. 10 vols*. The Universal Jewish Encyclopedia, Inc. New York, 1941, vol. 5.

Lapide, Pinchas, *The Resurrection of Jesus: A Jewish Perspective*, Minneapolis, MN: Augsburg Publishing House, 1983.

Levine, Samuel. *You Take Jesus, I'll Take God*, Hamoroh Press, 1980.

Lewis, Bernard, *What Went Wrong?: Western Impact and Middle Eastern Response*, Oxford University Press, New York, NY, 2002.

Lewis, C. S., *Mere Christianity*, HarperSanFrancisco, New York, NY, 1952.

Lewis, C.S. *The Screwtape Letters*, HarperCollins, New York, NY, 2001.

Lewis, C.S. *The Weight of Glory*, HarperSanFrancisco, New York, NY, 2001.

Lewis, C.S. *Letters to Malcolm*, Harcourt, New York, NY, 1992.

Lewis, C.S. *The Great Divorce*, HarperSanFrancisco, New York, NY, 2001.

Lewis, C.S. *The Problem of Pain*, HarperSanFrancisco, New York, NY, 1996.

Lewis, C.S. *The Joyful Christian*, Simon & Schuster, New York, NY, 1996.

Lewis, C.S. *The Four Loves*, Harcourt Brace & Company, New York, NY, Orlando, FL, 1988.

Lewis, C.S. *The Collected Works of C.S. Lewis*, Inspirational Press, New York, NY, 1996.

Liberman, Paul. *The Fig Tree Blossoms*, Harrison, Arkansas: Fountain Press, Inc., 1976.

(M)

Maimonides, Moses. *The Guide for the Perplexed*, Dover Publications, New York, NY, 1956.

Manuel, Frank E. *The Religion of Isaac Newton*, London: Oxford University Press, 1974.

McDowell, Josh. *Evidence That Demands a Verdict*, Campus Crusade for Christ, San Bernardino, CA, 1972.

McTernan, John. *God's Final Warning to America*, Hearthstone Publishing, Oklahoma City, OK, 2000.

McVey, Steve. *Grace Land*, Harvest House, Eugene, Oregon, 2001.

McVey, Steve. *Grace Walk*, Harvest House, Eugene, Oregon, 1995.

McVey, Steve. *Grace Rules*, Harvest House, Eugene, Oregon, 1998.

Michas, Peter. *The Rod of an Almond Tree in God's Master Plan*, Winepress Publishing, Enumclaw, WA, 2001.

Miller, Judith. *God Has Ninety-Nine Names: Reporting From a Militant Middle East*, Simon & Schuster, New York, NY, 1996.

Möller, Lennart. *The Exodus Case: A Scientific Examination of the Exodus Story—and a Deep Look Into the Red Sea*, Scandinavia Publishing House, Copenhagen NV, Denmark, 2000.

Moore, Phillip. *The End of History—Messiah Conspiracy, Vol. I*, Atlanta: Ramshead Press International Corporation, 1996.

Morison, Frank, *Who Moved the Stone?*, Grand Rapids, MI: Zondervan Publishing House, 1987.

Mordecai, Victor. *Christian Revival for Israel's Survival*, Victor Mordecai, Taylors, SC, 1999.

Mordecai, Victor. *Is Fanatic Islam a Global Threat?*, Victor Mordecai, Taylors, SC, 1997.

(N)

New Jerusalem Bible (The), Doubleday, New York, 1985.

Neusner, Jacob. *First Century Judaism in Crisis: Yohanan Ben Zakkai and the Renaissance of Torah*, New York: Abingdon Press, 1975.

Nye, Joseph S. Jr. *The Paradox of American Power: Why the World's Only Superpower Can't Go it Alone*, Oxford University Press, Oxford, England, 2002.

(P)

Parkes, James. *A History of the Jewish People*, Penguin Books, Baltimore, MD, 1964.

Patai, Raphael. *The Messiah Texts*, Wayne State University Press: Detroit, 1979.

Peters, Joan. *From Time Immemorial: The Origins of the Arab-Jewish Conflict Over Palestine*, Harper & Row, New York, NY, 1984.

Prayer of Manasseh (The), Revised Standard Version of the Bible, © National Council of Churches of Christ in America.

(R)

Rambsel, Yacov. *Jesus: The Hebrew Factor*, Messianic Ministries, Inc., San Antonio, 1996.

Rambsel, Yacov. *Yeshua: The Name of Jesus Revealed in the Old Testament*, Frontier Research Publications, Inc., Toronto, 1996.

Rambsel, Yacov. *His Name is Jesus: The Mysterious Yeshua Codes*, Word Publishing, Nashville, 1999.

Ritmeyer, Leen and Kathleen. *Secrets of Jerusalem's Temple Mount*, Biblical Archeology Society, Washington, DC, 1998.

Roth, Sid. *Time is Running Short*, Destiny Image Publishers, Shippensburg, PA, 1990.

Roth, Sid. *There Must Be Something More!*: The Spiritual Rebirth of a Jew, Messianic Vision Press, Brunswick, GA, 1994.

Roth, Sid. *They Thought for Themselves: Daring to Confront the Forbidden*, Messianic Vision Press, Brunswick, GA, 1999.

Roth, Sid. *The Last Lap: The Emergence of the One New Man*, MV Press, Brunswick, GA, 2001.

Ryrie, Charles. *Ryrie Study Bible Expanded Edition*, Moody Press, Chicago, 1995.

(S)

Scherman, Rabbi Nosson, *The Stone Edition Tanach, The ArtScroll Series®*, Mesorah Publications, Brooklyn, New York, 1996.

Schiffman, Lawrence, *Who was a Jew?: Rabbinic and Halakhic Perspectives on the Jewish-Christian Schism*, KTAV Publishing House, Hoboken, NJ, 1985.

Schlatter, Victor. *Showdown of the Gods*, Gazelle Press, Mobile, AL, 2001.

Seedman, Terrye Goldblum. *Holy to Yahveh: Yahshua*, Longwood Communications, DeBary, FL, 1996.

Sigal, Rabbi Phillip. *Judaism: The Evolution of a Faith*, Wm. B. Eerdmans Publishing Co., Grand Rapids, Michigan, 1988.

Singer, Isadore, ed. *The Jewish Encyclopedia. 12 vols.* KTAV Publishing House, Inc., 1964, vol. 9.

Sowell, Thomas. *The Vision of the Anointed: Self-Congratulation as a Basis for Social Policy*, Basic Books, New York, NY, 1995.

Strong, James. *The New Strong's Exhaustive Concordance of the Bible*, Thomas Nelson Publishers, Nashville, Tennessee, 1995.

(T)

Tabor, Dr. James D. *Restoring Abrahamic Faith*, Genesis 2000, Charlotte, NC, 1993.

(U)

Unterman, Alan. *Dictionary of Jewish Lore and Legend*. London: Thames and Hudson Ltd., 1991.

(V)

van Kampen, Robert. *The Sign of Christ's Coming and the End of the Age: A Biblical Study of End-Time Events*, Crossway Books, Wheaton, Illinois, 1999.

(W)

Williams, Larry. *The Mountain of Moses: The Discovery of Mount Sinai*, Wynwood Press, New York, NY, 1990.

Wilson, Ian. *The Blood and the Shroud*, The Free Press, New York, NY, 1998.

(Z)

Zacharias, Ravi. *Jesus Among Other Gods*, Nashville, TN: W Publishing Group, 2000.

Zlotowitz, Meir, translator, *The ArtScroll Tanach Series: Genesis, Volume 1(b)*, New York: Mesorah Publications, Ltd., 1986 and 1988.

Zondervan Pictorial Encyclopedia of the Bible (The), Volume 4, Grand Rapids, MI: Zondervan Publishing House, 1976.

Endnotes

[1] http://poll.gallup.com/content/default.aspx?ci=22885.

[2] Ryrie, Charles. *Ryrie Study Bible Expanded Edition*, Moody, 1995, p. 6.

[3] Exodus 20: 24.

[4] In this book, I capitalize the first letter in the word "Person" if I am referring to God. As the personification and the manifestation of Yahweh, Jesus is the essence, substance, and occurrence of Yahweh's divine nature. Thanks to Andrew Roth for recommending this clarification. Clearly, Jesus is no ordinary person.

[5] Philippians 2: 9-11. The parentheses are mine.

[6] Isaiah 45: 21-24.

[7] John 8: 58.

[8] Isaiah 43:11.

[9] Joel 2: 32, Acts 2: 21, and Romans 10: 13.

[10] Joel 2: 32, Acts 2: 21, and Romans 10: 13.

[11] Acts 17: 11.

[12] Kohlenberger, John III, *The Interlinear NIV Hebrew-English Old Testament*, Zondervan Publishing House, Grand Rapids, Michigan, 1987, p. xxxv.

[13] Scherman, Rabbi Nosson, *The Stone Edition Tanach, The ArtScroll Series®*, Mesorah Publications, Brooklyn, New York, 1996, p. xxv.

[14] Exodus 3: 14.

[15] Exodus 3: 15 from the *New International Version*. The parentheses are mine.

[16] *Encyclopedia Judaica* Jerusalem, vol. 7, Keter Publishing House, Jerusalem, Israel, the Macmillian Company, Jerusalem, 1972, p. 680.

[17] Weingreen, J.A. *Practical Grammar for Classical Hebrew*, Clarendon Press, 1939, pp. 6-7; Harris, R. Laird. *Introductory Hebrew Grammar*, Wm. B. Eerdmans Publishing Company, Michigan, 4th Edition, 1955, p. 16; Marks, John H. and Rogers, Virgil M. *A Beginner's Handbook to Biblical Hebrew*, Abingdon, Nashville, 1958, p. 7; and Horowitz, Edward. *How the Hebrew Language Grew*, Jewish Education Committee Press, 1960, pp. 333f.

[18] If you would like to know more about the correct pronunciation of God's Name, refer to the Encyclopedia Judaica, The Interpreter's Dictionary of the Bible, Unger's Bible Dictionary, The Jewish Encyclopedia (Volume 12), the Encarta Encyclopedia, or Clover, R. *The Sacred Name Volume I Third Edition*, Qadesh La Yahweh Press, Garden Grove, California, 2002, chapter 9.

[19] Encyclopedia Judaica, The Interpreter's Dictionary of the Bible, Unger's Bible Dictionary, The Jewish Encyclopedia (Volume 12), the Encarta Encyclopedia, or

Clover, R. *The Sacred Name Volume I Third Edition*, Qadesh La Yahweh Press, Garden Grove, California, 2002, chapter 9.

[20] Landman, Isaac, ed. *Universal Jewish Encyclopedia*. 10 vols. The Universal Jewish Encyclopedia, Inc. New York, 1941, vol. 5, p. 7.

[21] According to *The Jewish Encyclopedia* (Singer, Isadore, ed. 12 vols. KTAV Publishing House, Inc., 1964, vol. 7, p. 88), Galatinus was the confessor for Pope Leo the 10th.

[22] Many, if not most, Bible scholars believe Galatinus was the person responsible for interpreting the Name "Yahweh" incorrectly as Jehovah. However, there is some controversy about this question. No matter who made this mistake, we know the name Jehovah did not come into use until at least the 1400s A.D.

[23] Kohlenberger, John III, *The Interlinear NIV Hebrew-English Old Testament*, Zondervan Publishing House, Grand Rapids, Michigan, 1987, p. xviii.

[24] Genesis 4: 26.

[25] Genesis 4: 26 from *The New Jerusalem Bible*.

[26] Genesis 4: 26 in *The Interlinear NIV Hebrew-English Old Testament* by John Kohlenberger, III. The parentheses are mine.

[27] Genesis 4: 26 in *The Stone Edition Tanach, The ArtScroll Series®*, by Rabbi Nosson Scherman. The parentheses are mine.

[28] This quote is taken from a letter Rabbi Scherman sent me that is dated May 8, 2003.

[29] Matthew 15: 6.

[30] Psalm 22: 31.

[31] Psalm 22: 31.

[32] Psalm 30: 9.

[33] Psalm 73: 28.

[34] Psalm 145: 4.

[35] Psalm 145: 6.

[36] Psalm 22: 22.

[37] Psalm 78: 6.

[38] Psalm 96: 3.

[39] Psalm 80: 18.

[40] Psalm 83:16.

[41] Psalm 86: 11.

[42] Isaiah 26: 13.

[43] Psalm 86: 12.

[44] Psalm 92: 1.

[45] Psalm 96:2.

[46] Although *The New Jerusalem Bible* translates Yahweh's personal Name correctly when it appears unaccompanied by the title Adonai, it follows the editorial tradition of translating Adonai Yahweh as "the Lord GOD."

[47] Clover, R. *The Sacred Name Volume I Third Edition*, Qadesh La Yahweh Press, Garden Grove, California, 2002, p. 142.

[48] Until the destruction of the Temple of Yahweh in 70 A.D., these three groups competed with one another for dominance in Judaism. The Pharisees and the Sadducees were more prominent than the Essenes because they separated themselves from everyday life by retreating to the Dead Sea area to a village called Qumran. Following the Temple's destruction, the Pharisee sect took control of Judaism.

[49] *Mishnah* Ber., 9: 5 as translated by Herbert Danby, p. 10, n. 13.

[50] Jeremiah 23: 26-28 from *The New Jerusalem Bible*.

[51] Matthew 23: 13.

[52] Luke 11: 52.

[53] Sanhedrin 7: 5.

[54] Sanhedrin 7: 5.

[55] Evans, Michael D. *Beyond Iraq: The Next Move: Ancient Prophecy and Modern Day Conspiracy Collide*, White Stone Books, Lakeland, Florida, 2003, p. 119.

[56] Jeremiah 39: 10.

[57] Jeremiah 40: 7.

[58] Jeremiah 40: 14.

[59] Jeremiah 42: 2.

[60] Jeremiah 42: 10-16 from *The New Jerusalem Bible*.

[61] Jeremiah 43: 2.

[62] Jeremiah 44: 16-19.

[63] Jeremiah 44: 26 from *The New Jerusalem Bible*.

[64] Exodus 20: 7.

[65] Sanhedrin 11: 3.

[66] Danby, Herbert, trans. *Mishnah*. Oxford University Press, 1974, p. xvii.

[67] Most of these rationalizations are discussed in *The Sacred Name Volume I Third Edition* by R. Clover, Qadesh La Yahweh Press, Garden Grove, California, 2002, pp. xv-xvi.

[68] Joel 2: 32, Acts 2: 21, and Romans 10: 13.

[69] Acts 4: 12.

[70] Most of these Names for Yahweh are listed in Charles Ryrie's *Ryrie Study Bible Expanded Edition*, Moody Press, Chicago, 1995, pp. 2057-2058.

[71] Scherman, Rabbi Nosson, *The Stone Edition Tanach, The ArtScroll Series®*, Mesorah Publications, Brooklyn, New York, 1996, p. 145.

[72] Sigal, Rabbi Phillip. *Judaism: The Evolution of a Faith*, Wm. B. Eerdmans Publishing Co., Grand Rapids, Michigan, 1988, p. 7.

[73] Exodus 3: 4-5.

[74] Exodus 3: 6.

[75] Exodus 2: 14.

[76] Exodus 3: 15.

[77] Exodus 3: 15 in the *New International Version*. The parentheses are mine.

[78] Exodus 5: 1.

[79] Exodus 5: 2.

[80] Exodus 5: 23.

[81] Exodus 6: 6-8.

[82] Ryrie, Charles. *Ryrie Study Bible*, 1995, p. 101.

[83] Genesis 1: 3-28.

[84] Exodus 7: 17.

[85] Exodus 8: 1-2.

[86] Exodus 8: 10.

[87] Exodus 8: 19.

[88] Exodus 8: 22-23. Some Bible translations refer to the fourth plague as a swarm of lice or flies instead of insects, and the Tanach refers to it as a swarm of beasts. I searched diligently to find out how these various interpretations were reached but was unable to find a satisfactory answer. Thus, I used the *New American Standard* Bible as my source document. In any event, in this plague Yahweh is demonstrating His ability to take simple dust and turn it into something powerful with which to inflict punishment on mankind—in this case Pharaoh and all of Egypt. He was also demonstrating that He distinguishes between His people and everyone else.

[89] Exodus 9: 3.

[90] Exodus 9: 14-16. The parentheses are mine.

[91] "Deutero-canonical" simply means that it is not included in the Bible that Protestants use. Early church leaders accepted the book of Wisdom as Yahweh's divinely inspired word until St. Jerome and several other church leaders objected to its inclusion in the canonical Scriptures—the Protestant Bible. Be that as it may, Wisdom is a wonderful book that should be read by all Christians.

[92] According to *The New Jerusalem Bible*, Doubleday, New York, 1985, p. 1042, King Solomon wrote The Book of Wisdom. Although he is not named in the book itself as the writer, he is clearly indicated. For example, Wisdom 9: 7-8 says "You have chosen me to be king over Your people, to be judge of your sons and daughters. You have bidden me build a temple on Your holy mountain, and an altar in the city where you have pitched Your tent, a copy of the holy Tent which

You prepared at the beginning." Solomon is the person Yahweh commissioned to do these things. Wisdom 9: 12 says, "…I shall govern Your people justly and be worthy of my father's throne." Again, this verse indicates that Solomon is the writer of The Book of Wisdom, because he succeeded his father David to the throne of Israel.

[93] Wisdom 16: 17 from *The New Jerusalem Bible*.

[94] Wisdom 19: 6 from *The New Jerusalem Bible*.

[95] Wisdom 19: 18 from *The New Jerusalem Bible*.

[96] Wisdom 19: 20 from *The New Jerusalem Bible*.

[97] Exodus 9: 27.

[98] Exodus 10: 1-2.

[99] Exodus 12: 12.

[100] Exodus 11: 7.

[101] Exodus 12: 14 and 17.

[102] Genesis 2: 17.

[103] Exodus 12: 2-8 from *The Stone Edition Tanach*. The parentheses are mine.

[104] Exodus 12: 6. The parentheses are mine.

[105] Isaiah 53: 6 from the *The Stone Edition Tanach*.

[106] Isaiah 53: 10.

[107] Isaiah 12: 4-6.

[108] Möller, Lennart. *The Exodus Case: A Scientific Examination of the Exodus Story — and a Deep Look Into the Red Sea*, Scandinavia Publishing House, Copenhagen NV, Denmark, 2000, pp. 145.

[109] For more details about the Ipuwer Papyrus, read Möller's book *The Exodus Case: A Scientific Examination of the Exodus Story — and a Deep Look Into the Red Sea*, Scandinavia Publishing House, Copenhagen NV, Denmark, 2000, pp. 143-149.

[110] Exodus 12: 32.

[111] Exodus 12: 41.

[112] Exodus 13: 17.

[113] Exodus 13: 21.

[114] Exodus 14: 4.

[115] Exodus 14: 11-12.

[116] Exodus 14: 15.

[117] Exodus 14: 17-18.

[118] Exodus 14: 30-31.

[119] Exodus 15: 1-3.

[120] Exodus 15: 13.

[121] Exodus 15: 18.

[122] In Exodus 19: 9-15, Yahweh gives Moses instructions about what the Children of Israel should do to prepare for His arrival. He said He would descend on Mount Sinai "the day after tomorrow," or on the third day. The third day includes today, thus Yahweh would descend in two days.

[123] Exodus 19: 10-12.

[124] Exodus 19: 16-22.

[125] Shemos Rabbah 29: 9.

[126] Exodus 20: 2.

[127] Exodus 19: 5.

[128] Exodus 20: 2-17. It is Exodus 20: 2-14 in the Tanach. I have numbered the Ten Commandments to make it easy for readers to identify them, but they are not numbered this way in the Bible.

[129] http://win.niddk.nih.gov/statistics/

[130] For example, "Ancient Paths: The Sabbath" by Doug Trudell deals with this issue in great detail.

[131] See Matthew chapters 5, 6, and 7. These chapters discuss the Sermon on the Mount, and Jesus used this sermon to explain Yahweh's logic and His perspective on the Law.

[132] Exodus 32: 12.

[133] Ezekiel 20: 9.

[134] This information was included in an email from Melanie Snyder dated June 3, 2002.

[135] Habakkuk 2: 4 and Hebrews 11: 6.

[136] Leviticus 18: 24-25.

[137] Ezra 9: 11 from *The New Jerusalem Bible*.

[138] Ezra 9: 11 from *The New Jerusalem Bible*.

[139] Genesis 3: 8.

[140] Genesis 11: 27-32.

[141] Genesis 12: 7.

[142] Genesis 16: 5.

[143] Genesis 16: 8.

[144] Genesis 16: 9.

[145] Genesis 16: 10.

[146] Genesis 16: 13. The parentheses are mine.

[147] Genesis 16: 14.

[148] Genesis 17: 1.

[149] Genesis 17: 1-2.

[150] Genesis 17: 3.

[151] Genesis 17: 17.

[152] Genesis 17: 19.

[153] Genesis 17: 20-22.

[154] Genesis 18: 1.

[155] Genesis 18: 8.

[156] Genesis 18: 12.

[157] Genesis 18: 13-14.

[158] Genesis 26: 2-5.

[159] Ryrie, Charles. *Ryrie Study Bible Expanded Edition*, Moody Press, Chicago, 1995, p. 45.

[160] Genesis 26: 24.

[161] Genesis 25: 34

[162] Malachi 1: 2-3.

[163] Genesis 27: 38.

[164] Genesis 25: 28.

[165] Genesis 25: 23.

[166] For a complete explanation of this interpretation, see Peter Michas' book *The Rod of an Almond Tree in God's Master Plan*, Winepress Publishing, Enumclaw, WA, 2001, p. 113.

[167] Genesis 28: 13-15.

[168] Genesis 32: 24.

[169] Genesis 32: 28.

[170] Genesis 32: 30.

[171] Genesis 32: 28.

[172] Exodus 24: 10.

[173] Exodus 24: 11.

[174] Exodus 24: 10-11.

[175] Revelation 1: 12-16 and 4: 1-6.

[176] Numbers 22: 12.

[177] Numbers 22: 23.

[178] Jude 11.

[179] Joshua 5: 13-15.

[180] Joshua 5: 13-15.

[181] I want to thank David Chattleton, a former student of mine, for suggesting this wording.

[182] Judges 2: 1-3.

[183] Judges 6: 12.

[184] Judges 6: 13.

[185] Judges 6: 16.

[186] Judges 6: 22.

[187] Judges 6: 23.

[188] Judges 13: 5.

[189] Judges 13: 11. The capitalization of the first letter in "Am" is mine, but it is perfectly consistent with Yahweh's Word.

[190] Judges 13: 17.

[191] Judges 13: 18.

[192] Isaiah 9: 6-7. The parentheses and italics are mine.

[193] Judges 13: 16.

[194] Judges 13: 19.

[195] Judges 13: 20.

[196] Judges 13: 22.

[197] Judges 13: 23.

[198] 1 Samuel 1: 6.

[199] 1 Samuel 1: 10.

[200] 1 Samuel 1: 11.

[201] 1 Samuel 2: 11.

[202] 1 Samuel 2: 14.

[203] 1 Samuel 2: 16.

[204] 1 Samuel 2: 22.

[205] 1 Samuel 3: 11-14 from *The New Jerusalem Bible*.

[206] The meaning of the word "Messiah" is "Anointed One." David was a type of the Messiah, and he is referred to in the Bible as Yahweh's anointed one.

[207] 1 Chronicles 21: 1.

[208] This interpretation is from Radak and others. Radak is an acronym for Rabbi David Kimchi who lived from 1040 to 1105. His commentaries on the Tanach and the Babylonian Talmud are studied today by traditional Jews.

[209] 1 Chronicles 21: 9-12.

[210] 1 Chronicles 21: 13.

[211] 1 Chronicles 21: 15.

[212] 1 Chronicles 21: 16.

[213] 1 Chronicles 21: 17.

[214] 1 Chronicles 21: 18.

[215] 1 Chronicles 21: 25.

[216] Ryrie, Charles. *Ryrie Study Bible Expanded Edition*, Moody Press, Chicago, 1995, p. 656.

[217] 2 Chronicles 3: 1.

[218] 2 Samuel 24: 18.

[219] 2 Samuel 24: 24.

[220] 1 Kings 3: 5.

[221] 1 Kings 3: 9.

[222] 1 Kings 9: 2.

[223] 1 Kings 9: 3.

[224] Ecclesiastes 12: 13-14.

[225] 1 Kings 11: 9-11.

[226] 1 Kings 11: 1-3.

[227] 1 Kings 11: 5-7.

[228] Isaiah 6: 5 from *The New Jerusalem Bible*.

[229] Genesis 3: 14-15. The parentheses are mine.

[230] Genesis 3: 16.

[231] Genesis 3: 17-19.

[232] *The New Jerusalem Bible*, Doubleday, New York, 1985, p. 21.

[233] Genesis 6: 8.

[234] Ryrie, Charles. *Ryrie Study Bible Expanded Edition*, Moody Press, Chicago, 1995, p. 13.

[235] Genesis 2: 6.

[236] Genesis 8: 21.

[237] Genesis 9: 9-13.

[238] Genesis 12: 1.

[239] Genesis 12: 2-3.

[240] Genesis 13: 14-17.

[241] Genesis 15: 18-21. The parentheses are mine.

[242] Genesis 17: 4-8 from *The New Jerusalem Bible*.

[243] Genesis 17: 15-16 and 19-21 from *The New Jerusalem Bible*.

[244] Genesis 26: 2-5.

[245] Genesis 28: 13-15.

[246] Genesis 35: 10-12. The parentheses are mine.

[247] Exodus 6: 6-8.

[248] Exodus 23: 20-25.

[249] Exodus 23: 27-31. The parentheses are mine.

[250] Genesis 15: 1.

[251] Genesis 15: 1.

[252] Genesis 15: 2-3.

[253] Genesis 15: 5.

[254] Genesis 15: 6.

[255] Genesis 15: 9-10.

[256] Read Jeremiah 34: 8-22 to understand how important it is for us to live up to the terms of a covenant. Yahweh expects us to live up to our word, and He also expects us to obey His Word. Failure on our part to honor our word or to obey

Yahweh's Word is inviting disaster. Covenants are binding agreements no matter what happens.

[257] McVey, Steve. *Grace Land*, Harvest House, Eugene, Oregon, 2001, p. 81.

[258] Genesis 15: 12.

[259] Genesis 15: 17-18.

[260] Psalm 78: 22, Psalm 78: 32, and Psalm 78: 59-62.

[261] The three books on grace written by Steve McVey are *Grace Walk*, *Grace Rules*, and *Grace Land*, and Harvest House published all of them.

[262] McVey, Steve. *Grace Land*, Harvest House, Eugene, Oregon, 2001, p. 82.

[263] *The New Jerusalem Bible*, Doubleday, New York, 1985, p. 35. The parentheses are mine.

[264] Yahweh cannot die, because then the universe would stop running. The human form of Yahweh did die when He was hung on a tree, but His divine nature INSIDE Jesus did not and cannot die (see Isaiah 11:1-12, Isaiah chapter 53, Isaiah 63:1-14, and Psalm 51:1-11). In a nutshell, Jesus, who is Yahweh the Son, laid down his life voluntarily in submission to Yahweh the Father (see John chapter 10) to atone for our sins. Thanks to Andrew Roth for suggesting this clarification.

[265] Genesis 22: 2.

[266] Genesis 22: 5.

[267] Genesis 22: 8.

[268] Genesis 22: 8 from *Holy Bible From the Ancient Eastern Text*, George M. Lamsa's translation from the Aramaic of the Peshitta that was first published in 1933.

[269] Genesis 22: 14.

[270] Genesis 22: 14 from Holy Bible: From the Ancient Eastern Text, George M. Lamsa's translation from the Aramaic of the Peshitta.

[271] Ryrie, Charles. *Ryrie Study Bible Expanded Edition*, Moody Press, Chicago, 1995, p. 37.

[272] Genesis 22: 16-18.

[273] Scherman, Rabbi Nosson, *The Stone Edition Tanach, The ArtScroll Series®*, Mesorah Publications, Brooklyn, New York, 1996, p. 1781, and Kohlenberger, John III, *The Interlinear NIV Hebrew-English Old Testament*, Zondervan Publishing House, Grand Rapids, Michigan, 1987, p. 445.

[274] Exodus 20: 24.

[275] Deuteronomy 18: 18-19.

[276] 1 Samuel 13: 14.

[277] 2 Samuel 7: 12-13.

[278] 1 Chronicles 17: 14.

[279] 2 Samuel 7: 23 from *The New Jerusalem Bible*.

280 2 Samuel 7: 25-26 from *The New Jerusalem Bible*.

281 Jeremiah 31: 31-33.

282 Isaiah 42: 1-9.

283 Ezekiel 34: 1-31 and 36: 22-37.

284 Ezekiel 28: 12-15.

285 Isaiah 14: 12-14.

286 Genesis 3: 1.

287 Genesis 3: 3.

288 *The New Jerusalem Bible*, Doubleday, New York, 1985, p. 19. Also, see Scherman, Rabbi Nosson, *The Stone Edition Tanach, The ArtScroll Series®*, Mesorah Publications, Brooklyn, New York, 1996, p. 6.

289 Genesis 2: 17.

290 Genesis 2: 21-22.

291 Genesis 3: 4-5.

292 Genesis 3: 9.

293 Genesis 3: 10.

294 Genesis 3: 11.

295 Genesis 3: 12.

296 Genesis 3: 13.

297 Genesis 3: 13.

298 Deuteronomy 4: 29.

299 Isaiah 29: 13-14.

300 1 Chronicles 16: 8-11. The Hebrew word translated as "call upon" in verse 8 is *qara*, and it has several meanings. The Tanach interprets verse 8 as saying "declare His Name" instead of "call upon His Name." It could be interpreted "invoke His Name" as well. No matter how it is interpreted, we are commanded to declare, to call upon, and to invoke the Name "Yahweh." Both the Tanach and the Christian Old Testament make this point repeatedly.

301 1 Chronicles 28: 9.

302 2 Chronicles 7: 14.

303 2 Chronicles 15: 2.

304 Psalm 9: 10.

305 Psalm 40: 16.

306 Psalm 119: 2.

307 Isaiah 55: 8-9.

308 Isaiah 64: 6.

309 Jeremiah 23: 5-6.

310 Most Bibles translate the Hebrew word *tsidkenu* as righteousness and that is exactly what it means, but in a literal sense it means "saving justice." The notion

that righteousness is not free is key. Yahweh is holy and perfect, and He cannot abide sin. For us to be with Him, we must be spotless—without blemish. Since we cannot achieve this result on our own, Yahweh took it upon Himself to do it for us. He paid the price for our sins thereby fulfilling the requirement of the Law, and He is our Redeemer. Justice demands a price, and Yahweh paid that price for us and saved us. Therefore, He is our "saving justice" or our Righteousness—*Tsidkenu.*

[311] Isaiah 64: 6.

[312] Isaiah 45: 21-24.

[313] Isaiah 61: 10.

[314] Titus 3: 3-8, *The New Jerusalem Bible*. The parentheses are mine.

[315] Galatians 5: 2-6.

[316] James 2: 17-26.

[317] Psalm 37: 4-5.

[318] Psalm 49: 7-8.

[319] Psalm 49: 15. The parentheses are mine.

[320] Isaiah 8: 14-15. The parentheses are mine.

[321] Isaiah 28: 16.

[322] Isaiah 51: 1-2.

[323] Habakkuk 2: 3-4.

[324] Hebrews 11: 6.

[325] Proverbs 16: 25.

[326] Genesis 15: 6. The parentheses are mine.

[327] Kohlenberger, John III, *The Interlinear NIV Hebrew-English Old Testament*, Zondervan Publishing House, Grand Rapids, Michigan, 1987.

[328] Genesis 17: 11.

[329] Deuteronomy 30: 6.

[330] Genesis 22: 1-2.

[331] Romans 3: 20 and 31 from *The New Jerusalem Bible*.

[332] Matthew 17: 20. The parentheses are mine.

[333] Genesis 3: 15.

[334] Midrash Rabbah XXIII 5-6. As quoted in Dr. Moore's book *The End of History— The Messiah Conspiracy, Vol. I*, p. 9. The parentheses are mine.

[335] Jeffrey, Grant. *Jesus: The Great Debate*, Frontier Research Publications, Inc.: Toronto, 1999, pp. 230-239.

[336] The Appendix contains information on the fulfillment of all the prophecies listed in Exhibit 8.1. Jesus fulfilled all of them, and many more as well.

[337] To calculate this probability, simply multiply all 17 probabilities (i.e., probability 1 times probability 2 times probability 3....times probability 17).

[338] Psalm 22: 16.

[339] Levine, Samuel. *You Take Jesus, I'll Take God*, Hamoroh Press, 1980, p. 34.

[340] Brenton, Sir Lancelot C. L. *The Septuagint with Apocrypha: Greek and English, 9th Printing*, originally published by Samuel Bagster & Sons, Ltd., London, 1851. This version published by Hendrickson Publishers, 2001.

[341] A Targum is a Jewish commentary on the Old Testament, and it means translation.

[342] Eastman, Mark and Chuck Missler, *The Search for Messiah*, Fountain Valley: Joy Publishing, 1996, pp. 31-33.

[343] *Babylonian Talmud*, Sukkah 52a.

[344] A sage is a wise person. The word does not suggest or imply rank, title, or position, although many people consider sages to be wiser and more perceptive than ordinary people.

[345] "Talmudic times" refers to an era between the Babylonian captivity that began in 597 B.C. and about 400 A.D. During Talmudic times, Jewish Sages wrote about virtually every area of life, religion, custom, folklore, and law. Their writings in Hebrew and Aramaic contain approximately 2,500,000 words that are published as books called the Talmud, and they are studied today. The Babylonian Talmud is the best known and most authoritative of all the Talmud writings.

[346] Patai, Raphael. *The Messiah Texts*, Wayne State University Press: Detroit, 1979, pp. 166-167.

[347] Amos 8: 9.

[348] Ryrie, Charles. *Ryrie Study Bible Expanded Edition*, Moody Press, Chicago, 1995, p. 1400.

[349] Jeffrey, Grant. *Jesus: The Great Debate*, Frontier Research Publications, Inc.: Toronto, 1999, pp. 230-239.

[350] Isaiah 7: 14.

[351] *The New Jerusalem Bible*, Doubleday, New York, 1985, p. 1201.

[352] Isaiah 7: 14 from Scherman, Rabbi Nosson, *The Stone Edition Tanach, The ArtScroll Series®*, Mesorah Publications, Brooklyn, New York, 1996.

[353] Genesis 24: 43, Exodus 2: 8, Proverbs 30: 18, Psalm 68: 25, Isaiah 7: 14, and Song of Songs 1: 3 and 6: 8.

[354] Isaiah 7: 11.

[355] Isaiah 7: 12.

[356] Isaiah 7: 13.

[357] Isaiah 7: 14.

[358] Isaiah 9: 1.

[359] Isaiah 9: 2.

[360] Isaiah 9: 3.

[361] Isaiah 9: 6.

[362] Isaiah 11: 1.

[363] Isaiah 11: 2.

[364] Isaiah 11: 3-4.

[365] Isaiah 11: 4.

[366] Scherman, Rabbi Nosson, *The Stone Edition Tanach, The ArtScroll Series®*, Mesorah Publications, Brooklyn, New York, 1996, p. 968.

[367] Isaiah 8: 18.

[368] Psalm 2: 7-9.

[369] Midrash Tehelim, fol. 3, col. 4. As quoted in Dr. Moore's book *The End of History—The Messiah Conspiracy, Vol. I.*, p. 108.

[370] Psalm 8: 4-5.

[371] Psalm 69: 3.

[372] Jeremiah 31: 31-33. The New Covenant is mentioned by Isaiah and Ezekiel as well.

[373] Daniel 9: 26.

[374] Matthew 24: 15 and Mark 13: 14.

[375] Hosea 11: 1.

[376] Micah 5: 2.

[377] Targum Jonathan as quoted in Dr. Moore's book *The End of History—The Messiah Conspiracy, Vol. I.*, p. 119.

[378] The Jerusalem Talmud, Berachoth, fol. 5a, as quoted in Dr. Moore's book *The End of History—The Messiah Conspiracy, Vol. I.*, p. 119.

[379] Genesis 1: 3, 6, 9, 11, 14, 20, 24, and 26.

[380] Psalm 33: 4, 6, and 9.

[381] Psalm 103: 20.

[382] Genesis 3: 8 from the *Septuagint Tanach*. The parentheses are mine.

[383] Psalm 29: 3-9.

[384] From the Blue Letter Bible on the Internet.

[385] Jeremiah 1: 4.

[386] Jeremiah 1: 9 from *The New Jerusalem Bible*, Doubleday, New York, 1985.

[387] Jeremiah 1: 12.

[388] Psalm 18: 30.

[389] Genesis 15: 1.

[390] Genesis 15: 5. The parentheses are mine.

[391] Psalm 107: 19-20.

[392] Isaiah 53: 5. The parentheses are mine.

[393] Psalm 40: 6-7.

[394] Psalm 40: 7.

[395] Psalm 138: 2.

[396] Kohlenberger, John III, *The Interlinear NIV Hebrew-English Old Testament*, Zondervan Publishing House, Grand Rapids, Michigan, 1987, p. 500. Rabbi Nosson Scherman in *The Stone Edition Tanach, The ArtScroll Series®*, Mesorah Publications, Brooklyn, New York, 1996 translates this verse as follows: "…for You have exalted Your promise even beyond Your Name." The Hebrew word translated as "promise" by Rabbi Scherman in this verse is *imrah* (im-raw'), and it means word, speech, or commandment. It does not mean "promise."

[397] Jeffrey, Grant. *The Handwriting of God*, International Press, New York, 1996, p. 377.

[398] Jeffrey, Grant. *The Handwriting of God*, International Press, New York, 1996, p. 378.

[399] Hebrews 4: 12-13 from *The New Jerusalem Bible*, Doubleday, New York, 1985.

[400] John 1: 1.

[401] Genesis 1: 26.

[402] *The New Jerusalem Bible*, Doubleday, New York, 1985, p. 19.

[403] *The New Jerusalem Bible*, Doubleday, New York, 1985, p. 19.

[404] Genesis 2: 7.

[405] Scherman, Rabbi Nosson, *The Stone Edition Tanach, The ArtScroll Series®*, Mesorah Publications, Brooklyn, New York, 1996, p. 4.

[406] Scherman, Rabbi Nosson, *The Stone Edition Tanach, The ArtScroll Series®*, Mesorah Publications, Brooklyn, New York, 1996, p. 4.

[407] Deuteronomy 6: 4-5.

[408] Genesis 2: 24. The parentheses are mine.

[409] Numbers 13: 23. The parentheses are mine.

[410] Isaiah 48: 16.

[411] Proverbs 30: 2-6.

[412] Proverbs 30: 6.

[413] Proverbs 30: 4-5 from *The Stone Edition Tanach, The ArtScroll Series®*, Mesorah Publications, Brooklyn, New York, 1996.

[414] Scherman, Rabbi Nosson. *The Stone Edition Tanach, The ArtScroll Series®*, Mesorah Publications, Brooklyn, New York, 1996, p. 1612.

[415] Proverbs 30: 6 from *The Stone Edition Tanach, The ArtScroll Series®*, Mesorah Publications, Brooklyn, New York, 1996.

[416] John 3: 9-21.

[417] John 3: 4.

[418] John 3: 10-17.

[419] Isaiah 9: 6-7.

[420] Jeremiah 23: 5-6.

[421] Midrash on Lamentations 1: 16. The parentheses are mine.

[422] Genesis 15: 6. The parentheses are mine.

[423] Isaiah 59: 1-2.

[424] Isaiah 42: 1-9.

[425] Kac, Arthur W. *The Messianic Hope*, Baker House, Grand Rapids, 1975, p. 76.

[426] Isaiah 52: 3 through Isaiah 53: 12.

[427] 2 Samuel 7: 11.

[428] *The New Jerusalem Bible*, Doubleday, New York, 1985, p. 1165.

[429] Ezekiel 34: 23-24 and Ezekiel 37: 24-25.

[430] Zechariah 9: 9-10.

[431] John 1: 1-5. The parentheses are mine.

[432] A Gospel is a proclamation of redemption and salvation through Jesus the Messiah. This is the central tenet of Christianity. There are four Gospels in the New Testament: Matthew, Mark, Luke and John.

[433] *Bara* is the Hebrew word that is translated as *created* in Genesis 1: 1, and it means to create something from nothing.

[434] John 1: 10-14. The parentheses are mine.

[435] John 1: 17-18.

[436] Matthew 5: 27-28. The parentheses are mine.

[437] Matthew chapters 5, 6, and 7.

[438] Matthew 5: 17-18.

[439] Luke 16: 17.

[440] John 11: 48.

[441] The Talmud, Abodah Zarah 27b. The brackets are mine.

[442] For a complete discussion of this issue, you need to read Phillip Moore's *The End of History—Messiah Conspiracy, Vol. I*, Atlanta: Ramshead Press International Corporation, 1996, chapter 8. This quote is from p. 415 of the book.

[443] Exodus 15: 26. The parentheses are mine.

[444] The Talmud, Shabbath 14b.

[445] The Talmud, Sanhedrin X, 1. The parentheses are mine.

[446] Exodus 20: 8 from *The New Jerusalem Bible*.

[447] Luke 13: 12.

[448] Luke 13: 14 from *The New Jerusalem Bible*.

[449] Luke 13: 14.

[450] Luke 13: 15-16.

[451] Josephus was a Jewish general and historian who lived during the time of the Jewish revolt against the Romans in the Bar Kochba rebellion in the second century A.D.

452 Josephus. Book XX, Chapter X, 1.
453 Josephus. Book XV, Chapter III, 1.
454 Josephus. Book XVIII, Chapter II, 3; Book XX, Chapter IX, 4.
455 Talmud Yoma.
456 This passage is quoted from Moore, Phillip. *The End of History—Messiah Conspiracy, Vol. I*, Atlanta: Ramshead Press International Corporation, 1996, p. 71.
457 Matthew 23.
458 Matthew 18: 6.
459 Amos 5: 21-24.
460 Isaiah 29: 13-14.
461 Jeremiah 8: 8-9 from *The New Jerusalem Bible*.
462 Malachi 2: 8-9 from *The New Jerusalem Bible*.
463 Jeremiah 10: 21 from *The New Jerusalem Bible*. The parentheses are mine.
464 John 8: 5.
465 John 8: 7.
466 See John chapter 8 for the details of the exchanges between Jesus and the priests.
467 John 8: 49.
468 John 8: 52-53.
469 John 8: 54-56 and 58.
470 John 8: 58 from *The New Jerusalem Bible*.
471 John 11: 45-53.
472 John 11: 48.
473 John 5: 39-40.
474 John 5: 43.
475 John 5: 45-47.
476 A Messianic Jew is a Jewish person who has accepted Jesus as his or her Messiah.
477 Fischer, Raymond Robert, *The Children of God: Messianic Jews and Gentile Christians Nourished by Common Jewish Roots*, Olim Publications, Tiberias, Israel, 2000.
478 John 6: 35.
479 John 6: 41.
480 John 6: 48-49.
481 John 6: 51.
482 John 8: 12 and 24.
483 *The New Jerusalem Bible*, Doubleday, New York, 1985, p. 1763. The parentheses are mine.
484 John 8: 28.

[485] John 8: 30.

[486] John 8: 31-32.

[487] Psalm 119: 160.

[488] John 8: 37-38 and 44.

[489] John 10: 7-9. Some Bible translations use the word "gate" instead of "door."

[490] John 10: 14-18.

[491] Ezekiel 34: 7-16.

[492] John 11: 25-26.

[493] John 14: 6-7.

[494] John 14: 9.

[495] John 14: 6.

[496] John 15: 1and 5.

[497] Zacharias, Ravi. *Jesus Among Other Gods*, Nashville, TN: W Publishing Group, 2000, p. 89.

[498] John 12: 27-28.

[499] John 12: 44-45.

[500] John 17: 6.

[501] John 17: 11-12.

[502] John 17: 26.

[503] Dodd, C.H. *The Interpretation of the Fourth Gospel*, Cambridge University Press, 1958, p. 96.

[504] John 17: 22-23.

[505] Clover, R. *The Sacred Name Volume I Third Edition*, Qadesh La Yahweh Press, Garden Grove, California, 2002, p. 151.

[506] Sanhedrin 7: 5.

[507] Sanhedrin 7: 5.

[508] Matthew 26: 59.

[509] Matthew 26: 61.

[510] Matthew 26: 63.

[511] Matthew 26: 63.

[512] Matthew 26: 64.

[513] Luke 22: 69.

[514] Luke 23: 70.

[515] Clover, R. *The Sacred Name Volume I Third Edition*, Qadesh La Yahweh Press, Garden Grove, California, 2002, p. 158.

[516] Clover, R. *The Sacred Name Volume I Third Edition*, Qadesh La Yahweh Press, Garden Grove, California, 2002, p. 158.

[517] Matthew 26: 65.

[518] Matthew 26: 66.

[519] Sanhedrin 10: 11, J. Sanhedrin 7: 16 (25c, d), and B. Sanhedrin 43a and 67a.

[520] B. Sanhedrin 43a and 107b.

[521] Herford, R. Travers. *Christianity in Talmud and Midrash*. Reference Book Publishers, Inc., New Jersey, 1966, p. 55.

[522] Clover, R. *The Sacred Name Volume I Third Edition*, Qadesh La Yahweh Press, Garden Grove, California, 2002, p. 162. Also, see John 10: 25.

[523] John 10: 25. The parentheses are mine.

[524] For example, see Matthew 12: 40, Matthew 26: 61, and John 2: 19.

[525] Matthew 27: 63-64

[526] Mark 16: 9-11 and John 20: 11-18.

[527] Matthew 28: 9-10.

[528] Matthew 28: 16-20, Luke 24: 34 and 44-53, Mark 16: 14-18, Luke 24: 33-43, John 20: 19-25, John 20: 26-31, and John 21: 1-25.

[529] 1 Corinthians 15: 6.

[530] Morison, Frank, *Who Moved the Stone?*, Grand Rapids, MI: Zondervan Publishing House, 1987.

[531] Greenleaf, Simon, *The Testimony of the Evangelists: The Gospels Examined by the Rules of Evidence in Courts of Justice*, Grand Rapids, MI: Kregel Publications, 1995.

[532] Lapide, Pinchas, *The Resurrection of Jesus: A Jewish Perspective*, Minneapolis, MN: Augsburg Publishing House, 1983, p. 92.

[533] McDowell, Josh. *Evidence That Demands a Verdict*, Campus Crusade for Christ, San Bernardino, CA, 1972.

[534] Matthew 4: 7.

[535] Matthew 4: 10.

[536] Matthew 22: 43-44.

[537] Matthew 23: 37-39.

[538] Mark 12: 29-30.

[539] Luke 4: 18-19 and 21.

[540] Luke 4: 28-30.

[541] Acts 2: 1-12.

[542] Acts 2: 41.

[543] Acts 2: 5.

[544] Acts 2: 7.

[545] Acts 2: 8.

[546] Acts 2: 13.

[547] Acts 2: 15.

[548] Joel 2: 32.

[549] Philippians 2: 9-11. The parentheses are mine. See Isaiah 45: 21-24 for the Old Testament prophecy relating to this fact.

[550] Isaiah 45: 21-24.

[551] Acts 3: 1-3.

[552] Acts 3: 6 from *The New Jerusalem Bible*, Doubleday, New York, 1985.

[553] Acts 4: 22.

[554] Acts 3: 16. From *The New Jerusalem Bible*, Doubleday, New York, 1985.

[555] Acts 4: 7. From *The New Jerusalem Bible*, Doubleday, New York, 1985.

[556] Acts 4: 8.

[557] Acts 4: 8-12.

[558] Acts 4: 12.

[559] Isaiah 43: 11.

[560] Acts 5: 17-18.

[561] Acts 5: 28 from *The New Jerusalem Bible*.

[562] Acts 5: 30-32 from *The New Jerusalem Bible*.

[563] Acts 5: 33.

[564] Acts 5: 34.

[565] Acts 5: 34-40.

[566] Acts 5: 41 from *The New Jerusalem Bible*.

[567] Acts 9: 3.

[568] Acts 9: 4-6. The parentheses are mine.

[569] Acts 9: 13-14.

[570] Acts 9: 15-16.

[571] Romans 10: 13 and Joel 2: 32.

[572] Joel 2: 32. The parentheses are mine.

[573] Gorenberg, Gershom. *The End of Days: Fundamentalism and the Struggle for the Temple Mount*, New York, The Free Press, 2000, p. 68.

[574] The Babylonian Talmud, Yoma 39b, p. 186. The parentheses are mine.

[575] Colossians 2: 14 from *The New Jerusalem Bible*.

[576] Matthew 23: 37-39.

[577] Luke 19: 42-44 from the *New International Version*.

[578] Isaiah 30: 19 from *The New Jerusalem Bible*.

[579] Revelation 3: 12.

[580] Revelation 14: 1.

[581] Revelation 22: 4.

[582] Jeremiah 33: 15-16 and Ezekiel 48: 35.

[583] Revelation 13: 16-18. The parentheses are mine.

[584] Revelation 14: 9-11.

[585] Proverbs 18: 10.

[586] Revelation 19: 1, 3, 4, and 6.

[587] Revelation 19: 1-7. I have spelled "HalleluYah" correctly.

[588] Genesis 45: 3.

[589] Scherman, Rabbi Nosson, *The Stone Edition Tanach, The ArtScroll Series®*, Mesorah Publications, Brooklyn, New York, 1996, p. 115. The parentheses are mine.

[590] Lewis, C. S., *Mere Christianity*, HarperSanFrancisco, New York, New York, 1952, p. 65. The parentheses are mine.

[591] Matthew 13: 4.

[592] Matthew 13: 19.

[593] Matthew 13: 5.

[594] Matthew 13: 20-21.

[595] Matthew 13: 7.

[596] Matthew 13: 22.

[597] Matthew 13: 8.

[598] Matthew 13: 23.

[599] Micah 5: 2 and Genesis 49: 10.

[600] Isaiah 40: 3.

[601] Malachi 4: 5-6.

[602] Matthew: 17: 11-12.

[603] Isaiah 53.

[604] Isaiah 9.

[605] Matthew: 17: 11.

[606] Malachi 4: 1-3.

[607] Zechariah 9: 9.

[608] Psalm 41: 9 and Zechariah 11: 12.

[609] Zechariah 11: 13.

[610] Isaiah 52: 14.

[611] Isaiah 54: 5, Isaiah 50: 6, Isaiah 53: 7, Genesis 3: 15, and Isaiah 52: 14.

[612] Psalm 22: 16, Zechariah 11: 12, Zechariah 13: 7, Isaiah 53: 4-7, and Isaiah 53: 10.

[613] Isaiah 53: 9.

[614] Isaiah 53: 12 and Psalm 22: 18.

[615] Zechariah 12: 10 and Psalm 34: 20.

[616] Amos 8: 9.

[617] Isaiah 53: 12.

[618] John 19: 30.

[619] Ryrie, Charles. *Ryrie Study Bible* Expanded Edition, Moody Press, Chicago, 1995, p. 1719.

[620] Deuteronomy 21: 23.

[621] Isaiah 53: 9.

[622] Isaiah 53: 3.

[623] Isaiah 8: 14-15.

[624] Isaiah 11: 10.

[625] Psalm 16: 10.

[626] Psalm 118: 22, Isaiah 28: 16, and Zechariah 10: 4.

[627] Jeremiah 31: 31-33.

[628] Isaiah 42: 1-9.

[629] Ezekiel 34: 25.

[630] Psalm 110: 4. Also, see Isaiah 53: 12 where Jesus' role as intercessor is discussed.

[631] Scherman, Rabbi Nosson, *The Stone Edition Tanach, The ArtScroll Series®*, Mesorah Publications, Brooklyn, New York, 1996, p. 29.

[632] Ryrie, Charles. *Ryrie Study Bible Expanded Edition*, Moody Press, Chicago, 1995, p. 1466.

[633] This is the first time in the Bible El Elyon is used as a Name of Yahweh.

[634] Genesis 14: 18-20. The parentheses are mine.

[635] Psalm 110: 4.

[636] Psalm 110: 5-7. The parentheses are mine.

[637] Hebrews 7: 1-3.

[638] Hebrews 7: 4-11.

[639] Hebrews 7: 12-18.

[640] Hebrews 7: 18-19.

[641] Hebrews 7: 22.

[642] Hebrews 7: 24.

[643] Zechariah 6: 11-13.

[644] Jeremiah 23: 5 and 33: 15-16.

[645] Isaiah 4: 2-3 and 11: 1-5.

[646] Bruce, F.F. *Jesus and Christian Origins Outside the New Testament*, William B. Eerdmans Publishing Company, Grand Rapids, Michigan, 1984, pp. 64-65.